MODERN FRANCE

By F. C. Roe

MODERN TALES FROM FRANCE
TALES OF ACTION FROM MODERN FRENCH AUTHORS
TALES OF ADVENTURE FROM MODERN FRENCH AUTHORS

By C. A. Roe and F. C. Roe

SCENES DE LA VIE FRANÇAISE

MODERN FRANCE

An Introduction to
French Civilization

F. C. ROE

PROFESSOR OF FRENCH
IN THE UNIVERSITY OF ABERDEEN

LONGMANS, GREEN AND CO
LONDON · NEW YORK · TORONTO

LONGMANS, GREEN AND CO LTD
6 & 7 CLIFFORD STREET LONDON W I
BOSTON HOUSE STRAND STREET CAPE TOWN
531 LITTLE COLLINS STREET MELBOURNE

LONGMANS, GREEN AND CO INC
55 FIFTH AVENUE NEW YORK 3

LONGMANS, GREEN AND CO
20 CRANFIELD ROAD TORONTO 16

ORIENT LONGMANS LTD
CALCUTTA BOMBAY MADRAS
DELHI VIJAYAWADA DACCA

First published 1956

Printed in Great Britain
by T. and A. CONSTABLE LTD., Hopetoun Street,
Printers to the University of Edinburgh

To My Wife

PREFACE

THIS book is concerned with what France means to the Western World. Its aim is to set out some of France's contributions, permanent, recurrent or ephemeral, to civilization. We bring to the subject the harvest of forty years' study and close acquaintance with France and the French.

A country is to a great extent what its inhabitants make of it. An introduction to French civilization must of necessity begin with the people. We have sought to determine, however briefly, the complex elements, racial and others, which combine in the making of distinctive national characteristics. We have also sought to determine what traits in this character appear to us permanent: a difficult task made more difficult by the fact that a nation, like any living organism, lives in a state of perpetual transformation. If this phenomenon is more accentuated in France than in other European communities, it is perhaps due to her greater complexity. Some tendency, hidden from sight for a long time, may suddenly reappear owing to external or other circumstances and assume for a while a preponderant position; its subsequent disappearance does not mean its annihilation. Thus are the conservative and revolutionary spirit, whether in politics, literature or art, the mystic and the rationalist, the nationalist and the cosmopolitan.

The diversity of the people finds its most tangible expression in Paris, the crucible, the heart and the fireworks of France, a city where all contrasts meet, and somehow combine. This diversity, however, is matched and perhaps partly caused by that of the country itself; an epitome of modern Europe, a land still as agricultural as England was a century ago and whose industrial production offers many interesting features to dwellers in a country which knew the Industrial Revolution a century earlier. The one is still wedded to coal which brought her supremacy, the other, lacking coal, is harnessing her rivers. We are confronted with an equal diversity in the territories of the French Union, each calling for a different policy; it is, however, possible to recognize a general idea of colonial methods often very different from ours in practice if not necessarily in the ultimate aim.

The final section of Part I is devoted to French Institutions: Parliament, which under a deceptive external likeness to Westminster, hides a totally different conception of democratic representation often puzzling to the British. Other differences figure in local government, the system of justice, civil and criminal, the law relating to family relationships and administrative law. In these matters variation between French and English practice is indicated.

Part II beginning with education, deals with the scientific contribution from Descartes to the Curies, the artistic contribution from Poussin to the Jeune Ecole de Paris and the musical contribution from Lully to Françaix. A section is devoted to the cinema and to a bird's-eye view of the contemporary theatre. The final pages of the book do not attempt to recount the history of French literature but present five vignettes on diverse but characteristic French authors : Montaigne, Racine, Flaubert, Proust and Mauriac. However devoted to France and the French one man's life may have been, he can hardly hope to deal with all the contributions to civilization made by a country so rich in thought and expression, a nation with so long a cultural history. We have left aside, except for incidental remarks, sculpture, architecture, and philosophy. We trust that some entertainment as well as some useful information, with a fuller view of France's achievements, may have been brought to those who seek either pleasure or instruction in a deeper acquaintance with those often puzzling, fascinating and disturbing neighbours whose 'irreverent and perverse wit' so often scandalized our Victorian grandfathers.

CONTENTS

PART ONE

LIST OF ILLUSTRATIONS

Part One

Part One.

CHAPTER I

THE PEOPLE

WHEN the French perpetrate some piece of political friskiness or some startlingly original art form, popular opinion in the Anglo-Saxon countries is wont to explain this effervescence by allusions to the peculiarities of 'Latin blood'. Does this bland formula really help us to understand? The people of France speak a Romance language and their civilization represents part of the Roman heritage, but they are not a 'Latin race' and 'Latin blood' does not flow in their veins. A language-group —Latin, or Celtic, or even Indo-European—does not constitute a race, and no 'French race' exists.

From the earliest prehistoric ages, in fact, men have lived on French soil, and the mingling of races has been going on ever since. In France, prehistoric 'finds', more numerous and more varied than elsewhere, have been and are still being made, and the southern part of the country, with Northern Spain, may claim the glory of being the oldest centre of culture in Europe. The Mousterian culture, named from remains discovered at Le Moustier in Périgord, dates back, the anthropologists tell us, some fifty thousand or perhaps a hundred thousand years. The remains of Cro-Magnon man, whose wonderful drawings and sculptures may be seen in caves at Les Eyzies and Lascaux in Dordogne (in the latter the paintings are masterpieces and have earned for Lascaux the reputation of being the Sistine Chapel of prehistory), may be twenty or forty thousand years old. They date from an era when man lived by hunting the herds of reindeer and bison on the icy steppes which then covered France, in a period before writing, cloth or pottery had been invented. The language of these Palaeolithic hunters survives, some believe, in Eskuara, the language spoken by the Basques (probably an Iberian people), twenty thousand of whom live on the French side of the Pyrénées.

3

Prehistory passes into history, for France, six centuries before Christ. Not much can be averred with certainty about the Ligurians and Iberians whom the Celts found when, before the seventh century B.C., they invaded Gaul, but it is known that the Greeks founded Marseilles and Nice about 600 B.C. Still divided into independent tribes—Senones, Lingones, Sequani, Aedui, etc.—the Celtae (Celtic-speaking peoples who had arrived in successive waves from Central Europe) were the Gauls encountered by Julius Caesar when he completed, in 58-52 B.C., the conquest of Gaul begun in the second century B.C. These Gauls, like their predecessors in prehistoric times, probably represented already a racial mixture; skeletons of different and mixed types have been found in the most ancient caves.

The Gauls adopted the language, the way of life and the gods of the Roman conquerors, and in the second and third centuries A.D. became Christians. By this time they were Gallo-Romans. Their civilization was Roman: magnificent Roman roads linked their cities, which became Paris, Rouen, Nantes, Bordeaux, Toulouse, Rheims, etc.; their schools, at Autun, Bordeaux and Toulouse, produced Roman poets and orators; the Gallo-Romans tilled flourishing farms. After five centuries of Romanization the Roman boundary (*limes*) on the Rhine gave way and barbarians poured—or seeped—into Gaul from Germany. Some of these had no doubt acquired a veneer of civilization by contact with the legions, and much of the settlement was peaceful, the barbarians becoming farmers and soldiers. Various tribes settled down in Gaul, the Burgundians in the east, the Visigoths in the south, and the Franks in the north. These last gave their name to the country which became France. France, however, was not the land of the Franks, since most of the population consisted of Gallo-Romans, and the conquering Franks adopted the Latin tongue spoken by a population more civilized than they were themselves. The Gallo-Romans were not, like the ancient Britons, driven into the mountain fastnesses, and the Roman tradition was not broken, as in Britain, but remained a permanent strand in French civilization. (How much of the difference in outlook between French and English should be attributed to the unlike fate of the 'Celtic' population in the two countries?) At a later period (from the eighth to the tenth centuries) Norsemen invaded Northern France, settled on the Channel coast, and gave their name to Normandy. Thence, having in the course of a century and a half become Frenchmen, and more civilized than the Saxons in England, they set out to conquer the rough islanders in 1066.

During the Middle Ages the English in their turn invaded France—again and again—and for a long period they held Guyenne. Throughout the succeeding centuries foreigners filtered into France as soldiers, merchants and scholars; in the present century large numbers of political refugees of all classes from Germany, Spain and elsewhere sought sanctuary in that liberal country. Shortage of labour brought in immigrants from Poland for the mines of the north and east, and Italians came to work as navvies or bricklayers' labourers. More recently still—after the Second World War—North African labourers have come into the country to work in industry or on the land. France, which shows a power of assimilating aliens as remarkable as that of the U.S.A., puts no high barriers in the way of naturalization. In general, the second generation of immigrants becomes French and many distinguished Frenchmen bear foreign names.

The French take a very liberal view of what constitutes Frenchness: 'Est Français celui qui se sent tel et est content de l'être.' What could be more remote from the Germanic theory of race superiority? Yet it is piquant to remember that the theory of Nordic superiority was borrowed from France, where it had been evolved by the publicist and diplomat Count Joseph-Arthur de Gobineau (1816-82).

Like the British and most European nations, the French people represent a mixture of three main races or ethnic groups: Nordic, Mediterranean and Alpine. Nordics—tall, fair, blue or grey eyed, long faced, with a thin nose—prevail in the north and east, as well as in Normandy and Burgundy. The Mediterranean or 'Latin' type—dark, oval-faced, small and swarthy—lives mostly in the south and resembles the type so

B

frequently met with along the Spanish and Italian coasts. The broad-headed, round-faced, rather dark-haired and medium-built Alpine type, sometimes termed Celtic, constitutes the great bulk of the French population of the present day and spreads from the east as far as Central France.

No basic racial differences separate the population of France from that of Great Britain; but the three groups are mingled in different proportions. Britain has a higher Nordic content, France a stronger Celtic or Alpine strain. Characteristic types of each of the Alpine, Mediterranean and Nordic groups occur more frequently in some French provinces than in others, but few Frenchmen can, any more than most Britons, lay claim to be pure Nordics, pure Alpines or pure Mediterraneans. Purity of race does not imply superiority of intelligence; in fact, mongrels have a way of being clever. Varied heredity may bring richly diverse intellectual and artistic qualities, no less than diversity of character. Frenchmen like to think that each of these three ethnic groups, like the three fairies in the folk-tales, brings distinct gifts to the national heritage: the 'Latins' their lucidity, the Nordics their seriousness and the Celts their artistic nature and their anarchical individualism. To the inhabitants of the northern half of France it appears evident that Nordic seriousness, solidity and steadiness have been vouchsafed to them in richer abundance than to Frenchmen living south of the Loire. Just as the dour Caledonian looks upon the southern English as too talkative and too smoothly sociable, so does the northerner in France look with some disapproval upon the expansive, gesticulating Meridional. The southerner in his turn deplores the heaviness, the unresponsiveness, the lack of imagination of the northerner, condemned to live under cheerless, leaden skies, where existence itself calls for continuous effort.

Not only do north and south breed diverse social types, but every French province has been credited with producing its own variety of Frenchman. The Norman claims good sense with an unusual endowment of caution, the Breton is looked upon as singularly brave, straightforward and imaginative, the Dauphinois as uncouth and canny but inventive, the

Alsatian prides himself on his stolid calm, the Lorrainer sees himself as a man of action, thoughtful, adaptable and tenacious, and so on for the other provinces and districts. France, in a word, produces such a rich variety of types that it behoves the foreigner to be cautious in generalizing about national character.

This variety disguises but does not conceal an indubitable unity, for France has long been a highly organized and centralized country to a much greater degree and for longer than Spain or Germany. For centuries the people have been bound together in a State governed by the same sovereign. An age-long tradition, evolved by the French people, has in its turn moulded them, through home and school, through the Roman Church and, since the Revolution, through the conscript army. However diverse the types fashioned by the various provinces, and despite the conflicting influences of a highly disciplined and hierarchical Church and a Revolutionary tradition of freedom and equality, France looks upon herself, with justice, as the most solidly unified nation in Europe. Not only frequent contact but movement of individuals and families from one region to another has helped in the mixing and unification, for no province is cut off from its neighbours, as in Spain, by almost impassable mountain barriers. Love of the land of France acts as a powerful unifying influence. It has been sometimes said that, whereas English patriotism consists less in love of the land than in pride in being English, French patriotism is linked firmly with 'la terre de France'.

Are there any features which distinguish Frenchmen, as a nation, from citizens of other countries? Certainly no physical or physiological trait, scientifically measurable, has ever been shown to be specifically French, though long observation points to a singularly acute sense of taste to which their *cuisine* ministers. Have heredity and environment together endowed them with any psychological character of their own? The French themselves generally consider that they have, and their psychologists and geographers agree with Goethe that they are outstandingly sociable. 'La solitude nous pèse,' wrote a French psychologist, 'nous ne pouvons consentir à penser

seuls, à sentir seuls, à jouer seuls. Nous ne pouvons séparer la
satisfaction d'autrui de notre satisfaction propre.' [1]

Most Frenchmen obviously enjoy talking and hearing others
talk. Usually shyness and taciturnity hamper them not at
all and they contrive to give their fellow-men the impression
that they like them and that conversation with them affords
lively pleasure. They believe, with Montaigne, that 'le plus
fructueux et naturel exercice de nostre esprit' is conversation.
The strong silent man is no favourite among the French, who,
instead of crediting him with thoughts too deep for words,
tend to conclude that if he says nothing it must be because he
has nothing to say. They themselves delight in the play of
intelligence, in the give-and-take of ideas. Society and conversation afford them the joy on which they set most store—
the opportunity of pleasing.[2] The French seek to please by
the display of intelligence, tact, ready wit, delicate flattery or
fine irony. They do not all succeed—nor do they all try!

The long tradition of the French *salons* bears witness to the
pleasure they have always found in social life and to their skill
in bringing to a high level the art of living in society. Many
Parisian drawing-rooms still foster the art of conversation.
The social tradition left its mark on the French ideal of
conduct, expressed in the conception of the *honnête homme*, an
ideal implying *esprit*, judgment, knowledge and also 'l'habitude
de la conversation avec les dames, quelque expérience de
l'amour'. The corresponding English ideal, the gentleman,
puts character and conduct before the courtly graces. The
honnête homme generally found himself much more at home in
the drawing-room than his English counterpart; eighteenth-
century French travellers who came to London could not
conceive why the gentlemen of England preferred drinking with
their kind in club or tavern when they might have been
conversing with the ladies at some reception.

As social beings the French possess a unique asset in their
apparent gaiety, though it would be going too far to adopt the

[1] A. Fouillée, *Psychologie du peuple français*, p. 181.
[2] The taciturn may find consolation in retorting that this amiability is merely
a form of vanity or *amour-propre*, the desire to create an impression.

popular view that they are a gay nation. The glitter of Paris
hides a good deal of earnestness and even grimness, just as
there may be intense bitterness behind a flippant jest that sets
the table in a roar. In society the Frenchman, adroitly
amiable, seeks to give pleasure by stressing the lighter and
brighter sides of life. He realizes, of course, that the best way
of amusing himself lies in amusing others. The irrepressible
Dumas the elder, when asked whether he had enjoyed himself
at some frigidly pompous dinner-party, which he had succeeded in animating by his brilliant conversation, made the
delightful reply: 'Oui, mais combien je me serais ennuyé si
je n'avais pas été là!'

Long before Dumas's time an English writer had declared:
'Almost everybody is witty in France', and had gone on to
explain French superiority in this respect on culinary and
social grounds. 'A Frenchman never takes malt liquor, he
eats no butter, and his bread is light: the meat in France is
not nearly as fat as it is here and it is much better dressed:
the sauces are poignant, and not greasy; he eats a great deal
of soup and light vegetables; he drinks in moderation as much
wine and water as is necessary to dilute his dinner, and then
he takes as much good wine and liqueurs as is necessary to
heat his stomach, and quicken the circulation of his blood,
and no more. Add to this the pureness of the air, and the light
society of the most amiable women in the world, in which he
passes so much of his time, and you will see reasons enough
why his spirits should be quicker in their motions and more
refined than ours.' [1]

Mérimée declared that the secret of his countrymen's success abroad lay in this: they take trouble to amuse themselves
and in doing so manage to entertain other people. They
succeed with singular facility because their lively minds delight
to play on a variety of subjects so as rarely to exhaust a subject
—or a listener. They look upon pedantry as unforgivable,
and, despite their universal curiosity, they hate purely factual
conversations. A fact may be of interest if it can be used as
the springboard for an original or witty idea: in itself it has

[1] Martin Sherlock, *Letters on Several Subjects* (1781), pp. 77-8.

no value. For a Frenchman the exchange of batches of solid
facts unleavened by ideas does not rank as a conversation; nor
have they faith in

> the piling up of fact on fact, in the hope that
> Some day a road may be built of them and may lead some-
> where.[1]

Long-windedness and vagueness tend to irritate the Frenchman; to explain the obvious infuriates him. When Mme de
Staël called upon the philosopher Fichte to explain briefly
the system he had spent his life in elaborating, she cut him
short after a few minutes of laborious exposition, protesting
that she already understood the gist of the matter. Her conversational powers had been developed in a Parisian *salon*
and her Teutonic friends looked upon her, despite her Swiss
nationality, as the very type of 'la femme française'. She
possessed in a high degree the French qualities of universal
curiosity and a taste for general ideas. No conversational feat
surprises the British more than to observe Frenchmen promptly
and dexterously fitting newly learned facts into a general idea.
The French are impatient to find an explanation, a scheme
into which the facts will fit. Superficiality meets with more
indulgence than groping vagueness; it would no doubt be
possible in many literary and philosophical circles in France
to discover people whose mental attitude reflects that of the
illustrious lady who declared: 'Je comprends tout ce qui vaut
la peine d'être compris. Ce que je ne comprends pas n'existe
pas.'

The French look upon themselves and are commonly
regarded by others as the logical people *par excellence*. Their
precise and clear-cut language, their political ideas, their arts
have all been dubbed logical; an English historian of architecture described their mediaeval cathedrals as more logically
constructed than English cathedrals. What exactly do we
mean when we apply the term 'logical' to the French—often
with the corollary that we as a nation distrust logic? Is it
really logic that we mean? Do we not often rather imply

[1] C. Day Lewis, *An Italian Visit*, I.

abstraction, or ideology, or symmetry, or nothing more than a sense of form? Are we not merely expressing our conviction that many Frenchmen talk as if reality had a symmetrical recurrent pattern, as if the universe ran, so to speak, according to a scheme; as if events and situations recurred and were not unique? As Schlegel ironically remarked to Benjamin Constant: 'The French know so well everything they will say in every situation in life that they are very kind indeed to carry on with a life which is all so clear to them beforehand; it must bore them like a tale twice repeated.' [1]

Faced with a problem, the Frenchman tries to reduce it to first principles, to discover, that is, the pattern underlying it. 'Even the man in the street,' avers M. Siegfried, 'has a remarkable capacity for generalization, the faculty of seeing the principle implied in a question and the distant consequences that it may entail.' [2] The more intelligent the Frenchman, the greater will be his awareness of the pattern concealed by the complexity of reality. From these first principles he will deduce a solution in accordance with the underlying pattern. The Englishman tackles his problems rather more empirically. More fully aware of the diversity of elements in the problem than of its general, abstract character, he considers each problem as unique. He seeks a particular solution for that particular problem, not a general principle which should solve all problems of that type. He feels less convinced than the Frenchman that any discernible pattern exists. In human problems, at any rate, the Englishman rarely claims that his solution is reached by logic, for he considers that the motive forces behind much human behaviour are indefinable. It would, however, be possible to argue that a logical solution implies taking *all* the elements of a problem into consideration. If one does, can one offer more than an *ad hoc* solution, valid for the particular problem alone? Can it be more logical to abstract or extract a principle from the complexity of reality and claim for it universal validity?

The French method, illuminating a whole length of the

[1] B. Constant, *Journal Intime* (1804), p. 67.
[2] *Conferencia*, 1 February 1949, p. 70.

tissue of experience, shows the pattern, the general, the characteristic, the typical, and gives us the illusion that we know
more than the bare facts. For conversation, for the amuse-
ment of the mind, the disinterested search for the general
principles underlying a problem offers great advantages. But
does it afford better guidance for action? The practical
Englishman wants results that will work. As Emerson wrote:
'His is the logic which brings salt to the soup, the hammer to
the nail, the oar to the boat . . . he bows down to the earth
before a fact.' Let us not suggest unkindly that the Frenchman
shows more inclination to bow down before a theory than
before any fact, nor let us hastily conclude that intellectual
activity tends to flourish at the expense of wisdom. Let us
rather bear in mind that much theorizing in France remains
an intellectual exercise; many a brilliant upholder of capricious theories, designed to startle and amuse the practical man,
brings to the domestic and social problems with which real
life faces him a massive dose of sturdy common sense and
caution. We may agree or not with Lord Chesterfield and
Montesquieu, who concurred, after an argument lasting several
days (if we believe Diderot), that the French were cleverer
than the English, but that, on the other hand, they were devoid
of common sense! [1]

This liking for neat, symmetrical, 'logical' systems finds its
most striking illustration in the administration of the country.
The administrative machine which carries out the day-to-day
government of France appears to do its work successfully,
despite criticism, since it has run steadily for nearly a century
and a half. Political constitutions, even when elegant, carefully devised and abstractly perfect, have been less fortunate
and, with the exception of that of 1875—modelled for a con-
stitutional monarchy and illogically used for a Republic—
have not survived over any protracted period. The British,
who have been spared the ordeal of making a constitution for
their country and who tend to forget that the Dominions have
their written constitutions, sometimes aver that making a
constitution first is like putting on the roof before building the

[1] Diderot, *Lettre à Mlle Volland*, 5 September 1762.

house,[1] and show too frequently a proneness to look upon the French as doctrinaire in their politics and to stress the contrast with their own sturdy empiricism. Mid-twentieth-century Britain provided an ironical commentary on this attitude by electing a doctrinaire government at a time when France preferred an opportunist government (or more exactly a series of them), acting empirically, instead of choosing one of the extreme doctrinaire parties.

Generally speaking, however, British empiricism has clashed with French logic, particularly in foreign affairs. The French, for example, wished the *Entente Cordiale* of 1903 to be implemented by a clear understanding given by Britain that she would declare war if France were attacked. British politicians always preferred postponing any decision until the situation had actually arisen; who could tell in advance all the complexities that might be entailed? Frequent misunderstanding and mistrust have arisen from these conflicting habits of thought. At times each country has cast doubts on the other's sincerity.

In social life, too, divergent ideas on what constitutes sincerity may cause misunderstanding. The British, like Molière's misanthropist, believe that, when sincere, they express all they think. Many of them would rather be thought ill-mannered than insincere. The French, like Molière's Philinte, deplore such brutal frankness, holding that it may well be foolish to say all we think, though we should not say what we do not think. As Mme de Lambert put it: 'Il ne faut pas toujours dire ce qu'on pense; il faut toujours penser ce qu'on dit.' It may be that the observance of this maxim ensured the success of social life in France; alternatively, social life so fully developed may have imposed the observance of the maxim. Be that as it may, the French language possesses a wealth of formulas and phrases, often ironical, that permit, while avoiding any departure from the most urbane standard of politeness, the expression of the strongest disapproval.

By one of those strange anomalies which beset the study of national psychology, the nation that regards itself, and with some reason, as the most sociable, also prides itself on being a

[1] E. Bevin, 15 September 1948.

nation of individualists. Every nation, indeed, looks upon
itself as a nation of individualists. Nothing could be more
natural, for foreign nations, known less familiarly, appear to
conform to a mental as to a physical type, individual differences
being blurred by distance. Horace Walpole, travelling through
Europe in 1734, noted that the French and the Italians had
only national virtues and national vices, whereas in England
the variety of temperaments gave individuality to each citizen.

British political writers, convinced of French individualism,
see evidence of it in French politics and comment unfavourably
on the multiplicity of parties, indicative of an unwillingness
to sink minor divergences of view, mere *nuances* of opinion,
for the sake of achieving some major object of policy. Yet in
actual practice differences have to be sunk, for the government
of France must be carried on. Every French government
represents a coalition, for no one party is ever strong enough
to govern alone. All coalitions imply the sinking of differences,
compromise, elimination of *nuances*. The British, who deplore
the tenacity with which the French cling to their political
nuances, showed over a long period a deep attachment to
religious *nuances*. Each country has its specialities.

It has been remarked by a very shrewd observer that the
key to understanding the French character should be sought
in La Fontaine's Fables. The idea need not surprise us, for
French children learn their fables, as once English children
learned their Bible stories, at their mother's knee; in both
cases expressions and allusions to what had sunk early and
deeply into the mind became part of the language of everyday
life. No doubt at that age even precocious French children
do not bring profound philosophical meditation to bear on
these delightful stories, but what attitude to life, what view of
the world do the Fables engrave on the tablets of their memory?
La Fontaine, like that other purveyor of the average man's
philosophy, Molière, preaches a practical virtue, a virtue for
this world, a transitory world indeed, but to be taken all the
more seriously on that account. The Fables drive home the
idea that the outside world is full of perils, that adventure had
best be avoided, that 'le désir de voir et l'humeur inquiète'

may spell disaster. Wisdom counsels one to stay comfortably, safely and happily at home. Be moderate in your ideals, advises the fabulist; happiness lies in not straining after the sublimer virtues; the essential virtues are the social virtues: gratitude, mutual help, friendship; if you are ambitious, selfish or avaricious, you have strayed dangerously from the path of moderation. Life is precious, 'Il vaut mieux souffrir que mourir! . . .' but it is better still to avoid misfortune. The idea of duty no more obtrudes itself in La Fontaine's philosophy than in Molière's.

Let us not, however, rashly conclude that France prizes only mundane virtues or forget that she has had her puritans and her saints. Pascal and the Jansenists, St. François de Sales, and mystics who were no whit less French than Voltaire or Anatole France, remind us that otherworldliness has its share in the complex make-up of the French mind and character. In the same way the names of gallant explorers like Bougainville, Jacques Cartier, Cavelier de la Salle and dozens of others warn us not to conclude that La Fontaine's advice has always been taken and that the French are all averse to foreign adventure.

Not only does it take all sorts to make a world, as the popular dictum has it, it takes all sorts to make a nation. How best can one sum up the complexities of mind and character that distinguish the French people? Flinging out a net of generalization does not help very much, for as many fish slip out as are caught in its meshes. Shall we define the French as mercurial, impatient, lacking the faculty of sustained attention, as agog with intellectual curiosity laced with irony? As amiable social beings but compact of *amour-propre*? As thriftily and cautiously family-bound, or as individualists intent only on the enjoyment of everything this world can give? All these more or less contradictory epithets have been aimed at this enigmatic nation and here and there no doubt have struck home.

The newest label to be attached to the French mind and character is inscribed with the word 'introvert'—the technical terms of psychology have in recent years enjoyed a certain vogue. Even this comprehensive term would not apply universally, but if limited to the educated classes among townsmen would not, on the whole, be too wide of the mark. The introvert type abounds even in the classrooms of the *lycées*, and the instruction given in them may also conduce to reinforcing that habit of mind. The singular prestige that attaches in France to the intellectual, whether philosopher, novelist or artist, suggests that Frenchmen rate the thinker or the artist higher than the man of action; even statesmen like Edouard Herriot and Léon Blum earned more esteem for their literary achievements than for their political action. The smallness of the group of Frenchmen who have, by their personal drive, built up gigantic enterprises—like the Renaults and the Citroëns—and the meagre tribute of grudging admiration meted out to them in return, may be adduced as corroborative evidence. Expenditure of mental energy on cogitation leaves less copious supplies available for action; the man of action must focus his mental powers, not on the kind of analysis from which the intellectual hatches his books or his pictures, but on the outside world, with a view to solving practical problems. The extroverts, the 'go-getters', flourish less abundantly than in the New World, where they represent a different national ideal. If youthful ardour prompts us to irritated impatience with those who put meditation before vigorous and effective action, we might perhaps reflect on a maxim propounded by one of France's greatest thinkers, Pascal: 'Tout le malheur des hommes vient d'une seule chose, qui est de ne savoir pas demeurer en repos, dans une chambre.'

What do the French themselves regard as the characteristics of the average Frenchman, *le Français moyen*? This expression, first used by that shrewd observer Jules Lemaître (though often credited to Herriot), was defined by him in 1899 in terms which, with slight modifications made necessary by the half-century which has elapsed since then, would be generally recognized by his compatriots as accurate. 'The average Frenchman—bourgeois, peasant, independent workman or small employer—is pretty much the same in all our provinces,' avers Lemaître. 'He loves his country and the army instinctively without reasoning much on the subject and will not have a finger laid on them. He is genuinely imbued with the principles of 1789; he is a Liberal and not at all socialist. Private property is one of the things he prizes most, and I would even say, most blandly. In general he does not much care for *les curés*, but he is not intolerant. He lets his wife and daughter attend Mass; he thinks it a good thing that his children should take their first communion; he will allow himself to be buried by the Church just as he allowed himself to be married by the Church.

'On religion itself, the feelings of the average Frenchman are rather mixed. Generally speaking, he does not believe in the dogmas or else he avoids thinking about them. But, all the same, he vaguely feels that the moral teaching based on these dogmas counts for something in the conduct of his wife and daughter.

'Certainly the bourgeois—whose name is legion—and the same holds true of the peasant—looks on somewhat indifferently at injustices which do not affect him. Certainly too he is no fanatic, and in his view other people's freedom should be fully respected, provided it does not interfere with his own.' [1]

The Trends of Population

From the European as well as from the French point of view, France's demographic situation is a matter of major importance, all the more so because its ups and downs do not as a rule conform to the main European trend. Its fluctuations, closely related to complex moral and psychological factors as well as to social and economical ones, are therefore quite unpredictable by means of sheer statistics. In fact, the history of the last few years has caused demographic experts to reconsider their theories and revise their forecasts.

For the last hundred years or so, France has been held up as the classical example of 'depopulation'—a word often used loosely, for the only actual diminution of the French popu-

[1] *Journal des Débats*, 19 November 1936.

lation occurred between 1936 and 1946, partly as a result of the Second World War. It had become a commonplace to describe France as a 'demographic vacuum in a teeming continent', coupling this with remarks, uncomplimentary or sorrowful, on her irrevocable decadence. A comparison, however, between the census in March 1946 and that in 1953 reveals not only that the population of France was larger in 1953 than at any time of her recorded history, but also that it was growing more rapidly than that of several European countries, including Germany and Italy. Furthermore, this was not the result of massive immigration, but of an increase in the birth-rate.

The trend towards depopulation was in itself comparatively recent. Up to the end of the *ancien régime*, France's demographic situation was characterized by the high fertility of 'young' communities. Families, especially in the provinces, were enormous by modern standards. Fléchier in *Les Grands Jours d'Auvergne*, mentions families of eighteen as being by no means exceptional. Wars, epidemics and infant mortality took a heavy toll, yet France, in 1789, with her twenty-seven million inhabitants, had the largest population of any European country apart from Russia.

The losses sustained during the Revolutionary and Napoleonic wars, though heavy, were spread over twenty years, and do not appear to represent more than an accessory to the slowing down of the rate of reproduction that became apparent in the second half of the nineteenth century, alarming in the first decade of the twentieth.

This decline was relative rather than absolute. The population of France was still growing during the nineteenth century, in spite of the loss of Alsace-Lorraine, but while most European countries registered spectacular increases (Great Britain twenty-six million, Germany thirty-two million, Austria-Hungary twenty-three million, Russia seventy million) France lagged behind, with a modest increase of twelve million. Moreover, while a high birth-rate still prevailed in some regions, particularly Brittany and the North, by 1890, in forty-nine out of eighty-seven departments, the reproduction rate was below and in some cases well below replacement level.

At a time when the threat of depopulation, not caused by poverty or mass emigration, was an exclusively French problem, many reasons were put forward to account for this decline. Revolutionary inspired legislation abolishing primogeniture (*droit d'aînesse*) and dividing inherited property equally between all the children has often been looked upon as explaining the voluntary limiting of families in the rural areas—the 'only son' policy.

It appears more likely, since this phenomenon is not found only in France, that the causes are more complex. Four major factors suggest themselves: (*a*) social, personal and family ambition, a desire for better education, greater comfort and luxury, (*b*) economic—the rush to the town, low wages, shortage of houses, the need for the wife to work away from home, (*c*) political—a certain complacency after the social reform and progress due to the Revolution, and (*d*) psychological and moral—the Malthusian theories, the favourable picture given in books of an existence unhampered by parental responsibility, the attractions of feminine fashion, the adult point of view of a society with little use for children.

The thought of the teeming multitudes beyond the Rhine brought some uneasiness and larger families were encouraged by grants made by the northern industrialists and the *prix Cognacq*. At the turn of the century writers rediscovered the charm of childhood and the moral misery of the unwanted child.

The First World War, with losses of over one million and a half, and with the deficit in births during the war years and after, led to the hollow years (*les années creuses*) so disturbing to the French General Staff and the normal birth-rate was too low to ensure, as in Germany, a rapid recuperation. The recovery of Alsace-Lorraine, the massive immigration of foreign labour, masked for a while this disturbing situation. France's neighbours were still well on the increase while, from 1936 to 1939, there was in France a slight excess of deaths over live births—about thirty thousand per year. Much anxiety was publicly expressed, and a whole series of remedial measures was devised. The *Code de la Famille*, with the aim of relieving the burden of child-bearing and rearing, came into force in 1939; it had not yet had any effect when war broke out.

The French, mindful of the hecatombs of 1914-18, began the Second World War with deep misgivings. Curiously enough, the catastrophes of 1940-44—including the large-scale capturing of soldiers, the transportation of civilians, and general malnutrition—did not have such deplorable consequences as might have been expected. The birth-rate kept up. The infant mortality curve rose, however, and the tuberculosis death-rate among young men. The end of the war brought a striking increase in marriages, with a proportionate increase in birth-rate. The figures for 1953 included five hundred and fifty-five thousand deaths and eight hundred thousand live births, giving a surplus of births higher than that of Italy.

This increase has been attributed to the many social measures in favour of medium to large families; family allowances, increasing with the number of children, health services, tax reliefs, reductions on railways and buses, special discounts in the shops. These measures enable people to marry younger, at the age when fertility and optimism are at their peak. Let us note also that there is a new attitude towards family life: it is the rule, no longer the exception, for young mothers to look after their children instead of sending them away to foster mothers. Whether the present trend will continue is beyond prediction; it is making France a country in which the young will outnumber the old, not one in which the average age is disquietingly increasing.

READING LIST

Curtius, E. R. *Essai sur la France.* Paris, 1932 (Original German edition: *Französische Kultur*, 1930; English translation: *The Civilization of France*, London, 1932). Profound, philosophical approach, illuminating.

Gaultier, P. *L'Ame Française.* Paris, 1936.

Hamerton, P. G. *French and English.* London, 1889. Old fashioned but useful, and pleasantly written.

Huxley, J. S., and Haddon, C. *We Europeans.* London, 1935.
Madariaga, S. de. *Frenchmen, Spaniards, Germans.* London, 1928.
Sieburg, F. *Dieu est-il Français?* Paris, 1931.
Siegfried, A. *Tableau des Partis en France.* Paris, 1930. The first
chapter provides a brilliant analysis of the French character.

C

CHAPTER II

PARIS

FIRST and foremost, Paris is intensely alive. Even the most casual visitor can hardly remain insensitive to that quickening of tempo, that pleasant tingle of excitement, that subtle feeling of expectancy, of half-subdued ebullience which come to him, as it were, with the very air he breathes.

Paris moves neither with the frenzied rush of New York nor with the grim purposefulness of London, but with a rhythm all its own: a swift, irregular, apparently capricious rhythm, now dashing suicidally fast, now idling as leisurely as its own nonchalant river.

Paris is a city of moods. The joyous, light-hearted, champagne-like *griserie* of a fine April morning in the Champs-Élysées, green with new leaves, alive with the purr of expensive cars. The poignant, romantic melancholy of leaden skies and wet autumn twilight in the Luxembourg Gardens, among the russet horse-chestnuts and the white statues, with maybe here and there a couple of lovers sitting on a bench, rapt in each other. The indescribable loveliness of June: sunny, pearly haze, clear blue skies, fresh green leaves, the stone masks of the Pont-Neuf grinning in the sunshine, the silver Seine shimmering at the pointed prow of the Ile de la Cité, and, on the *terre-plein*, the equestrian statue of good King Henry the Fourth, bearded, armoured, with kindly eye and sardonic smile, keeping watch over his city. The ceaseless, hive-like activity in the dark, narrow streets around the *Halles*, the overheard snatches of talk, the good-humoured chat, the sudden vociferous arguments, the hundred and one incidents that make any street-corner in Paris look like the opening shots of a René Clair film. The silent, harassed crowds who jostle in the Métro corridors on their way home at night, and who stand in the packed carriages, swaying, reading, glancing at the headlines over a neighbour's shoulder or just staring into the rushing darkness outside. And always a woman knitting, knitting as for dear life, knitting in the Métro maybe as her great-great-great-grandmother knitted at the Revolutionary Tribunals, listening to Fouquier-Tinville denouncing Marie Antoinette.

And who can forget Paris in grim mood, teeth set, streets menacingly empty, shop-shutters closed and iron curtains down, groups of steel-helmeted police moving warily here and there, and one lone cyclist pedalling furiously, the width of the boulevard all to himself? Or Paris in thanksgiving mood, with the great bells of Notre-Dame booming?

At night, when the Eiffel Tower raises its small ruby head above the evening mists, Paris, seen from above, spreads like a gigantic carpet of lights. Not perhaps as magnificently exotic as the many-coloured tracery which dazzles the onlooker gazing down from the height of Brooklyn Bridge, but rather a carpet of twinkling stardust, sparkling with highlights, darker towards the centre, more brilliant along the brightly lit boulevards which encircle Paris in a girdle of golden throbbing light. Beyond them, another zone of stardust fades gradually into the faraway night, the wooded hills west and south, the open Seine valley eastwards and, northwards, the great, grim, industrial plain of St. Denis.

Paris means more to France than does Washington to the United States, or even London to England. Washington is overshadowed by New York, and London (although there is a trend that way) would not be universally recognized as the intellectual and artistic capital of Great Britain. Paris has no rival as the focus of national life in France. It is three or four times larger than any of the other great cities, and it stands out unmistakably as the political, economic, financial, social, artistic and intellectual capital of a country in which these activities are centralized to a degree as yet unknown elsewhere. The writer and the artist bring the treasures of their provinces to Paris, but success for them means success in Paris. For a civil servant or a *universitaire*, success means ultimately appointment to a post in Paris. Not without reason has it been said that an official or teacher can measure the precise stage he has reached in his advancement simply by counting how many kilometre stones separate him from Paris. Paris, and Paris only, gives the national or international stamp to French values. In some moods, Paris sees itself as the modern counterpart of Imperial Rome, whither all roads lead; at other moments it discerns nearer kinship with Athens, less stiffened with *gravitas* and *pietas* but with more feeling for art and beauty, more cultured and nimbler minded than the Eternal City contrived to be in the ancient world.

What is the secret of the attraction of Paris? What is there in its site or in its climate that has drawn to it all the threads of French life? What made the muddy little island *oppidum* of the Parisii grow into one of the world's capitals? Why did the early Capetian kings and later the Valois dynasty prefer Paris to Senlis, to Soissons or to Laon, all of which were quite as important at the time, or to Bourges, more central and less exposed to invasion?

In Roman times Paris—or rather Lutetia, as it was then named—by no means held first rank among the cities of Gaul. The chief city was Lyons—*Lugdunum*—and to this day the archbishop of Lyons bears the title of 'primat des Gaules'. The fall of the Roman Empire, the great invasions, brought a decline to the supremacy of Lyons. Paris, on the contrary, emerged from the dark ages with an aura of legend. Whether or not it was by divine intercession in the shape of the saintly shepherd-girl, Saint Geneviève, who encouraged the citizens, Paris had held back the hordes of Attila's Huns. Later, under the determined leadership of Robert the Strong, Count of Paris, the island city had successfully beaten off the Norman invaders.

Paris was becoming aware of itself as an entity; the city, more rapidly than any of the other French towns, was developing a collective and very distinct personality: alert, active, gay, quick-witted ('Il n'est bon bec que de Paris' sang François Villon), hard-working, independent, sceptical and *frondeur*. No city ever cheered its kings more lustily; no kings ever had more trouble than the French kings with their capital city: the 'big beast' (as Henry the Fourth called Paris) whose roar put kings' counsellors to flight and whose anger brought down thrones.

More than once invaded by foreign armies, more than once starved into submission, never completely subdued, Paris found new impetus in each crisis but remained basically the same. The French kings kept a wary eye on their capital; most of them resided in Paris from motives of prudence as well as by choice. Louis XIV disliked Paris, its narrow streets and thronging populace: they were an unpleasant reminder of the civil wars of his childhood. He loved open spaces and hunting, and also he was the great-grandson of Philip of Spain, who built the Escorial to live away from Madrid. He built Versailles and forsook Paris. Paris took its revenge a hundred years later by sweeping away king and monarchy.

Three times in the course of the nineteenth century Paris, and Paris alone, again shook off the régime: in 1830, 1848 and 1870. No wonder the Third Republic took no risks. The Second Empire had already cleared mazes of narrow streets in the heart of old Paris, hotbeds of rebellion—a few paving stones and articles of furniture and an overturned cart could turn these quarters into citadels. The Third Republic always garrisoned Paris with provincial, mostly Breton, troops, whose loyalty was never in doubt.

Much of Paris's early prosperity was undoubtedly due to its geographical situation as the centre of a network of waterways. Old prints show the Seine covered with boats. In times when roads were few, bad and unsafe, most of the transport was done by water. Long ago, in Roman times, the watermen formed a corporation important enough to be allowed to build an altar to Jupiter at the prow of the Ile de la Cité. During the Middle Ages the Guild of water-merchants was by far the most powerful of the Parisian trade-guilds. The Master of the Guild was *ex-officio* head of the Paris corporation as Prévost des Marchands, an office which in the course of time became equivalent to that of Mayor of his city. The official seal of the Guild represented a ship, and this seal, used for official documents, explains why the ship appears in the coat of arms of Paris to-day. This ship, with the addition much later of the Latin motto, '*Fluctuat nec mergitur*,' now symbolizes the city's trials and vitality.

Until the seventeenth century, Paris was really governed, for municipal matters, by the Prévost des Marchands, but as the city increased in size the government took away, as early as the fourteenth century, most of his prerogatives. Paris to-day is the only *commune* in France not administered by a mayor. It has, however, a municipal council, and the president of that council is the city's official representative. The usual powers of a mayor are shared between the Prefect of the department of the Seine and the Prefect of Police, both appointed by the government.

Paris has grown enormously since its early days, and it continues to grow. Spreading on both banks of the river, it has burst through line after line of fortifications: the mediaeval turreted wall built by Philip Augustus (now the site of the *grands boulevards*), the eighteenth-century 'tax-collectors' wall' (now the site of the *boulevards extérieurs*). Paris has caught up with the nineteenth-century defences, the *ceinture de forts détachés*. It has absorbed into its ever-expanding circle villages and hamlets which crowned the low hills rising around the magnificent curve described by the Seine near the point at which it is joined by the Marne. Most of them keep a tiny core of old-time life around their church and market-place. Nowadays on the green hills which surround Paris appear swarms of new red-roofed houses. Greater Paris (*l'agglomération parisienne*) casts its net as far as twenty-five miles from the capital. Towards the north, groups of *cités ouvrières* have sprung up, huge modern and unlovely tenements. But the Parisian's ambition, now as ever, is *un pavillon de banlieue*.

The Paris suburbs are entirely different, however, from the London suburbs, where the hall-mark is uniformity: rows and rows of houses exactly alike. Nothing could be more repugnant to the Parisian. For him no advantage in comfort and cheapness could make up for 'l'ennui qui naquit un jour de l'uniformité'. He does not submit very willingly to planning. He wants his house and his patch of garden to be unlike, not like, his neighbour's. These suburbs vary greatly, ranging from the new cheerful modern ones to the older ones of which Utrillo has caught the peaceful, wall-enclosed charm, to the manors and parks of the valley of Chevreuse, to the lovely boat-houses on the banks of the Seine or to the warren of untidy shacks that appear here and there on what is left of the ex-fortified zone. On the fringe of the industrial districts like Puteaux, Pantin, Villeneuve St. Georges there is housing slightly better than in the fortified zone, an intermediate zone of shoddy, mean, ugly tenements, interspersed with garages and *bistros*, but where a few trees, an occasional gravel walk, a few vine-covered arbours, speak of the outlying countryside and redeem some of the ugliness.

Paris is built mostly with the local limestone. Cream-white when new, age ripens it to a faint golden hue, as on the Pont-Neuf; smoke and rain darken it to a blackish grey, as on some parts of the Louvre. Paris, as a matter of fact, is not a colourful city; but there is a subtle harmony between the tints of the stone, the trees, the river, the grey-blue skies of the Ile de France, a harmony that varies according to season, weather and hour, ever tantalizing to painters. It may be noted that the smoke-abatement problem, though undoubtedly less acute than in London, has been tackled with great vigour and efficiency. No smoke-belching is allowed inside the precincts of the capital, and the prevalence of central, gas and electric heating over open fires reduces considerably the amount of smoke daily poured out into the air.

Architecturally, Parisian taste is definitely more sober than that of the French provinces. It bears the double stamp of the stern military architecture of the Middle Ages—of which the towers of the Conciergerie are the best example—and of the purity of the classical line. Compared to Chartres, Rheims or Rouen, Notre-Dame is austere, grave and sedate. The Renaissance architects Pierre Lescot and Du Cerceau, who built part of the Louvre, did not allow their fancy to run riot, as did those who built Blois or Chambord, or the Town Hall in Lyons or the inner façade of Josselin Castle. The classical age believed in keeping ornament strictly subordinate to the general design: witness Perrault's colonnade on the east

façade of the Louvre, the perfect dome which crowns the Invalides, the sober elegance of the Palais Royal, the dignified,
rather austere, ensemble of the Place Vendôme. The eighteenth
century softened this classical severity; it endowed Paris with
some delightful buildings, notably the Palais de l'Elysée, now
the residence of the President of the Republic. It is true that,
after the severe and rather heavy neo-Greek interlude to which
are due the Pantheon, the Madeleine and the façade of the
Palais Bourbon, a more ornate style came into favour under
the Second Empire. The Opéra, with its coloured marble
pillars and the well-known 'Dance' group of statuary by
Carpeaux, is the most striking example of this phase. A shade
soberer already are the Grand Palais and especially the Petit
Palais, both relics of the Exhibition of 1900. With the flamboyant exception of the Pont Alexandre III—of the same
epoch—the thirty bridges of Paris owe their beauty to boldness
of arch and simplicity of design.

The latest important building in Paris, the Palais de Chaillot,
whose severe classical simplicity is relieved by the grace of its
semicircular line, and which replaced in 1927 the much criticized over-ornate Trocadero, illustrates that same trend.
Exuberance finds an outlet in statuary groups, in fountains
and *jets d'eau*, an Italian fashion which found great favour in
France as far back as the sixteenth century.

As for the tall apartment houses, five to seven floors high,
where dwell most of the Paris population, they vary from the
old, narrow-fronted, huddled, shabby slices of tenements, of
which René Clair has popularized the rugged skyline and
fantastic irregularity, to the handsome and dull buildings of
the West End. In many of the most elegant thoroughfares
municipal regulations forbid any departure from the style of
architecture adopted and impose a proportion between the
width of the street and the height of the buildings.

Old Paris, tightly girdled within its walls, had dark, narrow
winding streets, as one can judge from the fact that the Rue
St. Honoré, one of Paris's oldest streets, ranked once as a broad
artery. Although there were many private gardens, Paris had
few open spaces. The largest of these was the old Place de

Grève,[1] now Place de l'Hôtel de Ville, which used to be the site for public executions.

As the town grew—westwards more than eastwards and on the right bank of the Seine more than on the left—attention began to be paid to the provision of broad open spaces and broad vistas that would show up the Paris monuments with greater effect. Such was the case under Louis XIV with the Esplanade des Invalides and under Louis XV with the Place de la Concorde. At an even earlier date, under Henry IV, interesting attempts were made in town-planning, in order to bring some harmony and regularity in that still-crowded, still-mediaeval town. Under Henry IV was planned the regular and pleasing Place Royale, now Place des Vosges, a charming, secluded, now rather forlorn square, surrounded by brick houses all alike, bordered with stone, roofed with blue-grey slates. (It is no paradox to say that while the French dislike uniformity they approve of unity of plan.) Contemporary with the houses of the Place des Vosges, some thirty houses, all conforming by order to the same pattern, were constructed on either side of the Pont-Neuf. Louis XIV, although he did not like Paris, took pains to embellish his capital. To him are due not only the Invalides but the circular Place Vendôme, with its mansions all of the same pattern, dignified, graceful, rather austere. The Place des Victoires, not dissimilar, belongs to the same period. To Louis XV is due the grandiose ensemble of the Place de la Concorde, with its twin palaces now the Hôtel Crillon and the Ministère de la Marine.

Napoleon found time to continue and sometimes to bring to fruition the work of his predecessors the French kings. He finished, for instance, the Palace of the Louvre. To him Paris owes, among other things, the Italianate Rue de Rivoli, with its perspective of arched galleries stretching from the Louvre to the Place de la Concorde. To him also Paris owes the magnificent vista spreading downwards and then upwards from the Tuileries to the Arc de Triomphe, that H. G. Wells called 'the noblest and most graceful perspective'. It is also the most

---

[1] Where men who were out of work used to congregate: hence the expression *être en grève*.

deceptive, as everyone who tries to walk from the Tuileries to the Arc de Triomphe may discover rather ruefully.

The most thorough changes in the aspect of the capital were, however, carried out under Napoleon III by Baron Haussmann. He swept away a maze of ancient streets and alleys and drove broad and straight avenues in all directions. To him Paris owes also the twelve avenues radiating from the Place de l'Etoile and those fanning out from the Opéra. Though much of the ancient and picturesque Paris thus disappeared, the city gained many majestic vistas in which every avenue leads to some impressive monumental structure. The Third and Fourth Republics, mostly for reasons of public health, have cleared away many 'îlots insalubres', often against stiff opposition on the part of the Commission of Historical Monuments. Under the Third Republic rose the white oriental dome of the Sacré-Cœur basilica which, from the height of Montmartre, looks down on the city. The various Exhibitions held within the last seventy years each left some monument as a souvenir: the Eiffel Tower (long reviled as an eyesore, and now part and symbol of Paris), the Grand Palais, the Museum of Modern Art and the Palais de Chaillot.

The slum problem in Paris remains serious, although the public powers and private organizations have between them made great efforts to reduce it. (The cartoonist Poulbot, with his humorous and poignant sketches of 'l'enfance malheureuse' did a good deal to awaken public consciousness and to help the efforts of the Anti-Slum League.) The situation is made worse by the great number of North African labourers whose standard of living is low, who, most of them, live in extremely wretched conditions and who, except for the fact that they do not usually bring their families with them, present a problem not unlike the Irish problem in Glasgow and Liverpool at the beginning of this present century.

Traffic—that headache of municipal and police authorities the world over—is traditionally fast in Paris. At peak hours, that is about noon, and again between four and eight in the evening, the main thoroughfares are streams of shining cars, six, eight or even twelve deep, alternatively stopped by the traffic lights to allow a spurt of hurrying pedestrians across the road, and urged on by the *agent's* white truncheon. As a preventive to traffic jams, Paris believes in speed. 'Get a move on!' the truncheon seems to say. 'Step on it, man! Don't block the way!' There seems to be no speed-limit in Paris, but as a matter of fact there is one: 60 kilometres per hour. (A story is told of a Parisian *agent* borrowed by Oslo to help organize traffic in the Norwegian capital and whose presence resulted, to his utter dismay, in the worst traffic jam of all, half the town having turned up to see the performance.)

A great deal of research, including helicopter surveys of the most crowded points, has been devoted to the control of traffic, to which new modes of transport—the motor-scooter for instance—bring every day a new problem. Every device has been put into action to ensure that traffic is fast and safe: traffic platforms, white cape, white képi, white gloves for the *agent*; crossing lights for the pedestrians, traffic lights for the cars. Some traffic lights are worked by hand, since, in the opinion of Paris traffic authorities, purely automatic time-control is a powerful factor in slowing down traffic and increasing the number of accidents. On the right bank of the Seine and along the Rue de Rivoli, however, traffic lights are controlled by a most ingenious robot, which synchronizes them according to indications given by a traffic meter. At the Préfecture de Police, on a huge plan of Paris, red, amber and green lights appear at the same instant as they appear all over the city, thus enabling the experts to judge, at any given time, the condition of the traffic.

Less majestic than his British counterpart, the Parisian *agent*, in his familiar cape and képi with his white truncheon, is equally efficient and helpful. It is impressive to see him patiently listening to the bemused provincial or foreigner, having courteously touched his képi with two fingers, his eye on the traffic, his left arm extended, controlling a surge of impatient cars.

G. B. Shaw was once asked by a Parisian journalist what struck him most in Paris. He answered that it was its provincialism. The journalist was nonplussed—as he was meant to be. Yet Shaw's paradox had some measure of justification, and there are moments when the Parisian, weary of life at high tension, turns with relief to some of the delightfully provincial corners in Paris: age-worn, sun-ripened stones, trees and peace. The Place Dauphine, the Ile Saint-Louis with its seventeenth-century mansions, its charming, quiet, tree-lined quays, some streets in Montmartre, or the Place Saint-Sulpice with its Jesuit church, its dim shops filled with *objets de piété*, an occasional cassocked figure flitting discreetly across the square.

The Ile de la Cité, cradle of Paris, although by-passed by the modern rush, yet escapes provincialism. It still holds the keys to the life of the capital. The old island stronghold of the early Capetian kings, now the Conciergerie with its neighbouring Law Courts, its northern façade grimly mediaeval, holds in one of its towers the cell in which Marie Antoinette was imprisoned. Above the Law Courts rises the lovely spire of the Sainte-Chapelle. This mass of buildings contains both the centre of legal life in Paris and the headquarters of the city police (the Quai des Orfèvres being the French equivalent of Scotland Yard).

On the island, too, stand the great buildings of the Hôtel-Dieu, the oldest and most revered of all Paris hospitals (the present building is comparatively modern, but the foundation goes back far into the early Middle Ages). Most impressive of all is the immense bulk of Notre-Dame, with its flying buttresses, its gargoyles and its forest of statuary, its west front with the Last Judgment in speaking images, its background of trees and greenery, and, inside, amidst the awesome gloom of its immense nave, the rays of purple, golden and crimson light which filter through the great rose-windows.

One of the secrets of the attraction of Paris is its diversity or rather its multiplicity. There are, as it were, several circles, superimposed, slightly overlapping, but quite distinct one from another. To the businessman the centre of Paris is the Bourse and its surrounding districts, a hive of commercial and industrial activity. To the statesman or politician it is the Palais Bourbon, the Luxembourg, the Quai d'Orsay. To the elegant society woman it is the Place Vendôme and the Rue

de la Paix, with their *haute couture* salons. To the tourist it is
the Opéra district, stiff with travel agencies, strident with
invitations to see Paris by day or Paris by night and offers to
unfold to innocent eyes from Wigan or Connecticut the
elaborate frivolities of the Folies-Bergère as well as the architectural treasures of the capital—a good alibi these, say the
knowing. To the theatre-goer it is the State-subsidized
repertory theatres: 'Opéra', 'Comédie Française', 'Salle du
Luxembourg', 'le Palais du Chaillot' the public of which presents
a very good cross-section of the Parisian population, or else the
other theatres—ranging from the highly cultural 'Atelier' to the
lighter and more spectacular historical shows of the 'Châtelet'.
The ordinary public is fond of revues, generally satirical, of
comédies de mœurs, of operettes, with, now and again, from a
sense of duty or 'for the children', *Athalie* or *Le Cid*.

To the scholar, to the scientist, to the historian, to the
student the centre of Paris is the *quartier latin*. In the world
there are many Universities, but only one *quartier latin*. It
occupies most of the left bank of the Seine up to the hill of St.
Geneviève, where once rose the palaces, the thermae, the
fountains and the temples of Gallo-Roman Lutetia. It is not,
however, to these vestiges of antiquity that it owes its name,
but to the fact that Latin was in the Middle Ages the language
of professors and students.

It contains not only the University of Paris, the Sorbonne,
(founded about 1250 by Robert de Sorbon, chaplain to
Louis IX, the saintly king and crusader), but some of the
Grandes Ecoles, research institutes and laboratories, the Collège
de France, the Institut and several libraries, including the
Bibliothèque Sainte-Geneviève, the Bibliothèque de la Sorbonne, and a little distance away, at the Institut, the Bibliothèque Mazarine. (The greatest of the Paris libraries, the
Bibliothèque Nationale, stands on the right bank, not very far
from the Comédie Française.)

The *quartier latin* provides the centre of French intellectual
life, abreast of scientific discoveries (the Centre de Recherche
Scientifique is housed there) but kept above inhuman techni-
cality by a long humanist and artistic tradition of culture.

It attracts students and scholars not only from every corner
of France but from every country in the world. At midday
and at dusk, its main artery the Boulevard Saint-Michel (le
Boul' Mich') all cafés and bookshops, is thronged with students:
longish-haired, pale, eager-faced youths, and short-haired
betrousered girls now sucked into the lecture-theatres of the
near-by Sorbonne, now pouring in crowds into the adjacent
streets towards the reading-room of the St. Geneviève Library,
towards the Luxembourg Gardens, towards inexpensive
students' restaurants, *pensions* and hostels.   They hail from
Europe, America, Africa, Asia.   A fortunate minority lives
at the *Cité Universitaire*, near the Porte d'Orléans, where
many countries have built for their nationals hostels in the
style, traditional or modern, of their own country.   The Cité
Universitaire provides for students a restaurant, public rooms,
a theatre, a ballroom, sports grounds and a library, the whole
set among green lawns and tree-planted gardens.

   To the north, across the Seine, on the outer rim of Paris,
rises another hill crowned with the white cupolas of a majestic
church: Montmartre. The name of Montmartre suggests nowadays the gaudy glitter of night clubs, the popping of champagne corks, and the crowds of bemused tourists whose chara-'
bancs, equipped with loudspeakers ('See Paris by night'),
crawl along the Place Pigalle.

   Montmartre—Mons Martyrum, the mount of martyrs, thus
named because it witnessed, according to legend, the martyrdom, among others, of St. Denis, patron saint of Paris—was
until some time in the last century a green hill crowned with
windmills, with a straggling village, orchards and a charming
old church.   Vineyards grew on its southern slope; one of
them survives as a local curiosity.   Parisians were wont to come
on Sundays to eat the 'galette' baked by the miller's wife and
drink the harmless local wine.   The ramshackle picturesqueness of Montmartre attracted impecunious artists in quest of
cheap lodgings, since artists were deprived of the free quarters
which the benevolent despotism of the eighteenth century had
granted to so many in the Louvre.   Montmartre gradually
became the centre of artistic and bohemian life.   The local

pot-houses were transformed into artistic cabarets and the renown of some of the artists drew to the *Chat Noir* or to the *Lapin Agile* the intelligentsia, the snobs and, later, fashionable society. These one-time cabarets have since become highly commercialized. They are night clubs calculated to bring a blush to the Anglo-Saxon cheek and to charm money out of South American pockets.

By that time most of the artists had packed up their easels and palettes and moved off to find a more congenial atmosphere on another hill. This time they chose their hill on the left bank: Montparnasse. Years ago their favourite café was the *Rotonde*, then a very ordinary Parisian café, but its walls were covered with canvases allegedly painted by customers and offered for sale. The motley crowd of artists and models who frequented the place were themselves its most picturesque element.

But even there the tourists have followed them from their former haunts. So they go on, playing hide-and-seek. There must be as many painters as there are students in Paris—tens of thousands of them. The man or the woman with an easel is such an everyday sight there that even street urchins hardly bother to look at his or her best efforts. It is easy to see what makes the atmosphere of Paris so congenial to artists: the numerous art galleries, the informality of life, the beauty or picturesqueness that surrounds them if they have but eyes to see, and, not least, the feeling of intellectual stimulation. Not all have any claim to be great or successful artists. Among those who do not succeed either in expressing themselves or in selling their pictures, many, after some grim years of *vache enragée*, will turn to a more profitable occupation, others will not abdicate and will persist and become old Bohemians, unsuccessful and impecunious, like decayed aristocrats who cling to their title.

To-day the intellectual throb of the capital makes itself felt most noticeably in the district that surrounds the old church of St. Germain-des-Prés. There congregate the existentialists, the futurist painters, the be-boppers, the adolescents with intellectual pretensions. The unofficial centre is a very bourgeois-looking café: *Le Café de Flore*. Already so many inquisitive visitors have crowded there, feasting their eyes on the sight of Jean-Paul Sartre thinking or Simone de Beauvoir writing, that it looks as if the history of Montmartre and Montparnasse may repeat itself a third time in St. Germain-des-Prés.

'Il y a deux peuples en France,' wrote Taine in 1863, 'la province et Paris, l'un qui dîne, dort, bâille, écoute; l'autre qui pense, ose, veille et parle; le premier traîné par le second, comme un escargot par un papillon, tour à tour amusé et inquiété par les caprices et l'audace de son conducteur.' This was no doubt partly true when Taine, himself a provincial, wrote it. But how far is the alleged divorce between Paris and the provinces a present-day reality?

Certainly the prestige of Paris in the provinces is enormous, for Paris ranks as the place where the rhythm of life is faster, competition fiercer, minds nimbler, life smarter and success more exalting. Other things being equal, the doctor from Paris, the lawyer from Paris, are, in the provinces, the object of the same reluctant consideration as, in English crime novels, the detective from Scotland Yard among the local constabulary. Also, Paris not only functions as the hub of French life, but has an international prestige, as one of the world's capitals. The seat of countless international conferences, Paris entertains, and knows how to entertain, foreign royalties and statesmen, and, in that respect, no other French city can compete.

On the other hand, those Parisians who, according to Taine, do the thinking and the daring are mostly ex-provincials. Only some thirty-five per cent. of the Parisians were born in Paris (and it is not among the authentic Parisians that one finds the tendency to ridicule or despise the provincials). It has even been affirmed that no family living in Paris survives beyond the third generation. Consequently, if this be true, Paris only persists because it draws continually new energy from the provinces. It is both the crucible and the fireworks of France.

The gap between Paris and the provinces described by

A French Family

Place de la Concorde by Night

Taine has also to some extent been diminished because of the ease and rapidity of modern transport.

The capital gives back to the provinces, in activity and stimulus, some of the strength derived from them. Many a remote province owes some great scheme, on a national scale, to the engineer from the Ecole Polytechnique; some improvement in activity to the Prefect from Paris.

The stimulating influence felt in the most remote provinces may sometimes develop a counter-movement against the uniformity which might result from too servile an adulation of the capital. The *député* who goes back to his constituency has to swallow some home truths as well as *vins d'honneur*. Regionalism, first a literary and artistic movement, has become in many places concrete reality as regards economic life. The main towns take some pains to assert and confirm that they are not mere satellites.

The capital, on the whole, has lent itself with very good grace to these manifestations of provincial vitality and originality. Paris loves, in turn, Breton or Provençal or Burgundian furniture, organizes festivals of provincial dance and song; it applauded *Mireille* at a time when the Arlesian national costume was already dying out and when *provençal* had let itself be degraded almost to the level of a *patois*. Parisian readers devour Mauriac's novels of the Landes and Colette's memories of Burgundy. Paris does not fear any competition, knowing that with one turn or twist of fancy it will set a new fashion and be ahead of them all. That is Paris, bubbling with new ideas, some good and some bad, Paris, gay, confident, sometimes over-confident, very old and ever young, sceptical and enthusiastic, iconoclastic and traditionalist. The poet Charles Péguy visualized the symbolic struggle of Paris as a majestic galley in which:

> Nos pères ont tenté le centuple hasard,
> Fidèlement courbés sur les rames obliques.
>
> Et nous, prenant leur place au même banc de chêne,
> Nous ramerons des reins, de la nuque, de l'âme,
> Pliés, cassés, meurtris, saignants sous notre chaîne;

D

Et nous tiendrons le coup, rivés à notre rame,
Forçats fils de forçats aux deux rives de Seine,
Galériens couchés aux pieds de Notre-Dame.

READING LIST

Cohen-Portheim, P. *The Spirit of Paris.* London, 1937.
Danzat, A. and Boumon, F. *Paris et ses environs.* Paris, 1928.
Demangeon, A. *Paris, la ville et sa banlieue.* Paris, 1934.
MacOrlan. *Voyages de Paris* (Ed. Nouvelle, France). Paris, 1954.
Poete, M. *Une vie de cité*, 3 vols. Paris, 1924-7.
Raval, M. *Histoire de Paris.* Paris, 1941.

Some recent books which give pictures of Paris are: *Paris tel qu'on l'aime* (Guide Odé); Cali, *Sortilèges de Paris* (an album of photographs published by Arthaud) and *Paris toujours* (published by Alpina).

CHAPTER III

FRANCE: THE COUNTRY

SOME years ago, a springtime whim of Parisian fashion filled for a few weeks the jewel-trays of the smart arcade-shops of the Rue de Rivoli with hundreds of tiny 'charms', six-pointed, star-shaped, made of gold, enamel or silver.

On closer inspection, the six-pointed shape turned out to be that of France, complete even to such details as the tongue-like projection of Givet on the Belgian frontier, opposite to the Cotentin peninsula on the Channel coast, a France cut loose from her continental moorings, France turned into an island—many a Frenchman's wistful dream. Holding it in the hollow of one's hand, one could visualize the long, lazy curve of the Loire, the meanders of the Seine, the almost arrow-straight course of the Rhône, the sharp bend of the Garonne. One could run the tip of one's finger along the edge of the long coast-line, from the grim, bleak North Sea shore to the Pyrenean cliffs of St. Jean de Luz, from Port-Vendres on the Mediterranean to the orange gardens of Mentone. For the mind's eye there would arise the azure barrier of the Pyrénées, the Alpine peaks, the forest-clad Vosges and the thick central knot of old mountains where the Gauls once held up for a while the advancing march of the Roman Legions.

Ancient Gaul extended over the whole area comprised between the Pyrenees, the Alps and the Rhine. Modern France occupies approximately five-sixths of that territory. Although she belongs to Western Europe, she is linked with Northern Europe by the North Sea routes and with Southern Europe by her Mediterranean fringe. Her eastern frontier is firmly wedged into Central Europe as if to balance the western peninsula of Brittany, flung like an arm into the Atlantic Ocean.

Before the construction of tunnels under the Alps, France afforded the easiest and shortest route between Northern and Western Europe and the Mediterranean. The discovery of America, the colonization of French West Africa, gave French

Atlantic ports their opportunity. Marseilles, the gateway to the East, assumed its full importance after the Frenchman Ferdinand de Lesseps had cut the Suez Canal in 1869. France, by her situation, is a turn-table between north and south, east and west.

Indeed, with the exception of her north-eastern frontier, the symmetry of her land-frontiers and sea-coasts seems so clearly to have been preordained by nature, there is such equal balance between hill and plain, such happy variety of climates, soil and production, that one is tempted to attribute such drawbacks as comparative scarcity of harbours, insufficient mineral resources, lack of protection from the north-east, to oversights by an otherwise bountiful Providence.

Reality is more complex. After all, France and her civilization existed long before she reached her present boundaries. It took, in fact, more than a thousand years—from the Treaty of Verdun in 843 to the acquisition of Nice and Savoy in 1860 —to reconstitute modern France out of the crazy jig-saw puzzle left in Western Europe by the breakdown of Charlemagne's Frankish Empire.

The geography of France is thus inseparably linked with her history. Nature gave her diversity, but her symmetry and her unity are the work of man.

This underlying unity goes very far back. Pre-Roman Gaul was a confederation of clans and peoples linked by kinship, language, customs and religion. Gallo-Roman civilization, with the help of the Christian Church, had struck such deep roots that even the great Germanic invasion of the fifth century could not obliterate it. Admittedly, it had worn rather thin at the edges; it had even practically disappeared in the north-east of Gaul, under the repeated onslaughts of the barbarians.

A linguistic map of Western Europe, showing the French-speaking zones outside France, illustrates this point. It is probably why, although the French kings never lost sight of the frontiers of Gaul as being France's natural and legitimate frontiers, France has never been able to establish herself permanently on the left bank of the Rhine, except in Alsace. Hence the insufficiency of mineral resources, since coal is mostly on the Belgian and German side of the border. Hence also the lack of protection to the north-east. Incidentally, it is to the most frivolous of her kings, Louis XV, that France owes one of her weightiest present-day economical assets: Lorraine and its fields of iron-ore.

In some subtle way, and in spite of much diversity, nature contributes to blend all parts of France into one distinct entity. There is not much, at first sight, to distinguish the chalk cliffs of Normandy from the English cliffs opposite, except their facing north-west instead of south; there is little, if any, difference between the French Northern Plain and the Belgian Plain, the French Alps and the Swiss Alps, yet the French landscape has a distinct quality of its own. One could not mistake even a green and hazy woodland scene of the Ile de France for an English landscape any more than one could mistake a Corot for a Constable. For one thing, the colour is not quite the same—moisture, ever present under an English sky, lends to colours a sharpness, an intensity, a richness of undertones, even sometimes an acidity, unknown in a drier atmosphere. The green of English grass hurts French eyes, and English eyes find French foliage a dull green. In the French landscape, light is more intense, colours more subdued, contours more firmly delineated.

On the other hand, with the exception of the sunny Côte d'Azur, sheltered by the Maures and the Esterel hills, one rarely finds in Southern France the crystal-like purity of the true Mediterranean sky, nor has the vegetation the *élégance un peu sèche* of the Southern European climes. In spite of the brilliant sunshine, the southern slope of the Massif Central and of the Alps retains a frequent mistiness of the atmosphere, an occasional darkening of rain-clouds, a more than frequent cold blast from the north, which make all the difference between the Provençal and the Italian landscape.

Geology

The form of France, her plains and mountain range, is the result of two main geological events. Foldings in the Primary age gave the ancient granite of the Vosges, the Ardennes, Brittany and the Massif Central—those mountains, worn and rounded by erosion, nowhere reach great heights. In Brittany, where erosion has been most severe, no summit rises higher than 1,400 feet.

The Pyrénées and the Alps, as well as the Jura mountains, arose in the Tertiary period, and owe to this comparative youth their greater altitudes and sharper outlines.

At the beginning of the Quaternary period there was intense volcanic activity in the Massif Central, where approximately 480 craters poured lava over the surrounding country. The numerous hot mineral-springs in the centre of France to-day bear witness to this terrifying prehistoric crisis.

Even these geological upheavals showed, in the phrase of the ancient geographer Strabo, 'intelligent anticipation'. They left plains and valleys, and also clefts to serve as highways between one region and another. The plains are covered with the thick slime deposited by the prehistoric seas or carried by the rushing waters of the Quaternary. Some are extremely fertile, the great northern plain, the plain of Beauce (France's granary), the Berry, the Languedoc, the valleys of the Rhône and of its tributary the Saône, etc.

Climate

Mediaeval poets sang of 'la douce France'—Du Bellay in his exile, longed for 'la douceur angevine'. Indeed, in those pleasant lands which formed the heart of ancient France, Touraine, Anjou, Ile de France, Vendômois, the sweetness of the air, the serenity of the sky mirrored in the gently flowing rivers, the brilliant yet not oppressive sunshine unite with the smiling landscape in that 'douceur', the memory of which wrung the poet's heart.

All France is not 'douce', however, nor always sunny or fertile for that matter—many regions are barren and uninhabited: the lower Alps, the plateau of Lannemezan in the south-west, arid, scorched by the sun and beaten by a relentless wind. France officially enjoys seven climates (eight according to Larousse), a fact all the more interesting since the country covers only one-eighteenth of the land space in Europe (530,000 square kilometres). In the western part of France the mild Atlantic climate, with its soft rains and warm winds, tempers the rigours of the winter and the heat of the summer. Some parts of Brittany enjoy an almost Mediterranean warmth in spite of their latitude—camellias, oleanders, and other southern shrubs thrive; Breton strawberries are ripe three weeks before those near Paris. In sheltered gardens, on the coastal zone of Vendée, it is not uncommon to see full-grown palm-trees.

As one travels eastwards, the climate becomes more continental, drier, with increasing extremes of heat and cold— Ushant, the most western of French Islands, has, in all, four days of frost per year, Nancy in Lorraine, although on the same latitude, has over ninety and Nice on the Côte d'Azur, fifteen. On the other hand, in the record of extreme temperatures published daily by the French meteorological bureau, Strasbourg and Belfort at the extreme eastern point as often as not top the list in summer, with temperatures equal to and sometimes higher than those of Perpignan in the south or of Algiers. The Parisian climate is half-way between the western and the continental: drier than Brittany, milder than Lorraine, extremely variable. The climate of the mountain districts is hard and extreme: the Mediterranean climate is warm, and dry on the coast. Inland, the valley of the Rhône is swept in winter by cold blasts of the north wind: the 'mistral'; springs are warm, summers hot and dry.

France has four main rivers—only one of which, the Seine, is entirely navigable. There is a very extensive network of waterways: rivers and canals. As everywhere else, the competition of the railways has been felt very severely by water transport—yet one sees many barges, single or in convoy, especially in the north and the east. Of late, the rising railway freight charges have brought some revival of this form of transport for heavy goods.

Each of these rivers drains a very large basin—the Seine is the most regular, although it is occasionally subject to

spectacular rises in the spring, when the Aisne from Lorraine
and the Yonne from the Morvan hills pour a spate of swollen
waters into her placid stream. The Loire is the longest of
French rivers (1,010 kilometres) and also the most irregular.
In summer, its lazy stream drags amidst sandbanks; in autumn,
it may rise in a few days to a mile-wide sheet of fast-flowing
grey water, sweeping away the riverside dams, flooding the
fields far and wide. For that reason, the towns bordering the
Loire are more often built on the right bank which is higher.
The Garonne is a torrential river from the Pyrénées; the Rhône
springs from an Alpine glacier and makes its way south, through
the Lake of Geneva, and through spectacular gorges between
which it even disappears from sight for a while. Both rivers rise
considerably in spring, when the mountain snows melt, and their
glacier-green water turns, in spate, to a muddy café-au-lait.
The Rhône is regulated to some extent by its main tributary,
the placid, smooth-flowing Saône—its other tributaries are as
fierce and torrential as the Rhône itself.

The Seine, the Loire and the Garonne end in broad estuaries
—the estuary of the Garonne (known as *Gironde*) and that of the
Loire, although they have to be continually dredged, provide
deep and safe harbours. Not so the estuary of the Seine, where
the current, meeting the advancing tide, gives rise to a tidal wave
known as the *mascaret*. Le Havre lies at the extreme entrance of
the estuary, but Rouen, the most important of French ports after
Marseilles, is some distance upstream. As for the Rhône, it
ends by dividing to form a broad delta enclosing a plain, the
Camargue, where wild bulls and horses still roam, and where
pink flamingoes come to rest on inland lochs. There is no port
at either of the mouths of the Rhône—Marseilles is a little
further east, a fine natural harbour dominated by rising
ground.

In many parts of France, particularly in the plains, the
porous nature of the surface soil accounts for the scarcity of
surface water. Wells, sometimes as deep as 200 feet, have to be
sunk to reach subterranean water. Where the surface is clay,
water stagnates, as in marshy, wooded Sologne. In the
Vosges, the Alps, the Pyrénées, water gushes everywhere. In

many cases it has been harnessed to provide hydraulic or electric power, which makes up to a considerable extent for the insufficiency of France's coal resources.

As in most countries of Western and Southern Europe, indiscriminate deforestation carried on for centuries has seriously altered the flow of the rivers. Gaul was covered with forests, mainly oak. A fifth of these forests remain, many of them State property. A great effort of reafforestation has been made within the last fifty years in order to combat erosion in the Southern Alps and in the Southern Massif Central. The French, as a rule, do not go in very much for quick returns; they prefer, to the planting of quick-growing conifers, the traditional type of mixed forest, mostly hardwood, which is not to be felled wholesale, but to be rationally exploited.

Variety in crops is also characteristic of the French countryside: wheat, vines, beet, potatoes, garden produce, orchard and forest. In the north there is a predominance of sugar-beet and oil-seeds, such as colza; flax is also extensively grown, both for seed and for fibre, but a good deal of the land is wheat land. The plain of Beauce is entirely given over to wheat, and parts of Languedoc to vine-growing. The valley of the Rhône is rich in orchards and the coastal zone of the Mediterranean in olive-trees, while Normandy in spring is a dream vision of rosy apple-blossom. Early fruit and vegetable growing has acquired a considerable importance, mostly in Brittany, and in the south of France. Roscoff in Brittany, Perpignan in the Eastern Pyrénées and Salon in Provence are the principal headquarters of this trade—garden produce intended mostly for Paris or for export.

Wheat, the most important crop, is cultivated more or less all over France. The national index of production to the square kilometre is not as high as in America or England, the reason being that, since bread is the staple article of French diet, wheat is cultivated in all sorts of soils: some on which the yield is very high, as in Beauce; some where it is quite low, as in Brittany and in the mountainous districts. Wine is the next crop in order of importance; it is produced south of a line from the mouth of the Loire to Givet in the Ardennes.

It ranges from the aristocratic *crus*: champagne, burgundy, to the homely and home-made *piquette*.

Most French soil is owned by peasants. In the few regions where monoculture prevails, large estates are the rule and modern methods of culture and storage are widely applied. Traditionalism remains firmly rooted, and the lone plough-man, with his team of horses or, as in Auvergne, of tawny-gold oxen, is still the predominant figure in the French countryside. Much criticism has been levelled at the peasant's routine and conservatism. But even from the purely economic point of view, peasant-tilled land can, in the long run, hold its own with land farmed by the more exhaustive modern processes. It does not become a dust-bowl. French land which has fed many generations is still in good heart, and ready to feed many more. The crux of the matter is that the peasant loves his land. To him, land is not just wealth to be mined, something to be exploited until it is exhausted, it is something alive, to be jealously cared for, cherished, increased if possible, and handed down to his children and to his children's children.

Variety of crops is to some extent forced on the small land-owner. If his hay crop fails, he may recoup himself on wheat, or wine, or failing that, on potatoes and garden produce, or on eggs and butter—also, it allows him to spread his labour over the whole year. This explains the variegated aspect of French countryside. In the north, where there are few hedges, the landscape, viewed from the air, presents the well-known 'sample-card' effect. Elsewhere, the effect is varied and pleasant.

Everyone who has travelled in France is familiar with the long stretches of straight, tree-lined roads. Some of them, although modern and tarred, are really old Roman roads. They all converge on Paris, from north, south, east and west, trundled over day and night by heavy, six or eight wheeled lorries. Road transport has in the last quarter of a century become an increasingly serious rival to railway transport. Railways fight this competition as best they can. On long-distance heavy transport they still hold their own; they have modernized their equipment, put into service passenger trains faster than any car (the 'Mistral', on the Paris to Lyons route, is one of the fastest if not the fastest train in the world). Many lines are electrified and the lines with a small amount of traffic are supplied with economical diesel railcars.

Villages

The aspect of French villages varies very much according to the region, to the climate and also according to the abundance or scarcity of water. In regions where water is scarce, as in the north or in Berry, or in the south, all houses congregate round the well or wells, or fountain. Where water is abundant, the houses straggle more and are surrounded with gardens, and there are numbers of isolated farms and hamlets.

American townships are built round the petrol pump and the bank office. Scottish villages are stretched along the roadside between the two rival kirks. French villages crowd round their church, whose spire rises above the huddled roofs, as if to watch and guard the flock. Some of these churches are very ordinary, some are surprisingly beautiful. In Brittany, as you enter the village you find a carved-stone Calvary depicting the scene of the Crucifixion. The market-place, the Mairie, the boys' school, the girls' school, and, in the smallest village, the memorial to the village dead in the 1914-18 war, some a plain stele, some ugly, some commonplace, all impressive and moving by the number of names of the young men who did not come back.

The style of house construction is influenced by the climate, as well as by the local materials. In the north, where stone and wood are scarce, most of the buildings are of brick. In Alsace and in the parts of Normandy where stone is scarce but wood plentiful, picturesque half-timbered houses abound. The peasant house in Brittany is low, built of granite blocks, often white-washed and thatched. The white limestone of the Loire valley and of the Parisian region, the yellow freestone of the Rhône valley, the white marble of the Pyrénées, the black lava of South Auvergne contribute to give to each of these regions their particular aspect. Roofs, high and pointed in the north, become progressively flatter as one travels south; the fine blue or purplish slate, the small flat Northern tile, are gradually replaced by the large rounded Roman tile. French towns are not very large by British or American standards— Paris with its 4,000,000 is by far the largest. Marseilles comes second and Lyons third.

The Regions

France was formerly divided into provinces. Under the *ancien régime* there was no forcible attempt at uniformization. The provinces kept their own individuality, their customs and costumes, their own weights and measures, their own dialects.

The French Revolution established a much more centralized form of government, abolished the province system and broke up the provinces into departments. Yet, in spite of the new division, aimed at breaking their oft-rebellious individuality, the provinces survived—their names, banned from official language, came back into daily use during the First World War. Through the communiqués the names of Artois, Flanders, Picardy, Champagne returned from their political exile, and also the names of *pays* (districts) such as Argonne, Wœvre, which the French themselves no longer knew, except locally. The reason why the General Staff had kept the old appellations was that they corresponded to a definite physical, and therefore strategic unit, while the department, an artificial creation, did not.

The least picturesque region of France, and also the richest, is no doubt the great northern plain, which extends, only slightly broken by the hills of Picardy, from Paris to the Belgian frontier. The landscape is monotonous—immense fields of cereals and sugar-beet, pasture-land cut up into squares by ditches. Thick, sticky, yellow soil. Here and there a clump of trees with a slightly forlorn château mirrored in the still waters. Towns of antiquity and ancient wealth, with ornate buildings denoting the neighbourhood of Spanish Flanders, Arras, Amiens, Douai. Further north, grim industrial and mining districts, long lines of workmen's houses, factory chimneys belching smoke, all that under dull skies and frequent rain. Flax, woollens, cottons, and, more recent growths, metallurgy, chemicals, glassworks, breweries, sugar-refineries—Lille, Roubaix, Tourcoing with their textiles; Lens, Douai, Valenciennes with their mines, provide much of the material of French industry. This plain, ravaged again and again by invaders, recovers every time, and becomes again a hive of industry, a sort of monument of what man can do, if he has the heart and the obstinate will, to make the best of a soil once very marshy, an unattractive climate, and the recurring devastation of war.

The Parisian basin, like the London basin, was once the bed of a sea. The area of this basin is about a quarter of that of France. Apart from the chalky cliffs of Champagne, there are no real heights, only pleasant rolling countryside, with gentle hills, often wooded—the whole region is linked by a close network of canals and rivers. The tall, slim, graceful poplars, whose roots love water, rise everywhere; screens of poplars are mirrored in the canals, poplar alleys lead up to an eighteenth-century château; poplars line the paved highroad, the ancient 'pavé du roi', so hard on modern tyres, which one still finds here and there around Paris.

Around Paris lies the Ile de France, an island in the sense that an escarpment eight hundred feet high, the cliffs of Champagne, protects it on the eastern side. It is round this province, the cradle of the French monarchy, that the rest of the provinces crystallized during the centuries that went to the making of Modern France. Apart from Paris itself, and its belt of industrial suburbs, this part of France is agricultural, with peaceful old towns and charming old stone bridges. East and slightly north lies Champagne, with its old provincial capital, Rheims, whose cathedral, the masterpiece of flamboyant Gothic art, was severely damaged during the First World War. Rheims is the centre of the champagne wine trade. The secret of the manufacture of this sparkling wine is said to be the exact proportion of the mixture of wine coming from Epernay, Ai, Sillery and other districts. The wine is left for five years to mature in the immense galleried cellars hewn out of the chalky

cliffs. Further east lies a desolate plain, with here and there
a flock of sheep, and an old shepherd wrapped in his thick
woollen cape.

To the north stretches the plateau of the Ardennes, a wild
tangle of marsh and forest, with canyon-like valleys and fast,
cold rivers. Further to the east lies Lorraine, a rough and
austere region. Yet, here and there in the valleys, wheat, hops
and vines prosper; the plum orchards of Lorraine are famous,
and the red-currant jelly made in the town of Bar has more
than local repute. Spinning and weaving have long been
staple industries, but her real and grim wealth is her fields of
iron-ore; the richest deposit in Europe lies around Briey,
Longwy and Nancy, a zone of smelting furnaces.

Nancy, the ancient capital of Lorraine, was very much
embellished in the eighteenth century by the last Duke of
Lorraine, Stanislas Leczinski, ex-king of Poland and father-
in-law of Louis XV. The Place Stanislas, with its ornamental
wrought-iron gates, is one of France's most treasured works of
art. The other main town is Metz, a grim, austere, impressive
and not unlovely fortress town. The country has been again
and again the scene of war and is dotted with fortresses, among
them the most famous in recent French history: Verdun.

Like Lorraine, Alsace is a country of forest-clad hills, but
its opulence, its rich cornfields and vineyards, its picturesque
half-timbered buildings, contrast with Lorraine's austerity
and solid grey-stone houses. Industrial centres lie around
Mulhouse and the charming town of Colmar. Strasbourg has
a variety of industries, a renowned university and a famous
cathedral, the pink stone 'Munster', which rises above a
picturesque Venice-like quarter of canals and old houses
called 'la petite France'.

The Belfort Gap, at the southern end of the Vosges, leads
the way through Franche-Comté into Burgundy at Dijon.
Between Dijon and Chagny, along the Saône valley, lie the
districts from which come the finest vintages in Burgundy:
Beaune, Meursault, Chambertin, etc. This Burgundy valley
was on the main trade-route of the Middle Ages, and a great
centre of religious life to which bear witness the Abbeys of

Cluny and Cîteaux, which had a lasting influence on mediaeval monasticism.

Dijon, once capital of Burgundy, is a fine city with a twin tradition of jurisprudence and good cooking—the Dukes of Burgundy were enlightened patrons of the fine arts, and a very original school of sculpture flourished in Burgundy during the fourteenth and fifteenth centuries—the church of Brou, with its exuberant lace work of carved stone, is one of the best examples of Burgundian art. A feature of Burgundian architecture is the ornate roofs, covered with shiny coloured tiles, in intricate patterns, mostly of black, green and gold.

To the south-east of Dijon the Jura mountains stretch from the Rhine to the Rhône—they are of calcareous limestone, wooded, with white cliffs. The largest town in the district is Besançon—Victor Hugo's native town—an old city, once belonging to Spain, which seems to retain something of Spanish gravity and stiffness. It is situated on the picturesque river Doubs, a tributary of the Saône. Besançon had the first factory in Europe for making artificial silk, but its main industry is watchmaking. The little town of St. Claude is well known to all pipe-smokers for its superfine briar pipes; it also manufactures scientific instruments, optical glass, furniture, and specializes in diamond-cutting.

South of Burgundy, on the untraced frontier between Northern and Southern France, lies the capital of the silk trade, the city of Lyons. With a population slightly under half a million (this figure does not include the busy industrial suburbs), the ex-capital of Roman Gaul ranks as the third French city. Set between hills and across two rivers, the mighty Rhône and its tributary the Saône, with tree-lined quays, numerous bridges, and a fine Renaissance town-hall, the city is mostly built in great regular blocks, square and massive, which betray the influence of the south.

It is an austere, hard-working town. Though it manufactures chemicals, machinery, cars and a number of other products, it is first and foremost the town of silk. There silk is brought in bales of pale, golden, gossamer-thin thread; there it is spun, dyed and woven into heavy damasks, shimmering satins, tulles, watered-silks, crêpes of every description. The invention neither of artificial silk nor of nylon has shaken Lyons' supremacy; it has adopted both. Its superiority does not lie in mass production, but in creative design as well as in expert workmanship. Silk-weaving is not done only in Lyons, but also in the whole surrounding country, in family and village factories. The little town of Tarare is well known for its muslins and embroideries, and St. Etienne, to the north-west of Lyons, holds the practical monopoly in France for the manufacture of silk ribbons as well as—strange to say—of small arms and bicycles. East of Lyons, Savoy and the Dauphiné are entirely mountainous. In Savoy, the Mont-Blanc massif, the highest summit in Europe, 15,781 feet, overlooks the Lake of Geneva. As in Dauphiné, the landscape is magnificent, the country poor. Most of Dauphiné is covered with forests. A few crops and some dairy farming were the only resources until winter-sports became fashionable, and many a small hill-village became a winter resort.

Central France

South-west from Paris lies the great plain of Beauce, level and treeless; in summer an undulating sea of golden wheat as far as the eye can see. Two tall spires pierce the distant horizon: those of the magnificent cathedral of Chartres which one can see for miles and miles around. As we continue southwards, we come to the garden of France, Touraine, to the harmonious landscape of the Loire country and of the valleys of its tributaries: the Loiret, the Loir, the Cher, the Indre: the beloved land of Ronsard and Du Bellay, the garden of kings. The Valois kings liked the Loire valley; they enriched it with many beautiful Renaissance châteaux: Valençay, St. Aignan, Langeais, Chenonceaux, Chambord, Azay-le-Rideau, Amboise, Blois, surrounded by woods, parks and flowing waters.

Further south and a little to the east, after the flat expanses of Berry—whose capital Bourges is a very ancient town, the 'Avaricum' of pre-Roman Gaul—the heights of the Massif Central begin to rise. To the east, the *monts du Morvan*, covered

A Kiosk

The River Doubs

with forests—to the south lies the marvellously fertile valley of Limagne, alongside a range of extinct volcanoes, the 'chaîne des Puys'. We are in Auvergne, a country of fertile valleys and dour, lonely, secretive Highlands. Numerous hot mineral-springs—Vichy, Néris, Mont-Dore, Chatelguyon—as well as a few industries bring wealth to an otherwise not very rich country. South Auvergne villages are built in black lava, squat houses under their bright orange-red roofs clustering around their ancient Romanesque church, with elaborately carved portals and semicircular chapels, also roofed with red tile. The terraced hill-town of Thiers, the French Sheffield, built in black lava, is an impressive sight.

To the north-east lies one of the main industrial centres of France, round the towns of Le Creusot, St. Etienne, St. Chamond. To the south-east, the Cévennes range rises, flanking the Massif Central like a bastion. They have a severe grandeur, and constitute an impressive wilderness. There, in the seventeenth century, the Huguenots fled to hide from persecution. It is poor, dour country: the narrow terraced fields held by dry-stone walls yield meagre crops.

Further south still, the mountains open, and, all of a sudden, there lies the southern, sunny, fertile plain.

Western France

Normandy and Brittany have the same mild and moist climate—otherwise, they are as different from each other as the fair-haired, blue-eyed, long-headed *Normand* from the stocky, dark-haired, round-headed *Breton*.

Normandy is one of the richest of French provinces—its thickly wooded hills, green hedges, lush pastures dotted with sleek cattle, its prosperous farms, surrounded by apple orchards, speak of the fertility of the soil and of the mildness of the climate. The whole of Normandy might be regarded as the 'home farm' of the Parisians; its dairy products, milk, cream, butter and cheeses—among them the well-known Camembert and Livarot—are supplied daily to the Parisian market. The descendants of the Vikings, the sea-rovers who conquered

E

England in 1066 and later Sicily, who took part in the Crusades and left their mark on many lands overseas, seem to have settled down comfortably to enjoy the good things in which their land abounds. They remain, however, a seafaring breed. They have created the great ports of Le Havre, Rouen and Cherbourg. Rouen, one-time capital of Normandy, is the second French port after Marseilles (according to some authorities, it comes before Marseilles), one of the wealthiest cities in France, and her most important link with America. It has iron works and oil refineries, and it is the great cotton, sugar and coffee market for France. A great deal of trade with North America goes, however, to the great Channel port of Le Havre, headquarters of many shipping companies, and particularly of the Compagnie Transatlantique. It has ship-building yards and important oil refineries. Cherbourg, a naval station, is a port of call for transatlantic lines.

The Second World War left a trail of terrible devastation in Normandy. Le Havre, mostly razed to the ground, is being re-built; the historic quarters of Rouen, its fine cathedral, suffered grievously; the town of Caen was three-quarters destroyed and many villages annihilated.

Brittany, a Duchy which became French in 1491 by the marriage of young Duchess Ann to the French King Charles VIII, was for long a somewhat isolated part of France. It had never been Romanized or Germanized, and a Celtic language is spoken. It is a granitic peninsula, with the wildest coast of France, a rocky, rugged coast beaten in winter by the Atlantic gales, strewn with reefs, islets and isles, but with many harbours. From St. Malo and Paimpol, Concarneau and Douarnenez, fishermen sail to Newfoundland for cod; tunny and sardines are fished all along the Bay of Biscay. These Breton fishermen form the most important element in the French navy. Brest, with its natural harbour, the finest in Europe, invisible from the sea, the greatest French naval station, was almost completely destroyed during the Second World War. So was Lorient. There are two ports on the Loire: Nantes, some distance up the estuary, an old-established port, with a traditional link with the French West Indies and Central

America, and St. Nazaire, the port on the sea (coupled with the great shipbuilding yards of Penhoet) which competes with Le Havre and Bordeaux for American trade.

Inland, there are ancient forests, and, on the windswept uplands, desolate moors covered with gorse and broom. In the clayey soil of the lowlands, cattle thrive in the meadows, and the apple-orchards rival those of Normandy. Rennes, one-time capital of Brittany, is in the lowlands. The northern coastal belt, with its mild winter climate, its early spring, is thickly populated and the soil, fertilized by seaweed, gives valuable crops of early vegetables and strawberries.

Celtic Brittany has often been compared to the Highlands of Scotland. Both regions provide bonnie fighters, both patronize the bagpipes,[1] both show extreme devotion to their natural leaders, and in both there has been a remarkable display of loyalty to a lost Royal cause: in Brittany and in Vendée, the rebellion after the execution of Louis XVI; in Scotland the Jacobite risings. It is interesting to remember that in the fifth century a large number of Celtic-speaking Britons emigrated from Cornwall and Wales to Brittany, bringing their language with them. This emigration no doubt strengthened the 'Celtic' nature of the province.

The Breton is often a mystic, and still more often an artist. The remarkably expressive figures of the stone 'calvaires' of Breton villages, the elaborately carved furniture, the marvellously ornate local costumes—mostly on their way to disappear —give Brittany a very high place among the arts and crafts of the French provinces.

South of Brittany, the Atlantic coast is flat and marshy, with *marais salants* (salt marshes). The only good harbour is La Rochelle, an old port which is rapidly developing in combination with the neighbouring harbour of La Pallice. The coastal zone of Vendée and of Poitou is a network of streams and canals, clumps of trees, thick hedges. Further inland stretch the 'Bocage' of Vendée, also green with trees and thick hedges. The former capital of Limousin, Limoges, is known all over the world for its fine porcelains. It is also a great shoe-making

---

[1] The native *biniou* has now almost been ousted by the Scottish variety.

centre. The Limousin is mostly granitic with a poor soil. In the pasture-lands among the woods, graze flocks of sheep.

South-western and Southern France

The Pyrénées form a very real barrier between Spain and France, much more difficult to cross than the Alps. The mountain passes or 'ports' are at both extremities: the eastern end is guarded by Perpignan, the western by Bayonne. The Pyrénées attract many tourists, particularly on the western coast: Biarritz, St. Jean de Luz; and at the spas: Luchon, Bagnères, Cauterets, etc. The mountain streams constitute an important supply of hydro-electric power.

The valley of the Garonne and of its tributary the Dordogne, as well as their estuary, form the claret region, and the trade in these wines is concentrated in the great port of Bordeaux. Bordeaux has also a great export trade of resin from the Landes and pit-props for England. The South of France is mostly agricultural, with the exception of the wool industry in the small towns of Castres and Mazamet, and of the coal-mines of Decazeville. The upper valleys of the Dordogne and of her tributary the Vezère are among the most anciently inhabited spots on earth. There, at the time when the great glaciers were receding, the Palaeolithic hunters of Cro-Magnon and Lascaux roamed the primeval forest and adorned their cave-dwellings with impressive pictures of auroch, reindeer, mammoth and bison.

East of the Garonne and west of the Rhône spreads the plain of Languedoc, much of which is devoted to the growing of the vine, but there are mulberry and olive-trees, and, inland, some sheep-farming. The main towns are Montpellier, with its ancient University, and Roman Nîmes, which has preserved its antique monuments: arena, temple and terraced gardens. South of Nîmes, Aigues-Mortes, a mediaeval walled town, was once a port from which the saintly king, Louis IX, sailed for the Crusade. It is now inland, as the sands from the Rhône delta have progressively silted the sea-coast. The only ports of this coast are Port Vendres and Sète.

A little to the east of the delta, the great port of Marseilles has grown round a fine natural harbour, within a half-circle of hills—Marseilles, founded by the Greeks around 600 B.C., has been a busy port for the last two thousand years, and has probably always been noisy, lively and colourful. The destruction by the Germans during the Second World War of the squalid but quaint mansions of the Vieux Port—the Lacydon of the Greeks—a once aristocratic quarter, later inhabited by fishermen and their families, has robbed Marseilles of much of its homely, friendly, Southern picturesqueness. These antique dwellings are being replaced by modern blocks of flats: the huge skyscraper block of flats built by Le Corbusier stands like an island in the eastern part of the town. Together with the houses of the Vieux Port disappeared the metallic 'pont transbordeur', rather an eyesore.

Marseilles is the headquarters of a busy trade with North and West Africa, with the Near and Far East and with Oceania. It is the headquarters of several shipping and passenger lines and France's main link with the countries of the former French colonial Empire, now the French Union. North of Marseilles lie the valley of the Rhône and the sunny land of Provence, where thyme, marjoram and lavender grow thick on the hills. On the windward side of the farms stand lines of closely planted cypress-trees to protect the gardens from the biting north wind, the 'mistral' which sweeps down the Rhône valley. Avignon, the walled city of the Popes, is surrounded by olive-groves; orchards thrive; wheat, wine, fruit and olives are the basis of life in this region. Rome has left its mark on Provence. The huge aqueduct called the Pont du Gard, the arena at Arles, the Roman theatre at Orange, bear witness to the solidity and durability of Roman buildings.

From Marseilles the coast road eastwards, the 'Corniche', passes Toulon, naval base and arsenal, and then continues to wind with the hills on one side, the blue sea on the other, under a cloudless sky. This is the Côte d'Azur, or French Riviera, a continuous chain of delightful beaches and bays, fishing villages, small ancient towns, and luxurious modern villas, shining white among palm-trees, cacti, mimosa with golden blossom, acacias, rosy tamarisks and all sorts of exotic, semi-tropical plants. Through the old Roman town of Fréjus, through Cannes and Antibes, to Nice, Monaco and Mentone, we reach the Italian frontier just before Ventimiglia. All along the coast and specially around Grasse, the perfume town, spread fields of violets, carnations, tuberoses, and almond-trees. Orange and lemon trees, peach-tree orchards, are seen everywhere. The Riviera has been for over a hundred years a favourite resort of visitors attracted by the delightful climate and the beautiful scenery.

Monaco, a small independent principality, occupies a particularly favoured peninsula, and its Casino, with its roulette and baccarat tables, is not the least attraction of the Côte d'Azur. About a hundred miles off the Mediterranean coast lies the island of Corsica: the 'Isle of Beauty'. The Genoese, to whom the island belonged, had infinite trouble with the islanders and sold Corsica to France in 1768, one year before Napoleon Bonaparte was born in Ajaccio. The Corsicans speak an Italian dialect. They are most of them poor, but very proud and extremely clannish; family feuds last for generations. Many Corsicans emigrate to France to enter the army or the administration. The island is mountainous and very picturesque, but the soil is poor. Most of the interior is covered by the *maquis* or bush of aromatic shrubs. Tourist traffic continues to develop in the island. The chief towns are Ajaccio, the administrative capital, and Bastia, the commercial capital.

READING LIST

Brangwyn, J. *Reasons for France.* London, 1939. A very readable study of provincial France. Illustrated.

Fleure, H. J. *The Peoples of France.* London, 1920.

George, P. *Géographie économique et sociale de la France.* Paris, 1946. Very readable. Illustrated.

Granger, E. *La France.* Paris, 1932. An excellent geographical study.

Ogrizek, D. *La France, Paris et les Provinces.* Paris, 1948. A gay, popular account, with numerous amusing coloured illustrations.

Vidal de la Blache, P., in E. Lavisse, *Histoire de France*, t. I.

CHAPTER IV

FRANCE AT WORK

Le seul peuple fort est le peuple qui travaille, et le travail seul donne le
courage et la foi.   ÉMILE ZOLA

I

TWENTIETH-CENTURY England, sometimes described as an
enormous and delightful park studded with unlovely industrial
cities, bears everywhere the disfiguring marks of the Industrial
Revolution. France resembles a garden in which millions of
peasants dig, plough, hoe and weed from sunrise to sunset.
Save in the north and north-east, in parts of the Paris region,
and in smaller patches elsewhere, France shows few of the
stigmata of the revolution which, since about 1760, changed the
face of England. One might make a journey through a whole
province and return home believing that no industrial revolution had ever occurred in France. This impression would not
be quite accurate, for an industrial transformation, in a milder
form, did happen, though about a century later than in England
—after 1870 instead of after 1760. It would not be at all
fantastic to maintain that the pattern of life in France to-day
was determined by the 1789 Revolution rather than the
Industrial Revolution. By confiscating first the rich and
extensive Church lands, then the broad acres of the *émigrés*,
by dividing them into small lots and selling them to the
peasants, by abolishing feudal dues and thus turning many
tenants into owners,[1] the 1789 Revolution made France a land
of small farmers, masters of the fields they tilled, and consequently ardently attached to the soil . . . as well as to the
Revolution. England, it has been said, is a nation of farm
tenants, France a nation of farm owners. In England, during
the hundred years or so following 1760, thousands of landless

---

[1] In 1789 almost half of the French soil already belonged to the peasants.
See *Géographie Universelle*, vol. VI, 2, I, p. 146.

men, many of them victims of the enclosure of common land, left the countryside for ever and trooped to the towns, their hearts beating with hope that the new factories would assure them better conditions of life. In France, though there, as elsewhere, the population of the rural districts trickled into the urban centres,[1] no such mass movement ever took place. While in England the factories and the towns grew apace, and mechanization moved forward with great strides, on the other side of the Channel, industry, though registering some progress under Louis-Philippe and Napoleon III, grew but slowly, and mechanization was applied later and on a more modest scale. By the middle of the nineteenth century half of England's population was already urban. At that date three-quarters of the French people still lived in the country, not more than a quarter were town-dwellers. Only to-day, half-way through the twentieth century, has France reached the degree of urbanization, fifty per cent., that England attained a century ago. England, meanwhile, has seen her rural population shrink to a mere twenty per cent. at most. For nearly a century, under the spell of industrial and commercial expansion, England neglected her agriculture, which was gradually ruined by free trade, particularly after 1875, when the British farmer could not compete with cheap American wheat. She freely imported her foodstuffs and paid for them by the colossal earnings of her exported manufactured goods and by her financial and insurance services. During the same period France remained sturdily agricultural. By her high tariffs she protected her farmers from foreign competition and she grew enough foodstuffs to feed her whole population.

France cultivates a very high proportion of her soil—out of a total area of 550,000 square kilometres no less than 200,000 are ploughed—and a vast area is used for pasturage. France tills as much arable land as Germany and more than Italy. The broad plains of the northern half of France, cut into a patchwork of green and gold squares and strips, furnish more than half the cereal crops and allow of more intensive cattle-raising than does the southern half of the country, much of whose

---

[1] Noted by François Quesnay, the physiocrat, as early as 1757.

sunbaked soil is less fertile and provides less fodder than the northern plains.

Variety is the keynote of French agriculture. Farm life could be sketched in a long series of contrasted pictures: the damp fertile plains of Flanders, where, under a leaden sky, stretch endless acres of sugar-beet, potatoes, root-crops; the hot sun beating down over the rich, level fields of golden grain spreading for miles around Chartres, whose twin cathedral spires dominate the fertile plain of Beauce; the lush green pastures of Central France with the grazing herds of the characteristic white Nivernais cattle; the tiny vineyards and fields nestling on the terraced slopes of almost barren mountains in Auvergne, Ardèche or Savoy, where, after a storm, the peasants, with a hod or basket of soil on their backs, climb painfully up the slope to replace the earth swept away by the rain; spick-and-span Burgundy vineyards impeccably aligned along the Saône—or, further south, the red soil of the vineyards on the slopes of the Rhône, some of the labourers, after a lifetime of hoeing, looking no less gnarled and bent than the stumps of the vines themselves; the market-gardener on the very outskirts of Paris, in blue overalls and old straw-hat, treading gingerly, watering-can or hose-pipe in hand, among the bell-glasses and the frames, and by dint of constant tending, succeeding in raising magnificent crops; the village shepherd of the Cévennes, sounding his rustic horn every morning to summon sheep and goats from their byres, leading them to the mountain pastures and bringing them back in the evening, each animal turning into its own stable as the procession tinkles through the village street. Such are a few of the infinitely varied aspects of agricultural life in France. The wheat-farmer, the grazier and the wine-grower, all agriculturists, lead very different lives. Many farmers, those who run mixed farms, manage to be, on a small scale, wheat-farmers, graziers and *vignerons*; they grow not only wheat but vegetables, make butter and cheese from the milk of their cows and goats, keep pigs and chickens, grow fruit in their orchard and make their own cider or wine. This self-sufficiency represents the ideal of the French peasant, and not a few of them achieve as great a measure of self-sufficiency as can be attained in the modern world.

British and American economists, mostly no doubt town-bred, incline to look somewhat scornfully at what they term old-fashioned and wasteful modes of agricultural production. Convinced that mass production and high specialization applied to agriculture can achieve an enormous output at a lower cost, they deplore the expenditure of energy in small-scale mixed farming; they see no future for French agriculture unless it becomes industrialized and abandons its conservative ways. They point out that while the average American farmer, raising a single crop and employing the latest machinery, provides enough food for fifteen people, the average French farmer, working on a small farm without much help from machines and dispersing his efforts in mixed farming instead of specializing in one crop, grows enough food for only six people.

At a first glance it might well seem that this way of looking at the problem expresses plain common sense. Would it not be better to reorganize French agriculture on entirely modern and mechanized lines and produce more food more cheaply? Or is this view based too exclusively on statistics? Does it take into account the human elements in French agriculture? The peasant likes mixed farming, he experiences a lively satisfaction in working towards self-sufficiency; he appreciates variety in his occupations and finds pleasure in what he looks upon as a fuller life. He has, it is true, little leisure, but leisure is less precious to a man who loves his work than to one who finds nothing but boredom in a monotonous task. Would the peasant be happier if his day were filled by one ever-repeated farm operation? If agriculture were rationalized and could be run with a fraction of the labour employed in France to-day, would the superfluous farm labourers, drafted into industry, lead happier lives? Would they be better citizens? Would France show more stability if her agriculture were efficiently operated by a very reduced number of highly mechanized specialists and the men displaced employed otherwise? Judging by the discontent with their lot so often expressed by factory workers in France, the country would probably be less stable and less happy. The successive governments who have protected the farmer by tariffs, and fixed a price that has allowed him to sell his crops advantageously, evidently realized that the agricultural population, by assuring social stability, had earned these favours. Moreover, if agriculture were forced to become a mass-production industry, France would no longer be France, for the peasant, independent, leading a life which, if hard, is balanced and healthy, forms the very backbone of the French nation. Were his numbers drastically reduced, the essential character of the country would be modified.

How does the peasant live? Though his agricultural work offers the charm of variety, his life follows a simple pattern. His recreations are few: he attends Mass on Sundays at the village church—in many districts he talks with his cronies over a bottle of local wine in the café while his wife and children listen to the service. Once a week, he or his wife—sometimes both—jog along in their cart to the nearest village or little town and sell their butter, eggs, poultry and vegetables in the market. The wife buys from the *marchands forains*, also in the market-place, the few necessaries their farm cannot provide—clothes and pots and pans. The only other breaks in the year-long round of monotonous toil are family events—baptisms, weddings, funerals, and the first communion of the children when they reach the age of twelve. In the wine-growing districts the traditional festival of the grape-gathering brings a day or two of merry junketings.

The peasant's life is hard, much harder than that of the English farmer who lives in elaborate comfort and sometimes even rides to hounds. The Scottish crofter, living a simple, austere life on his modest holding, provides a nearer parallel. The peasant rises with the sun and sets off for field or vineyard, where he toils in the sunshine or rain until sunset, knowing nothing of the forty-hour week. When he returns home because he can no longer see to work, he eats his evening meal —generally soup with a crust of bread and a bottle of wine, and goes to bed, for light must not be wasted and he must rise early next morning. An element of drama—of tragedy even—lies behind this undramatic existence: the ever-present possibility of sudden disaster owing to rain, frost or hail, which may destroy his vines or flatten his crops.

The peasant's wife works no less strenuously than her husband: she gets up first and prepares the breakfast—soup made with vegetables, with a little home-fed bacon added; in some districts the soup is laced with red wine. She helps her husband in the fields or vineyard, makes the butter and the cheese, milks the cows, carries her husband's dinner to him at his work. Until recent years she had to bake her bread every fortnight; and she does the washing, sometimes at the village wash-house (*lavoir*), where, as she scrubs, she may exchange gossip with her neighbours sometimes at the edge of a river or a lonely pond.

When they are not at school, the peasant's children must also give a hand on the farm—if it be only watching over the cows and goats as they graze at the roadside. Grandfather and grandmother work too, as long as they can walk. Sometimes you may see on a hillside an old woman of eighty staggering along under a bundle of faggots, for coal is expensive and the cooking is mostly done in a huge pot over a wood fire.

Many of the smaller farmhouses consist of two plain, sparsely furnished rooms and a loft. The children sleep in the loft, the farm labourer, if there be one, in the barn. One of the rooms serves as kitchen, and in the poorer districts as dining-room and bedroom as well; the other is a store. The type of farmhouse varies with the province; 'the unadorned Lorraine farms turning their backs on the barns, separated from the road by a broad open space covered with manure; the smiling Alsatian dwelling with many windows, framed by climbing vines and decked with scarlet geraniums; Savoy chalets in which animals and people live in common in the tiny ground-floor rooms as though crowded under the weight of the hayloft; white cottages of the wine-growers in Touraine, flanked by a cellar that is the most indispensable room of all; little Flemish farms, neat as a new toy; high and sombre Corsican houses, disdainful of any graces, refusing even the modest ornament of a festoon of wistaria; Basque *etche*, whitewashed every year at midsummer; Provençal *mas* browned by the sun, often with an oil-press and a silkworm-rearing house, and always sheltered by an African lotus, a plane-tree or the glossy trunks of tall cypress trees.' [1]

The peasant, whose physical and mental type differs according to his province from the tall, blond, heavily built Northerner to the small, dark and wiry man of the centre or the south, looms large in the population figures in France; out of a total of some forty million inhabitants, over seven million men and women are actively engaged in agriculture. About five millions own their farms. An average farm covers only fifteen acres or less, and many are worked by the owner, with his wife and family but without outside help. Quite a considerable number of farms, partly as a result of the laws of inheritance (as in parts of mediaeval England), consist of several separate strips, perhaps five or more, not contiguous, sometimes in different parishes. One of the reasons for the continuation of this dispersion may be that the peasant likes to ensure variety of crops, and a strip on a hillside may prove useful if the other strips lie on the plain. Because of the smallness of the units and the dispersion of effort, the yield does not attain the production level that can be reached per man in large enterprises specializing in a single crop. On a big farm alone can all the farming operations be carried out on a sufficiently extensive scale to warrant full mechanization. In the Camargue, that once-neglected plain in the extreme south where bulls and horses still wander wild, estates extending over several hundreds of acres now grow vines, maize and rice, using drills, harvesters and machines for cutting maize, all of the latest American pattern. One estate at least has powerful electrically driven pumps for irrigating its rice-fields and sows the rice from a Piper Cub aeroplane.

This example goes to show that, despite the conservatism of the French farmer, whose traditional habits and age-old customs no modern system can transform in an instant, France has here and there adopted novelties imported from abroad.

[1] E. Granger, *La France*, p. 199.

The Camargue, Normandy and Flanders, all areas where thrive great estates, adopt modern methods more readily than regions of small farms. In many places the 'large contented oxen heaving slow' and the wiry Percheron horses have made way for the more prosaic but swifter-moving tractors. Like most rationalization, this change means less self-sufficiency, for it entails dependence on imported fuel-oil. The considerable wealth amassed by the peasants during the war and post-war periods of food-shortage raised their standard of living and made these primary producers less refractory to a certain measure of mechanization, and Marshall Aid has brought valuable help in re-equipping the country. In view of the diminutive size of the average farm, each with a wide range of different crops, the purchase of the varied machines required by each farmer would not be justified. Modernization therefore usually takes the form of co-operation. A group of neighbouring farmers unite to found a co-operative society and thus share the purchase of expensive machinery which each member of the group can use in turn.

By 1946 several thousands of farm co-operatives had been founded—some of them dating from pre-war times—and by 1950 they had acquired no less than 150,000 tractors, half the total number estimated as necessary for the whole country, and an impressive figure if compared with the 35,000 in use in 1939. It says much for French initiative that in 1946 no less than 90 per cent. of French farms had electricity laid on as against 15 per cent. in U.S.A.[1] At the same time it must be admitted that most French farmers use this advantage only for lighting and quail at the prospect of the expense involved in installing electrical machinery.

The French peasant, tilling his ancestral lands from time immemorial, has in the course of the centuries learned many precious lessons about the unwisdom of exhausting the soil which nourished his forebears and which must provide for his descendants. He faces conditions quite unlike those faced by the transatlantic farmer, whose concern is simply to raise the maximum yield from prairie-land. Traditional

[1] J. Fourastié and H. Montet, *L'Economie Française*, p. 64.

practice and a sturdy conservatism in his agricultural, if not in his political, outlook, make the peasant reluctant to try out new and strange experiments. He shows no great zeal for the wholehearted adoption of industrialized farming, but he now admits that more mechanization is inevitable. Projects on foot aim, not at monoculture, but at increasing and improving the yield of a whole range of products which the variety of the climate and soil makes possible; at encouraging, for instance, the production of fruit, vegetables, chickens and eggs, cheese, *foie gras* and honey on farms which so far have cultivated cereals and root crops. Fresh and dried vegetables, *primeurs* and fruit bring in already each year a sum which is four-fifths of that obtained for the annual wheat crop. It is proposed to organize the sale of agricultural produce under a national mark guaranteeing its quality. Among its very varied products French agriculture favours those crops typical of a rich country—wheat, sugar-beet, milk, butter, beef and wine; potatoes and rye, which provide the staple food in poorer countries, have less attraction for the farmer in most parts of France.

France intends to develop agricultural research and to bring it into closer touch with the practical problems of the farmer. It will concentrate its attention on increasing the yield of the soil per man-hour. Everyone recognizes that any wide adoption of new and complicated machinery—tractors, electric motors, irrigation pumps, etc.—will mean equipping the peasant with a higher standard of technical education.

II

Though, like other countries, France has for long been gradually urbanized, she has so far succeeded in maintaining the balance between agriculture and industry. This happy equilibrium enabled her to surmount, with greater ease and less unemployment than more industrialized countries, the severe economic crisis that burst upon the world in 1929 and which began to affect France only at the end of 1930. How did France contrive to maintain a balance that England lost

so long ago? Why was the rhythm of her economic development so slow? The answer certainly cannot be that the
French lacked the inventive mind or a feeling for technical
progress. On the contrary, France, before any other country,
applied industrial methods to the production of soda, of sugar
from beetroot and of coal gas.[1] Several geographical factors
hindered industrial transformation: the distance separating
the ports and the industrial regions of an earlier economy from
the coalfields and ironfields; the coal and iron not being found
in proximity to one another; the rivers, except the Seine, not
being naturally suited to navigation; the canal system remain-
ing, despite the urgent admonitions of Napoleon I, inadequate
during part of the nineteenth century. All these hindrances
played their part. But perhaps the most cogent reason of all
for the slow pace of industrial development lay in the inex-
pensiveness of human labour in France and the very high cost
of fuel. Nevertheless, some great industries were developed:
the industrial belt in the north, with its collieries—grimly
remembered by soldiers of the First World War—had long
produced vast quantities of steel, as well as weaving enormous
quantities of wool and cotton; in the north-east, Lorraine,
which also manufactures textiles, extracts from her soil millions
of tons of iron-ore and potash; in the extremely active industrial region near Paris, textiles, metallurgy and chemical
products hold an outstanding position. All these industries,
organized in large units, represent an important part of
France's export trade.

In the present century France displays a vigorous spirit of
initiative, a quality to which some foreign critics appear to
have been blind, in solving one of her long-standing problems
—the shortage of motive power which retarded her industrial
development. Coal has always been insufficient in quantity
for the needs of industry, and the electric power generated from
coal was already equalled before the Second World War by
hydro-electric power. First used by the celebrated M. Bergès
as early as 1869 in paper-works in the Dauphiné, the power of
the Alpine torrents, at a period when electricity could be

---

[1] See also Chapter VIII (Science and Inventions).

The Château of Chenonceaux with its Formal Gardens

Vineyards in Champagne

transported only over very short distances, brought industries —particularly the manufacture of aluminium, soda and calcium carbide—into mountainous regions in which, though they had long possessed small workshops and home industries, rustic life had hitherto been undisturbed. Now that no distance limits the transport of electric current—is there not a project, put forward in 1952, for the linking-up of the French and British systems for mutual aid?—the 'white coal' from the Alps (*la houille blanche*) employs some of its power to drive the trains and to feed far-off factories. The mighty Rhône has already been dammed in several places and immense power-stations constructed. Since the completion of the barrage at Génissiat near Bellegarde, the railway line from Paris to Lyons has been electrified and will in time be electrified as far as Marseilles (electric trains drawing their power from the Pyrénées already make the complete journey from Paris to Bordeaux). The latest project, well in hand, as the traveller by road to the south may see, is the colossal undertaking on the Rhône near Montélimar, at Donzère-Mondragon, which is expected to attain the stupendous output of two thousand million kilowatt-hours—a quarter of the whole French production of hydro-electric energy in 1935. The triple task of these gigantic barrages and miles of canals will be to provide power for the electrification of the railway as far as Mar-seilles, besides the power needed by industry, to improve the Rhône for navigation, and to irrigate the countryside around the Rhône valley.

The leap forward in electrification provides unmistakable evidence of French energy and initiative. So indeed did a French commercial venture of last century. It is often for-gotten that, whereas she lagged behind England in applying to industry and to wholesale trading the principles of con-centration, in retail trading France was in the van of progress as early as the middle of last century. To France must be credited the invention of those great emporiums, *les grands magasins*—the *Bon Marché* was the pioneer—created not by powerful combines endowed with vast resources but by the modest efforts of traders gifted with commercial shrewdness.

F

One simple principle ensured the success of these vast stores: buy on credit and sell for cash. This allows an immense turn-over on a very small capital, for the customer has paid for the goods long before the date on which the manufacturer's invoice has to be met.

In considering the industrial and commercial scene in France as a whole it behoves us to keep in mind French achievements in heavy and large-scale industry, her success in creating the first examples of the *grands magasins* and her present-day vigour in developing hydro-electric power-stations on the grand scale. Nevertheless, in industry and in commerce as in agriculture, the keynote is variety of production and the scale of enterprise appears to be more often the family scale than that of the huge anonymous concern. Nor is this surprising when one considers that numerous Frenchmen of peasant descent are engaged in business. Many of them, it has been truly said, still wear, morally speaking, the ancestral smock. These men have played an important part in moulding the business life of the nation into a shape which everywhere betrays its peasant origin. The peasant, ploughing his lonely furrow, willingly limits his horizon and acquires an indivdualist outlook; the rhythm of his life has a slow and steady beat; his ambition, in general, does not soar above a moderate fortune, painfully amassed by unremitting thrift; counting on himself, he distrusts large-scale enterprises. The *petite bourgeoisie*, which with the peasantry forms the warp and woof of the French population, shares many traits of character with the farmers: their thrift, their preference for small-scale activity and for variety, their concern with family interests. As the peasant's aim in life has always been to acquire a fresh strip of land to round off his inheritance, so the petty bourgeois saves up (or did until catastrophic devaluation of the franc made saving look silly) to provide a modest dowry for his daughter and a very moderate pension to live upon frugally when he retires to his native village, there to tend his vines and his garden.

Given the general outlook on life of the peasant and the petty bourgeois—the most numerous classes in France—little surprise can be felt that in France the small workshop did not rapidly evolve into the huge factory, nor did the substitution of machinery for manual skill take place so universally and so rapidly as in England. French industry, slower to concentrate its efforts, gave extraordinary importance to variety. Hereditary traits offered a dogged resistance to attempts at concentration, either commercial or industrial; the individualism of the peasant was shared by the workman and by the small employer too. The typical French workman is the artisan, that is the man who makes a complete object and whose task calls for skill, taste and inventiveness, not the performance of a few uniform actions endlessly repeated.

These traits appear most conspicuously in branches of French industry, like the luxury trades, that are most characteristic of the nation. Yet even in some of the few large-scale enterprises foreign observers have pointed out specifically French features—the family spirit, for instance. Thus the three colossal firms of Peugeot, Schneiders of Le Creusot and Les Petits-Fils de François de Wendel are family concerns, using outside capital but controlled by descendants of the founders. Another characteristic of French large-scale industry, noted by British and American critics, is the attempt at self-sufficiency or 'integration'. Instead of farming out to sub-contractors the supplying of accessories or components of a motor-car, for instance, French firms like Renault (now nationalized) prefer to carry out the whole complex series of diverse operations themselves, without the help of contractors.

Many moderate and small-scale industries are managed like a bourgeois household and their policies reflect the principles of sound household management: to live strictly within one's means, and to put aside for future emergencies whatever can be spared. Vigorous initiative of the kind which, if successful, would lead rapidly to a huge fortune, but if unsuccessful would mean a headlong plunge into bankruptcy, ranks in France not as brilliant business capacity but as sheer recklessness, highly blameworthy, for any recourse to the bankruptcy court would besmirch the family honour. The French businessman has his place in the community marked out for him already by his social origin. If he wishes to keep his standing, he cannot afford to act in a manner that his business acquaintances would regard as unbecoming: not only bankruptcy but the savage crushing of a competitor or the doing of a number of things which in some other communities might pass as 'smart business' would spell social disaster. His pattern of behaviour, not the size, make and number of his motor-cars, the type of house he lives in and his sumptuary expenditure in general, will determine his social importance. Sinclair Lewis's American businessmen—Babbitt or Dodsworth for instance—appear to be less trammelled by old-world traditional ethics than Balzac's César Birotteau, but of course they belong to a later generation.

Nothing in France would scandalize Mr. Babbitt more profoundly than the unwillingness shown by certain industrial concerns to expand their production to the utmost. He would express pained surprise on learning that firms in France could show reluctance to ask the banks for long or medium-term credits—and equal astonishment no doubt when he discovered that (except perhaps in Lyons, where co-operation between banks and the silk trade is traditional) the banks on their side evinced scant enthusiasm for granting them. Mr. Babbitt's up-to-date business creed avers that the greater the total production the greater the service to the community—with its obvious corollary: the increasing wealth which the businessman amasses in producing on an ever-expanding scale automatically measures the value of his service. This view, which should prove comforting to the successful manufacturer, does not seem to commend itself universally to the French industrialist. If he considers he is making sufficient money already—and such cases have been known—he prefers to keep the even tenor of his way and can with difficulty be spurred into attempts at doubling his production, and perhaps his income, simply because the golden opportunity lies just ahead. He probably remembers studying Horace's *Satires* in his schooldays at the *lycée* and recalls the doubt propounded by the Augustan poet as to whether, after all, taking one's money out of a bigger pile really does afford the possessor a more delicious thrill.

The cautious attitude, so often made a reproach to the

French businessman, may be dictated to him by the nature of his clientele, and most French manufacturers work mainly for their compatriots. French customers have never shown as much willingness as Americans to absorb all the novelties made available—nor is the same high-pressure salesmanship turned on to force them to do so. Household 'gadgets' like refrigerators, washing-machines, television sets and the like would perhaps have less value also in impressing the neighbours! Not only would the income of the average household not run to luxuries of this type, but most families would probably prefer to spend what money was available on finer food and wine—mechanical delights come far behind in the ideal of a high standard of living. In matters of dress the Frenchwoman wants individuality and personality; she finds a handsome ready made frock, exactly like thousands of others, less desirable than a dress-length chosen by herself, and cut by herself or her dressmaker to suit her particular type. Most French families buy only what they can afford, and not always that; the old-fashioned principle of living within one's income condemns the buying of luxuries on the instalment system.

No more characteristic example of French industry could well be found than the silk trade, centred, not in Paris—where of course much of the made-up silk is sold—but in Lyons, a sedate, hard-working and rather austere city which, at the point where the swift imperious Rhône joins the gentler Saône, rears its severe six-storey houses, separated in the older quarters by narrow streets. In the factories, generally of medium size, both real and artificial silk (*la rayonne*) are woven on power-driven looms. The skill of the silk worker and the ingenuity of the designer together give Lyons silk goods their particular *cachet*. The rich, elegant and discerning purchasers of the world luxury market insist on distinction and novelty in the wares they buy, and the designers must be perpetually creating something new. With such a trade small-scale production alone can cope, for factories must be capable of swift adaptation when fashion decrees a sudden change. In the period between the two wars, a silk manufacturer enamoured of mass production built a huge new factory outside Lyons with a village for the workers. He soon encountered trouble, for rapid changes at the dictates of fashion proved both difficult and onerous to carry out on this huge scale. And what was to be done with the miles of silk material of a design on which fashion had turned her back? The factory still stands, looking rather forlorn, just 'ticking over' and providing an object lesson not lost on the Lyons' silk manufacturers (*les soyeux*).

Many of the *soyeux*, partly in order to maintain maximum adaptability, do not weave all their silk in their own factories, but send much of the silk thread to weavers (*les canuts*) whose looms are installed in their homes in the Croix Rousse quarter, where the tall ancient houses, honeycombed with windows (good light is essential), look down over the steeply sloping streets towards the Rhône. Most of these looms are driven by electricity, the old hand-looms, used for the richest flowered brocades, having now practically disappeared. Silk weaving is by no means confined to the city itself, since no less than 20,000 of the 39,000 power-driven looms in use are scattered among the villages in the Isère valley along the road to Grenoble. Parcels of silk, of tulle, of gold and silver thread are despatched to workers in cottages in Bourgoin, La Tour du Pin and dozens of tiny hamlets. At the bottom of the orchard of a well-built comfortable-looking cottage you see a small brick building rather like a garage or an outhouse. This is the workshop or *atelier*, and from it comes the clanking of one, two or three power-driven looms. Though he wears blue overalls, the weaver looks more like a farmer than a factory hand. He divides his time between the *atelier*, his neat garden, his orchard and his modest vineyard. When weaving booms, his wife and son join him in the workshop; fortunately the rush of work comes mostly in the winter months when garden, orchard and vineyard make little call on the family's time. In the off-season he works alone at one of the looms while his wife does the housework, and he puts in as many hours as he can spare with his son in the garden or vineyard. The balance of indoor and outdoor employment appears to ensure a happy, healthy life for the weaver and for his family. No doubt he could earn higher wages and spend fewer hours at the loom were he working in a town factory, but he enjoys his independence and prefers his country life to a cramped existence in the town. The spread of industry to these Alpine valleys represents no new phenomenon, but has been going on for the last hundred years; its object was not the philanthropic desire to assure a happily balanced life for the workman, but was economic; water power was everywhere available there and labour was less expensive than in the city.

The linking-up of industry with rural life, a traditional practice which France has not, like England, abandoned, has done much to prevent the desertion of the countryside. This practice flourishes not only in the Lyons region but in many areas and in many trades. In the Jura, at St. Claude, briar pipes are turned on the lathes in small workshops; high-grade watches, of which the parts are manufactured at Besançon and Morteau, are mounted and finished in village workshops or at home. In the Pyrénées, villagers in their *ateliers* pursue century-old crafts and shape all kinds of objects from felt, leather and rope. In North-west France the farmers, skilful with their hands, use their spare time to fashion articles of wood, leather and other materials. Textiles in amazing variety are spun in the villages on the northern plain, especially in the department of the Somme. In the Massif Central, around the little old-world town of Thiers (sometimes called the Sheffield of France), each valley shelters a factory—many of them have no more than a dozen cutlers working in them. These men, who make the blades of the knives, work lying flat on their faces in front of the grindstone. As their bodies remain almost motionless and winter chills their bones, some of them train a dog to lie all day long on the small of their backs so as to preserve them from rheumatism. In village homes in the Thiers region (e.g. St. Rémy-sur-Durolle), wives, daughters and even grandmothers work at a little bench near the window. They turn and polish the horn or ebony handles of the knives —without, however, neglecting to perform their household duties. These old rural forms of industrial activity have been given a fresh lease of life by the coming of electric power into the country districts, particularly in the mountainous regions, where it has generally replaced the water power which first attracted industry to these secluded dales.

Paris also has its small workshops, indeed in that city 15,000 establishments of less than twenty employees work for the textile and clothing trades.[1] In the district lying around the Bourse, a quarter largely devoted to textiles, dozens of *ateliers* employing a score of girls and women, fashion, with delicate skilful fingers—and, no less indispensable, with inventive minds —the little ornaments to adorn women's hats and dresses. Again the *articles de Paris* (Paris novelties), inimitable elsewhere, which are displayed for instance in the elegant little shops under the arches of the rue de Rivoli and which fascinate the foreign tourist, mostly come from similar workrooms, made by hand by artisans who almost deserve the name of artists. These charming trifles are certainly better known as typical products of French industry than the machines and implements of all types that pour out from the huge factories engaged in heavy industry in and outside Paris, though among these machines are handsome motor-cars and aeroplanes, examples of the recognized manual skill of the workman.

With regard to the luxury trades, which loom so large in the list of French exports, the French claim, not without reason, that the beauty of Paris itself, the symmetry of its singularly graceful buildings, the enchanting perspectives afforded by the artistic layout of avenues and squares, and no doubt other even less tangible elements, play their part in forming the taste of the workers. The influence of the incomparable setting, its formative value for artisans and for artists, is recognized outside France. A New York jeweller whose craftsmen have been trained in Paris regularly sends them back there for a short spell every few years lest they lose, if not their skill, their inspiration. Another example of the prestige of Paris in this respect comes from the city of Lyons, a provincial city once the capital of Gaul, not given to adopting a subservient attitude towards the capital to which it sends its silks. Every week a team of window-dressers travelled down from Paris to Lyons to arrange the window-displays in one of the big shops, for the

[1] P. George, *Geog. écon. et sociale de la France*, p. 167.

management maintained that no one but a Parisian actually living in Paris could unfailingly achieve the *chic*, the impeccable taste required.

In any study of the characteristics of French industry it is impossible not to stress the variety and inventiveness revealed most clearly in the successful export of light, beautiful and expensive articles such as luxury textiles. Exports of this kind, fashioned for a limited clientele, run the risk of becoming in times of crisis the earliest sacrifices to economy. France, therefore, without neglecting these aesthetic and profitable products, which have long enjoyed world-wide renown, must, declare the experts, if she means to survive in the post-war world dominated by mass production, cater for the needs of the mass, at home and, if possible, abroad. Success in this 'century of the common man' can be won only by the adoption of modern and mechanized production. Moreover, the safety of France herself in the conditions of the modern world calls for expansion of heavy industry. After the Second World War the government adopted a National Plan for Modernization and Equipment, perhaps better known as the Monnet Plan, from the name of its administrator, M. Pierre Monnet. This legislation aimed at the expansion of the national output, over the four-year period 1947-50, to a point 25 per cent. above the 1929 figure. This programme has been applied to the six basic industries regarded as vital in the country's economy: coal, electricity, steel, cement, agricultural machinery and transport. At the same time farm-produce, housing, exports and the equipment industry also call for expansion. The Monnet Plan is giving its results now. The activities of the National Centre of Scientific Research, a governmental agency for co-ordinating the researches of a considerable body of French scientists, should bring much help in the future development of industry.

How far has the nationalization of sections of French industrial activity helped or hindered the success of the Monnet Plan? The answers to this question vary according to the political views of the speaker. The mines were nationalized in 1944-46, and under their new name—Les Charbonnages de

France—have markedly increased their output. French air-
lines, gas, electricity, the principal insurance companies, the
Bank of France and the chief deposit banks became national
enterprises in 1947, after which the wave of nationalizing
fervour appears to have receded. Criticism turns mostly on
political interference in the management and on the vast sums
called for to meet deficits. It remains to be seen how far these
nationalized concerns will realize the greater output, greater
economy and the increased contentment among the workers so
vociferously promised by their champions. But every traveller
in France must have been vividly impressed by the way the
French railways (S.N.C.F.), nationalized as early as 1938,
coped with the utter devastation suffered by the whole system
during the war years. They repaired bridges [1] and permanent
way, rebuilt stations and carried out a thousand tasks with
despatch and efficiency, as well as electrifying hundreds of
miles of track on the main lines. No more convincing evidence
could be adduced of the survival of that traditional zest for
work, which, with order and thrift, has always been the most
prized virtue among the bourgeoisie and the peasants.

The changes in France since the Second World War, and
particularly the devaluation of the franc, have made necessary
a system of social security; personal thrift can no longer
guarantee to provide adequately for spells of ill-health, for the
exigencies of a large family, or even a modest competency for
old age. France, therefore, in 1946, instituted a system of
nation-wide social security. Unlike the British system, the core
of which is the provision of unemployment benefit, the French
scheme attributes first importance to family allowances, the
reason being, of course, that, while Britain was obsessed by the
memory of years of mass-unemployment, France, where labour
is scarce, not redundant, had no such memories and was
haunted by the decline in the birth-rate and the spectre of
depopulation. France claims that, contrary to what happens
elsewhere, her own system of social security is based, not on
taxation, but exclusively on the contributions of the bene-
ficiaries. Unemployment pay falls, not under the social

---

[1] It was estimated that more than 6000 bridges were destroyed.

security scheme, but under *assistance* (State relief). France, like Great Britain, is taking shape as a Welfare State (*L'Etat Providence*).

In the modern world no country, be its agriculture and its industry never so nicely balanced, can provide from its own resources everything necessary to its existence. France still needs coal, though she does her best to replace it by hydro-electric power; in spite of well-tended forests, she has to import timber and wood-pulp; the far-flung territories of the French Union provide hardly any petrol or fuel-oil and France imports large quantities of both; she depends on imports from abroad for raw materials—wool, cotton and silk—for her textile factories. From the U.S.A. she receives machine-tools and chemical products.

Her agriculture furnishes many of the exports with which France pays for these imports: from the French vineyards wine and liqueurs have flowed for centuries to transform meals into banquets the world over—did not the Bordeaux wine-trade send its vintage clarets to grace English baronial tables as early as the twelfth century, when England held Aquitaine? France's fresh and dried fruits and early vegetables bring in vast sums from abroad. Not all her exports, however, are luxury products. From Lorraine come iron-ore and potash in vast quantities; bauxite (aluminium ore) mined close to the ancient and picturesque site, near Arles, of Les Baux, from which it gets its name, represents a huge share of the bulky exports, among which figure also cast-iron and steel. Many distinctive motorcars are also exported. No less than a quarter of French exports (among them textiles and machines) are despatched to her overseas territories. They, in their turn, supply the mother-country, among other produce, with oils and fats. France counts on greatly expanding this colonial trade, while realizing that, even when the territories have been developed, she will still need to import much from the outside world. She must therefore continue to encourage tourists who bring in millions of foreign currency, to develop mass production of heavy goods, and to cultivate, even more intensively, those luxury products, from field, vineyard and artisan's workshop, which cheer the

hearts and the eyes of dwellers in latitudes more austere. No
country perhaps has appreciated French luxury for longer,
perhaps none appreciates it more, than France's best customer,
Great Britain. As Voltaire put it in his eulogy of luxury,
written over two centuries ago:

> Ainsi l'on voit en Angleterre, en France,
> Par cent canaux circuler l'abondance.
> Le goût du luxe entre dans tous les rangs:
> Le pauvre y vit des vanités des grands;
> Et le travail, gagé par la mollesse,
> S'ouvre à pas lents la route à la richesse.[1]

[1] *Défense du Mondain ou l'Apologie du luxe* (1737).

CHAPTER V

INSTITUTIONS

Parliament

THE Revolution and the Empire made modern France with her unified and centralized institutions. It would be unjust, however, to ignore the part played by the kings of France in welding the country into a politically unified area. Roman Gaul, broken up by the barbarian invasions, became, after the civil wars of the seventh century, a jigsaw puzzle of two or three hundred independent states, ruled by dukes or counts, bishops or abbots. Clovis, crowned King of the Franks in 481, Charlemagne and Hugh Capet, all helped in the work of unifying France. The process of extending the Royal domain went on right through the Middle Ages. Beginning with a small fief around Paris, the kings persistently increased their domain by conquest, by negotiation and by marriage. Despite the set-backs caused by the Hundred Years War and by the religious strife of the sixteenth century, France, in Louis XIV's time, had achieved her present hexagonal shape, recovering in great measure the hexagon of Roman Gaul, bounded on the land side by Alps, Pyrenees and Rhine. The seventeenth century saw France the most united, centralized and powerful country in Europe. The political unity of France achieved by the monarchy was reaffirmed by the voluntary act of its inhabitants when, at the *Fête de la Fédération* on 14 July 1790, fourteen thousand delegates from all the towns and provinces, including Alsace, took a solemn oath of loyalty to the nation.

The piecemeal manner in which the France of the *ancien régime* had been built up left much to be done before centralization could be regarded as complete, for the component territories retained many of their ancient customs and distinctive usages. Legal systems in particular survived in bewildering variety. While the more Germanic north widely practised

customary law, Roman law continued to be administered in
many regions of the south. Voltaire complained that when a
man travelled in France he changed laws almost as often as
he changed post-horses. The centralized and uniform institutions which regulate life in modern France all date from
the deliberations of the Revolutionary assemblies and the
vigorous action of Napoleon.

Parliamentary government in England developed slowly but
continuously from the thirteenth century. In France, after
an early start, it succumbed to the Royal power. Although
the States General in 1356 had proclaimed the right of the
nation's representatives to vote taxes, this national assembly
met infrequently and, after the 1614 session, the States General
were not summoned until the fateful meeting of 1789. The
parlement de Paris, which played an important rôle under the
ancien régime, was not an elected body but rather a High Court
of Justice having the right to register the Royal edicts; its
opposition could be overcome by the King through a procedure known as a *lit de justice*. Parliamentary government
began with the Revolution. Manhood suffrage, proclaimed
in the Constitution of 1793 and again in 1848, was finally
established by Louis Napoleon after the *coup d'état* of 1851.
Universal suffrage, applying to women as well as men, came
only in 1944 (Ordinance of 21 April of the Committee of
National Liberation). It was inscribed in the Constitution
of the Fourth Republic in 1946.

The Constitution of 1946 reproduces many features of the
1875 Constitution under which the Third Republic had been
governed until its disappearance in 1940. Worked out by an
assembly in which three parties were each strong enough to
insist on attention being paid to its views, the 1946 Constitution
marks a compromise between individualism and State socialism, a compromise also between single-chamber government,
desired by the Left since the Convention, and double-chamber
government, which the Left regards as a vestige of aristocratic
régimes. After reaffirming the Declaration of the Rights of
Man of 1789, the Constitution guarantees to women in all
spheres rights equal to those of men, recognizes the right of

every citizen to obtain employment and the right to strike,
and declares that any property or undertaking possessing
or acquiring the character of a public service or of a monopoly
must come under collective ownership.

The Fourth French Republic is a parliamentary democracy.
Though it has two chambers, only one of them, the National
Assembly, is a sovereign chamber; the Council of the Republic,
replacing the former Senate, plays, as its name implies, a
purely consultative rôle. The titular head of the State is the
President of the Republic. The actual powers of government
belong to a Cabinet of Ministers directed by the President of
the Council of Ministers, who is the Prime Minister (though
this title is not the official one). The Cabinet is responsible
to the National Assembly.

The president of the Republic lives in the Elysée Palace,
once the dwelling of Mme de Pompadour, and migrates
in summer to the Château of Rambouillet. Elected for seven
years by the two chambers meeting as Congress at Versailles,
he can be re-elected only once. Top-hatted and tail-coated,
he presides, with some pomp and circumstance but without
the picturesque mediaeval pageantry of Royalty, at national
solemnities. He promulgates the laws, appoints ambassadors
and high administrative officials, signs and ratifies treaties
and takes the chair at the Council of Ministers, i.e. the formal
meetings of the Cabinet. Besides being Head of the Republic,
he holds the Presidency of the French Union, into which the
French Empire has been transformed. All the Presidential
decrees must be countersigned by the Prime Minister and one
other Minister, for the Cabinet, not the President, wields in
reality the executive power. The President of the Republic
takes no part in parliamentary conflicts, he remains above the
strife. At each change of government the President chooses,
after consultation with the Presidents of the two Chambers,
the new Prime Minister, but the chosen candidate can only be
appointed after the National Assembly has expressed, by an
absolute majority, its confidence in him and his Cabinet.

In theory, every citizen, except those belonging to families
who have once reigned in France, may aspire to the Presidency

of the Republic. In practice, under the Third and Fourth Republics, the Presidents have invariably been parliamentary figures, but not usually outstandingly powerful and energetic men. History has taught the French to fear a *coup d'état*—they have not forgotten the two Napoleons and General Boulanger. No French President could say of his office what the American President Woodrow Wilson said of his: 'The President is at liberty, both in law and conscience, to be as big a man as he can.'

The sovereign Chamber, the National Assembly, sits, as did the former Chamber of Deputies, at the Palais Bourbon, a building in the classical style, with Ionic columns and symbolically adorned with statues of Liberty, Public Order, Reason, Justice, Prudence and Eloquence. The 619 Deputies representing France, Algeria and overseas territories are elected by direct universal suffrage. At present a modified system of proportional representation is in use but encounters strong criticism. Every Frenchman and Frenchwoman over 21 years old is entitled, unless deprived of political rights, to vote for a list of candidates for the National Assembly. The candidates must be at least 23 years of age. Every five years the Deputies must face their electors again. Elections take place on a Sunday so that voters may perform their civic duty without losing time from their work. Political life in France revolves almost entirely around the National Assembly. The Assembly alone directly represents the people, who are regarded as the real sovereign power in the State. The Assembly alone votes laws; on it depends the choice of the Ministry that is to govern and the resignation of the Ministry when the Assembly loses confidence in it.

Facing the semicircle formed by the Chamber at the Palais Bourbon, stands the rostrum (*tribune*), on to which members mount when they wish to address the House, for they do not speak from their places as is the Westminster usage. Each member sits at his desk, which has a lid which he can bang when he wishes to demonstrate hostile sentiments. The Speaker (*Président de l'Assemblée*) occupies a seat above the rostrum and Left and Right wing parties sit on the left and right of the

The Dam at Sarrans

The Chamber of Deputies
(Le Palais Bourbon)

Chamber looking towards the rostrum. The extreme Left is occupied by the Communists, disciples of Marx and Lenin, working towards the realization of a classless society and striving to avoid the formation of any bloc hostile to Soviet Russia. Next come the Socialists, professing either the humanitarian and democratic tradition of Jaurès or the more 'scientific' socialism of Jules Guesde. The third major party in the Assembly is that of the Catholic Democrats, the M.R.P. (*Mouvement Républicain Populaire*), a new party which emerged under the Fourth Republic. The M.R.P. carries on the tradition of Lammenais and Lacordaire and strives towards achieving a society in which the 'rights of man' can be combined with the Christian outlook on life. It professes to share the Socialist zeal for nationalizing key industries, the Socialist hostility to private monopolies and the Socialist attitude towards domination of the worker by the capitalist; but it strongly resists Socialist anti-clericalism as applied to the schools and it opposes any action against religion.

The Radical-Socialists—neither Radicals nor Socialists but bourgeois anti-clericals—who so often formed the nucleus of any governing coalition in the days of the Third Republic, once more constitute a major party. Like the English Liberals of the nineteenth century, the Radical-Socialists oppose State control, defend private enterprise and claim that the businessman has a right to lawful profits. The party has always espoused the cause of the 'small man', favouring the small business and declaring itself the friend of the small farmer. Its anti-clericalism separates it from the Conservative parties, such as the *Fédération Républicaine*, which is nationalist, clerical, authoritarian in home affairs but, like the Radical-Socialists, favours economic liberalism. This last-mentioned doctrine forms the main plank in the platform of M. Paul Reynaud's *Alliance Démocratique*, which is Right-Centre. The Rally of the French People (*Rassemblement du Peuple Français*, R.P.F.), founded by General de Gaulle, appears in the rôle of a pressure group rather than as a parliamentary political party. It severely criticizes parliamentary government, calls for a Constitution admitting a more authoritarian government under a

G

powerful President, fiercely hates Communism, yet is averse to
any systematic agreement with Great Britain and the U.S.A.

The Council of the Republic replaces the more powerful
Senate of the Third Republic, which it succeeded in the
seventeenth-century Palais du Luxembourg, once the home of
Marie de' Medicis, Henry IV's Italian queen. Since the end
of 1948 the councillors have been given official permission to
describe themselves on their visiting-cards as *Sénateurs*, but
their powers compare very unfavourably with those of their
predecessors. In no circumstances can the Council bring
about the fall of the government, as the Senate could and did.
Bills are indeed sent up from the National Assembly to the
Council, just as bills were sent up from the Chamber of
Deputies to the Senate. If the Council expresses a favourable
opinion or if no opinion is expressed within a stated time, the
bill becomes law. If the opinion is unfavourable and amendments are proposed by the Council, the bill is given a second
reading by the National Assembly. The Assembly may reject
wholly or in part the Council's amendments, but in this case
the Assembly's vote must be by an absolute majority.

The 320 members of the Council of the Republic must be
35 years of age (the minimum Senatorial age was 40); while
some are elected by Algeria and French overseas territories, the
greater number represent metropolitan France. These are
elected by indirect suffrage: municipal councillors choose
delegates who, with the General Councillors[1] and Deputies of
the *département,* form the electoral colleges which designate the
Councillors of the Republic.[2] These Councillors are elected
for six years; every three years half of them retire but may
of course offer themselves for re-election. They may bring
forward bills, but any bill they sponsor is simply laid on the
table of the House and transmitted, without debate, to the
National Assembly. Any bill sponsored by a Councillor must
not entail a decrease in national income or an increase in
national expenditure.

[1] The French *conseillers généraux* correspond approximately to the British County
Councillors.
[2] Members of both Chambers receive a salary. France decided to pay her
Members of Parliament long before Britain did so.

In addition to the two Chambers, several bodies share in the government of France but in a purely consultative capacity. The Council of State (*Conseil d'État*), founded in 1800 and housed in the Palais Royal, gives its views on the drafting of parliamentary bills before they are submitted to the Assembly and examines them afterwards to integrate them into the framework of existing laws. A newly created Economic Council may be, and in certain cases must be, consulted by the government about bills that affect the economic condition of the country.

Parliamentary government has not evolved in France into the British pattern of a clear-cut conflict between two powerful parties, each with serried battalions of highly disciplined troops. Although, with the Communist example before their eyes, French political parties have strengthened their organization and discipline, the multi-party set-up prevails under the Fourth as it did under the Third Republic. English political writers explain the multiplicity of parties by the mode of polling adopted (proportional representation) and prefer the United States system, which favours the English device of simple majority polling and has the two-party organization. They forget that France had used simple majority polling for legislative and senatorial elections during the Third Republic and abandoned it because it failed to produce a durable parliamentary majority. The interesting problem is surely *why* the multi-party system has so long flourished in France. The explanation must be sought in the psychology of the French people. Temperamentally they are individualists, and the geographical variety of the country accounts in some measure for the diversity of outlook. While undoubtedly opinions can be classed in two main groups, the Right with its belief in the known and tried, the Left eager for progress and experiment, a wide range of intermediate positions exists, each held with something of the fanaticism of men convinced that their view expresses ultimate truth.

The French appear to prefer a system that calls for skill on the part of the temporarily dominating majority and would look askance at a strong party forcing its policy through by

mere strength of numbers. Were France to have two powerful
political parties, the supporters of the minority would regard
themselves as totally disfranchised and would feel in consequence that they had an intolerable grievance against the
majority. Differences between Right and Left in France have
normally been more violent than in Great Britain, and a strong
government by one of two powerful parties would offer more
dangers than advantages. Even to-day many men of the Right
entertain the hope of utterly extirpating the men of the Left
. . . and vice versa! A two-party parliament works satis-
factorily enough if the two opposing parties have sufficient
common ground, and that has so far been more obviously
the case in Great Britain than in France. Moreover, the committee habit and the discipline of games, both of which bring
home early to the British boy and girl the conviction that good
form implies the acceptance of the captain's choice or the
majority decision, are not features of French school life. Instead,
however, of girding at France's inadequate notion of parliamentary democracy and concluding that her political set-up is
all wrong, it would be fairer to bear in mind that, under the
parliamentary régime as practised by the Third and Fourth
Republics, France appears to flourish and that most Frenchmen,
though as prone to complain as we are ourselves, seem to find
life very tolerable. When we deplore their political instability,
let us remember that to the seventeenth-century Frenchman
it was England that appeared to be politically unstable and the
English whose political temperament was condemned as over-
exuberant. Generalizations about a country's politics may not
be valid for more than a few generations.

The governments of the Palais Bourbon, compared with
those at Westminster, show great instability, most of the
Ministries of the Fourth as of the Third Republic counting
their existence in months rather than years. Under the two-
party system as practised in Britain, the government is the
agent of the majority in the House of Commons and, since the
Whips apply party discipline strictly, the Ministry in office
can look forward confidently to receiving continued support
from its majority. When, as in France, many parties exist,

none of which numbers enough members to afford an absolute majority, every government is perforce a coalition. Coalitions show less stability than homogeneous parties. Since the Chamber of Deputies, under the Third Republic, was only dissolved when it had completed the four years for which it was elected, the Deputies had every inducement to wreck the government. In the reshuffle likely to occur at the formation of a new Ministry, some of the Deputies previously disappointed had a chance of securing a portfolio; Deputies were tempted to fling out a Ministry in which they had not been included in order to replace it by a combination in which they might be. If, on the contrary, the defeat of the government had implied dissolution of the Chamber, each Deputy, having to face his constituents again, would have run the risk of losing his seat.

With the problem of achieving government stability in mind, the makers of the 1946 Constitution provided for dissolution. But they defined the conditions justifying dissolution with such precision that, though a whole series of governmental crises and defeats occurred in 1948, the exact situation justifying a dissolution according to the Constitution never arose. It looks as though France still prefers, as she has preferred so long, that the Assembly, representing by directly elected mandataries the sovereign people, should be stronger than the government. The French people always fear that a government tends to become tyrannical; in the hearts of those not in power smoulders a jealous distrust of those who are, and they strive to the utmost to prevent the government settling comfortably down into permanent authority.

Not only has the Ministry to cope with the varying moods of the powerful National Assembly, it has also to hold its own against the numerous Commissions or standing committees which the Assembly appoints to deal with practically every department of government. These general Commissions (there are nineteen of them) comprise not only representatives of the government parties or groups but of every political group in the Assembly according to its numerical strength. Every bill, including the budget, comes before the appropriate Commission for examination. When a Commission feels ill-will towards the government, it can twist bill or budget into a very different shape from that intended by the government. The Commissions also supervise the activities of the various Ministries and can make their criticism felt. As the Commissions remain in office during the whole five years of the parliamentary session, they have more permanence than any government, for no government lasts five years. They look upon themselves as more fully representative of democracy than the government; are they not directly elected by the sovereign Assembly emanating from the sovereign people? Here again we see very clearly that, in France, power belongs to the elected Assembly rather than to the Cabinet and that parliamentary government in France means government by parliament and not, as at Westminster, government by a party.

Local Government

In England, local government grew up spontaneously during the centuries and, like parliamentary government, forms part of the national tradition. In France, local government started very early and, even before the Hundred Years War began, many towns had acquired the right to administer their own affairs. The Royal power scented possible danger even in this modest measure of decentralization, and Henry IV and Louis XIII left little independence to any of the communes. Louis XIV deprived them of the right to choose their own mayors. At the Revolution dawned an era of liberty, and the Constituent Assembly created 44,000 communes, giving to each the right to elect a municipal council and a mayor enjoying wide powers. Bringing this devolution of authority to an abrupt end, Napoleon established a system even more strongly authoritarian and more highly centralized than anything the *ancien régime* had known. The *intendants* and *subdélégués*, who had administered the provinces for the monarchy, were replaced by prefects who were to govern the newly created departments, by sub-prefects for the arrondissements into which the ninety departments were divided, and by mayors to rule the communes. All these officials were appointed, of course, not by the people but by the government. These

agents of the central government supervised all the details of
the national life. In setting up this very centralized and hierarchical administration, Napoleon no doubt found his inspiration in the example set by the Roman Empire.

This organization, now hallowed by time, still functions
to-day. The Third Republic modified the authoritarian
mechanism in some slight measure in 1884, when the communes
obtained the right to elect their mayors and municipal councils.
But, on the whole, 'local government' still depends on the
Ministry in Paris, and officials, nominated in Paris, are despatched into the departments and arrondissements, forming
a nation-wide network to administer taxes, roads, education
and the manifold activities which constitute local government.

Each of the ninety departments, neatly divided into arrondissements, cantons[1] and communes, is governed by a prefect,
whose title recalls the *Praefectus Urbis* of the Romans. A
political officer, he discreetly watches the state of political
feeling in his district and reports his observations to the
Minister of the Interior, who has nominated him and who
can dispense with his services if he sees reason to do so. The
prefect controls all the government machinery, is responsible
for the appointment of officials, including roadmen and
teachers, and he signs the orders for all payments. He may
even make arrests when necessary. Limits to his powers are
set by the local Deputies, whose criticisms he cannot afford
to ignore, and by the General Council of the Department
(*Conseil Général*), a body elected by the citizens to work in
association with him. (The nearest British equivalent is the
County Council.) Between 200 and 300 Deputies are members
of these *conseils généraux*. At the half-yearly meeting of the
council the prefect sits beside the chairman, but does not vote.
A smaller body, a committee chosen by the council and known
as the Departmental Commission, ensures a more continuous
attention to finance. Though the prefect must carry out the
decisions arrived at by the General Council, the council do not
appoint the officials who carry out the work in the department.

---

[1] *Arrondissement* is a main administrative district and a *canton* a sub-division
of an *arrondissement*.

The organization of the arrondissement, with its sub-prefect and its *Conseil d'arrondissement*, is exactly similar to that of the department. The canton has no official or council in charge of its administration, but is the seat of the justice of the peace (*juge de paix*).

France has about 38,000 communes, and they range in size from cities like Bordeaux and Lille to tiny villages. At the head of each commune officiates a mayor, elected by the municipal council; he may be a Minister (like M. Herriot in Lyons), a Senator (a third of the present Senators serve as mayors in their communes), a businessman, a workman or a peasant. Besides being the elected representative of his commune he transmits, as a government functionary though unpaid, orders from the Ministry in Paris, and petitions from his *administrés* to Paris. Officially head of the municipal police, he appoints the *agents* in his town, or, if his is a rural commune, he chooses the humble *garde-champêtre*. He administers the property of his town or village; handles the multifarious tasks concerned with housing, street-cleaning and the rest; prepares, in consultation with his council, the municipal budget; keeps the registers of births, marriages and deaths; and takes the chair at the frequent meetings of the council. One or more elected *adjoints* take some of the burden from his shoulders and, in the country, he usually can count on the village schoolmaster to act as his secretary. In every commune the official acts of mayor and council, including the municipal budget, are subject to revision by the prefect of the department, and if not approved by him are sent back to the mayor and council for reconsideration.

There is no mayor of Paris, where the duties of mayor are performed by the Prefect of the Seine and the Prefect of Police. Minor mayoral functions are performed by the mayors of the twenty arrondissements into which the city is divided for purposes of municipal government. Paris has a municipal council, but the mayors have no place in it; the chairman of this council enjoys considerable prestige. The city of Lyons also has a special régime. These exceptional arrangements reflect the central government's fear that the mayor of a large city might become too powerful.

In the nineteenth century, local government in France and England offered a striking contrast. On one side of the Channel flourished a 'natural' system, native to the soil, with its roots deep in the past: the natural leaders of the people, the local aristocracy—lords or squires—in their traditional setting, administering local government—dispensing justice to their villagers, founding schools, cottage hospitals and clubs; in the towns, the mayors and corporations ruling their boroughs undisturbed by Whitehall. On the other side of the Channel, teeming cohorts of functionaries were despatched from Paris by an anonymous authority, men without roots in the 'artificial' districts they were sent to govern—a centralized bureaucracy on the Roman model stifling all local initiative.

These violently contrasted pictures in black and white of idyllic paternalism on the one hand and on the other a grim, impersonal bureaucratic discipline imposed by the capital, were obviously somewhat overdrawn by complacent Victorians. To the English villager the squire, especially when as J.P. he administered the laws concerning game, at times appeared in the guise of a tyrant. Many worthy French citizens felt no small satisfaction at the thought that local affairs were being looked after by competent and impartial officials from Paris instead of being the preserve of neighbours about whose competence and honesty they entertained the gravest doubts. Yet the two pictures contain a modicum of truth about the diverse systems. The essential difference between local government in the two countries lies in the firmer grip maintained by the national government in France over the administration of local affairs. The influence of central officials on local government has recently increased. The English government left—and still leaves—to unpaid amateurs (e.g. the County Councils and the Education Committees) extremely wide powers. These unpaid amateurs themselves appoint and control the paid officials who carry out the actual work of local government. The State in France has always shown marked reluctance to allow responsibility in such matters to locally elected bodies, doubtless because it feared lest local interests should overshadow the interests of the nation as a whole. In nine-

teenth-century England the belief was widely held that
responsibility might safely be given to private initiative and
that, indeed, the less the State meddled in local government
the healthier would be the national life.

In an age when England, like most European countries,
continued to follow the traditional aristocratic pattern of
government, France provided the first example of the modern
form of State: centralized, democratic, equalitarian. Having
long looked upon this novel creation as unnatural and probably unworkable, England is now moving, with unwonted
precipitation think some, with a speed justified by the urgency
of the situation according to others, towards the French type
of centralized and equalitarian State. In England to-day the
State undertakes more and more activities that were once left,
not wholly unsuccessfully perhaps, to private initiative or to
the public spirit of the citizens. Not only education, but public
assistance, the health service, gas, electricity, the coal-mines
and some forms of transport have become national enterprises.
In England much more of the work in these vast schemes falls
to be done by local and municipal bodies than devolves upon
them in France. However, since the State pours ever-increasing
subsidies into the municipal coffers, Whitehall acquires ever
greater power in the direction of municipal policies. In the
interests of uniformity the locally elected bodies find their
activities more closely directed and more strictly supervised.
Though no civil servant is despatched from Whitehall to govern
borough or county as the prefect governs his department,
numerous inspectors and auditors swoop down on the provinces,
armed with brief-cases bulging with instructions, and carry out
much the same task as that performed by the prefect in France.
It is an arresting thought that whereas France aimed, in 1789,
at liberty, equality and fraternity and carried out two supplementary revolutions, in 1830 and in 1848, to effect democratic
reforms not fully established by the first revolution, the
island, so long and until so recently aristocratically governed,
was destined to anticipate France in founding the Welfare
State or, as the French call it, *L'Etat Providence*.

Justice

Under the *ancien régime* the French judicial system, with its *parlements*, its *baillages*, its *sénéchaussées*, its remnants of manorial justice high and low, presented a spectacle of almost inextricable confusion. Attempts were made, particularly under Louis XIV, to introduce some order into this feudal chaos by codifying existing laws, but great diversity survived until the Revolution. Then this heterogeneous judicial structure was swept away with the rest of the *ancien régime*. In 1790 the Constituent Assembly decreed that a general code of simple and clear laws should be compiled dealing with every aspect of relationship between citizens—all of whom were now equal. Napoleon, in 1804, carried out the reforms decided upon by the Constituent Assembly. The Code Napoléon became henceforth the law of the land. Though this was the first legal code founded on the principle of equality among citizens, not all the laws were new, for it embodied laws that had proved their worth in practice, including customary laws of the *ancien régime* and principles taken from Roman law. But a new spirit breathed in it, and for that reason the Code Napoléon commended itself to many foreign nations. Germany, Italy, Belgium, Holland, Rumania, Egypt, Japan and Turkey used it as a basis for their legal systems, and it was adopted by several South American states.

Eight codes cover the various departments of law, the two most important, the Civil Code, concerned with property and inheritance and completed by the Code of Civil Procedure, and the Penal Code, under which cases are tried according to the rules set down in the Code of Criminal Procedure. English law, never codified, has been gradually built up partly from statutes (Acts of Parliament), partly from common law, unwritten, based on customs recognized by the Law Courts, on previous judicial decisions and on authoritative statements in ancient learned tomes like those of Coke and Blackstone. But in the French courts nothing, in principle, counts except the written word of the code. In practice, decisions on the interpretation of obscure points of law made by one Court are invoked by other Courts in the interests of uniformity, though these decisions have no statutory validity.

Other features differentiate the administration of justice in the two countries. In France the bench is not recruited from among experienced members of the bar. Judges and barristers belong to two distinct professions. Less well paid than English judges, French judges are more numerous. Justice costs less. There appears to be no French parallel to the ironical *obiter dictum* of an English legal luminary: 'The law is open to all—like the Ritz Hotel!' The French do not, like the English and the Americans, entrust a single judge with the responsibility of making decisions; in all courts, except the *cabinet du juge de paix*—the lowest rung of the ladder—three judges at least must concur in any judgment for it to be valid.

In Anglo-Saxon countries many people believe that in French criminal trials the accused is presumed to be guilty until he has proved his innocence. This is not so. French law, like English law, puts the burden of proof upon the prosecution. 'Une règle absolue dans notre droit contemporain', states a standard work,[1] 'est que le doute bénéficie à l'inculpé.' How then has the widespread belief to the contrary grown up? It is, declares an expert, because French procedure *appears* to aim primarily at obtaining a confession (*un aveu*). French law permits the prosecutor to prove the guilt of the accused by any method which is logically probative, any method which will result in the Court's having the *intime conviction*—a firm and settled persuasion—of that guilt. In English criminal law the Crown is bound by stricter rules of evidence. The bad character and even the previous convictions of the accused cannot be admitted as evidence, nor can the accused be required to answer any questions whatever. It is, continues the expert, the necessity laid upon the French accused to give an explanation which has led ill-informed English observers to conclude that in France the prisoner is presumed guilty.[2]

[1] Donnedieu de Vabres, *Droit criminel*, 91240, quoted by C. J. Hamson.
[2] C. J. Hamson, 'The Criminal Process in England and France', in *The Times*, 15 and 16 March 1950.

In the French criminal courts the English system of examination-in-chief, cross-examination and re-examination is unknown. No bewildered witness has to face ruthless cross-examination by a skilled advocate seeking to entangle him. It is the presiding judge, not the prosecutor or the defending counsel, who interrogates the prisoner and the witnesses.

Anglo-Saxons are often puzzled by the part played in French criminal justice by the examining magistrate, known as the *juge d'instruction*. When a person has been arrested or is suspected of a crime, the *parquet* (i.e. the public prosecutor and his deputies) calls upon the Court to inquire into the accused's guilt. The judge chosen for this examination (in the provinces often a young man who is learning his profession) is called the *juge d'instruction*. He has the right to detain the accused for not more than twenty days on his own authority. He first interrogates the accused (*l'inculpé*) as many times as he considers necessary, but always in the presence of the accused's counsel. He then hears and questions the witnesses without the accused and his counsel. Finally, the accused is confronted with the witnesses. If the *juge d'instruction* finds a case against the accused, he sends the document to the Public Prosecutor and, after consultation, the matter is dealt with by the *Chambre des mises en accusation*, which may commit him for trial at the Assizes. This procedure has been criticized as constituting a private trial which may prejudice the accused before his public trial. French lawyers claim that this system works out less unfavourably for the accused than would an inquiry made by the police, who are not, like the *juge d'instruction*, controlled by the Council of State. In England until 1933 a grand jury inquired into the guilt of an accused person before he was indicted on a charge. Since the grand jury was abolished, prosecutors are often specially nominated members of the local police, as readers of detective novels are no doubt aware.

The French judicial system fits neatly into the system of land divisions. Canton, arrondissement and department have each their own tribunal, and the highest Court sits in the capital. The humblest Court, that of the justice of the peace (*juge de paix*) functions in each canton. The *juge de paix* is not, like the English J.P., an unpaid amateur but a government official, and he administers both civil and criminal justice. When a civil case comes before him he must try to reconcile the parties at variance, and no case may be taken before the Court of First Instance until the *juge de paix* has made this attempt at reconciliation. He can, when small amounts of money are at stake, settle summarily a variety of minor disputes—damage to crops, quarrels between neighbours, differences between hotel keepers and travellers, and so on. In his *cabinet* a more homely and paternal atmosphere reigns than in the higher courts and he is less strictly tied down by legal formalities. When acting *au criminel*, i.e. as a police-court magistrate, he judges minor infractions of the law (*contraventions*) such as cycling without lights, driving a car without a licence, etc. He can fine offenders and can commit them to prison for fourteen days or less. In the more important cases appeal may be made to the Court of First Instance. In both civil and police-court cases the *juge de paix* sits alone.

The three or more judges who constitute the *Tribunal de Première Instance* in the chief town of the arrondissement wear a black gown and a silver-embroidered toque. In its civil capacity the Court (corresponding to an English County Court) deals with matters such as sales, contracts, mortgages and divorce. The plaintiff's case must be set out in written documents by an *avoué* (solicitor, attorney-at-law). The *avoué* does not usually plead, but if a party in a lawsuit wishes the case to be argued he may engage an *avocat* (barrister), Both *avoué* and barrister wear toque and gown; the barrister's black gown has a stole or *épitoge* worn over the left shoulder.

When sitting as a criminal Court (*Tribunal correctionnel*), this Court judges such offences as theft, fraud and assault. The Court can inflict a maximum penalty of five years' imprisonment. The accused (*le prévenu*), who may or may not be in custody, is interrogated by the presiding judge, on whom devolves the duty of discovering the truth about the accusation. The witnesses for the prosecution and for the defence are then heard but are not cross-examined by counsel. The public prosecutor thereupon rises to make his indictment and call for the application of the law to the accused. He is followed by the barrister briefed for the defence, who attempts to put his client's case in the most favourable light. The Court has no jury and the judges pronounce their verdict after, or without, deliberation in private.

The twenty-five Appeal Courts (*Cours d'appel*) in metropolitan France hear appeals both in civil and criminal cases. Five judges, who hold the title of *Conseillers à la Cour*, wear black gowns, but on great ceremonial occasions they don the scarlet robes that, under the *ancien régime*, distinguished judges who tried crimes. These judges re-try cases coming up from the Courts of First Instance, taking into account matters of fact and matters of law. Whereas in the lower Court the *procureur de la République* and his *substituts* forming the *parquet* act as public prosecutor, in the Appeal Court the *parquet* comprises an *avocat-général* as well as a *procureur-général*, each with his deputies. The *parquet* is also known as *la magistrature debout*, the judges who try the case being called *la magistrature assise*. The Appeal Courts do not receive appeals from the Assizes.

At the Assizes (*Cour d'assises*), held quarterly in each department, but fortnightly—practically in continuous session—in Paris, sit three judges, and a jury is empanelled. Sinister figures succeed one another in the dock: murderers, assassins, men charged with arson or armed burglary. Their misdeeds rank as *crimes*, not mere *délits*. The Court has power to pronounce the death sentence (decapitation by the guillotine, not hanging), sentence of imprisonment with hard labour, and penal servitude. Procedure at the Assizes resembles that at the *Tribunal correctionnel*, except that an *avocat-général* appears as public prosecutor or 'Counsel for the Crown' and that the jury pronounces the verdict. This need not be unanimous, a majority verdict suffices. The judges, after deliberation, announce the penalty corresponding to the finding of the jury. Juries, particularly those of the Seine department, have the reputation of being susceptible to eloquence, and on occasion murderers for whom their counsel has made a heart-rending plea on sentimental grounds (*crimes passionnels*) have been known to escape with a surprisingly mild punishment. Women may be condemned to death, but gallantry, if not the law, makes it customary to commute the sentence to one of imprisonment. French journalists at times gird at British ruthlessness with murderesses.

The Assizes deals not only with crimes but with cases which concern the freedom of the Press, e.g. libel by a newspaper on a government official or a Minister. Journalists would rather stand for trial before a jury of ordinary citizens at the Assizes than face a tribunal composed of government functionaries.

Appeals from the Appeal Courts or from the Assizes go before the *Cour de Cassation*, the supreme Court of Appeal. This august body examines only matters of law (procedure, etc.), not matters of fact. If the procedure of the lower Court shows some irregularity, or if the judges had failed to respect the law, the judgment is quashed (*cassé*). The case goes back for re-trial by another Court of the same standing as the Court in which the disputed judgment was pronounced.

First offenders in France usually benefit by the *loi de sursis* or Bérenger Law (1891), which provides that, when the Court so decides, the offender may be exempted from serving his term of imprisonment or other penalty if he does not appear before the Court during the following five years. On a second conviction the initial penalty is added to that which he then incurs.

France possesses a special commercial and industrial juris-diction. In a number of towns disputes between employers and workers are taken before the *Conseil des prud'hommes*, an elected conciliation board comprising an equal number of masters and men. Their status corresponds to that of the *juge de paix* and he is called in to take the chair when deadlock occurs. In towns with no *Conseil des prud'hommes* the *juge de paix* deals with cases relating to wages, dismissals and other industrial disputes. Appeals come before the Commercial Court (*Tribunal de commerce*), also an elected, unpaid body of tradesmen and retired tradesmen. The Commercial Court judges disputes about banking transactions and sales, and it receives declarations of bankruptcy.

COURTS OF LAW

Territorial Div.	Number	Criminal	Civil	Industrial and Commercial	Administrative
Group of Departments	1	COURT OF CASSATION			COUNCIL OF STATE
Department	25	COURT OF APPEAL			Regional Council
	90	Assize Court			
Arrondissement	279	*Tribunal of First Instance* (a) Correctionnel;	(b) Civil	*Commercial Court*[1]	
Canton	3027	*Juge de Paix* (a) Tribunal de simple police	(b) au civil[2]	Council of Trade Arbitrators (Conseil des prud'hommes)	

[1] There are 214 in industrial and commercial towns.
[2] *i.e.* exercising civil jurisdiction.

H

Administrative Law

No system of administrative law exists in English-speaking countries. Indeed, until recent years they were wont to boast that there lay the secret of their freedom. Their public officials, amenable to common law and liable to be tried in the ordinary courts of justice, found in this common status a reminder that they were the servants of the public, not its masters. In France, any charge against a government official, any complaint against a government order must be judged by special tribunals. Ever since 1790 judges have been forbidden to interfere in any way with the operations of administrative bodies. If any English police-car, while chasing a burglar, runs over and injures a bystander, the driver may be charged before any ordinary civil Court, and if convicted will have to pay compensation. If the driver of a French police-car is equally unfortunate, he will appear before a special administrative Court, and the State will pay any damages awarded. These special administrative Courts—the Regional Councils and the Council of State—are composed of State officials.

English jurists long scented danger in the existence—in France as in most Continental countries—of special tribunals, since they put government servants in a privileged position, beyond the reach of the common law of the country. The legislators of 1790 certainly intended to protect the agents of the government. In practice, however, the Council of State deals out such even-handed justice that it has won universal approval. Far from providing shelter for peccant officials, it acts as the protector of the rights, the liberty and the property of the private citizen against the Administration. Recourse to the Council of State involves neither much difficulty nor great expense. The lower administrative Courts, the Regional Councils (functioning for a group of Departments instead of for one like the Prefectoral Councils they superseded), deal with a vast number of cases, including innumerable appeals from taxpayers indignant at the amount of their tax assessment.

Many legal authorities in Great Britain to-day no longer

follow the great Dicey in scorning special tribunals as a deplorable Continental aberration but incline to the view that such Courts would be useful in their own country. The State now carries out an increasing number of public services and intervenes so fully in the life of every citizen that some lawyers doubt whether ordinary Courts are suitable tribunals for interpreting modern social legislation and whether they afford the best means of protecting the citizen against the State. Do ordinary Courts of law, it is asked, adequately protect the citizen whose land is threatened with compulsory acquisition? Would he not be better served by Courts specially competent to deal with conflicts between citizen and State? Tribunals outside the ordinary Courts and covering special fields have in fact already come into existence: the Railway-Rates Tribunal, the Market-Board Tribunals and, in 1943, the Pensions Appeals Tribunals. These Courts have grown up sporadically, in the typical English fashion, to meet specific needs; no uniform and symmetrical system has been evolved comparable to that which renders such signal service in France.

Law on Marriage and Inheritance

Law relating to marriage and inheritance recalls the rôle of the long Roman occupation in fixing the traditional pattern of French life and offers some interesting features. The family, despite individualistic trends, remains the basic element in French life. Much of the legislation concerning marriage reflects, though to a less degree than formerly, the Roman principle of making the head of the family all-powerful. Until 1938 the law declared that the wife owed obedience to her husband, and though this formula has now been dropped from the marriage ceremony in its civil form, the husband may forbid his wife to exercise a separate profession and has the right to supervise her correspondence.[1] Until recently, a son or daughter required, up to the age of 25, parents' consent to marry, though after reaching the age of 21 consent could be dispensed with after notification. At present only minors

[1] Code civil, article 1388.

require parental consent to marry. Court action for compensation for breach of promise of marriage is practically unknown in France.

Church and State in France adopt a different attitude towards marriage. The Roman Church looks upon marriage as a sacrament; the State regards it merely as a civil contract. The latter insists that the civil ceremony must precede any marriage in church; a priest who celebrated a wedding before the couple had been officially united by the mayor or his substitute would incur legal penalties. The ceremony at the *mairie* is brief and simple. The mayor, wearing around his waist his gold-tasselled, blue, white and red sash of office, reads the relevant articles (212-215) of the Civil Code, the couple make their declaration, the parents signify their consent if called upon to do so, the wedded pair, the parents and the two witnesses sign the register, and then the mayor may or may not make a speech. This short official ceremony fulfils all the legal requirements. If the families desire a religious marriage, the party then proceed to the church, which stages a more elaborate ceremonial, generally followed by Mass. The Church's attitude to the civil marriage may be inferred from the priest's use of the word 'Mademoiselle' when he addresses the bride.

Many French girls receive a dowry (*une dot*) destined—as among the ancient Romans—to assure the financial stability of the newly founded family. Before the wedding a marriage contract is drawn up by the *notaire*, a public officer who gives legal validity, by registering them, to contracts, wills, sales and other acts. The future bridegroom usually expects the amount of the dowry to bear some relationship to his social position and salary scale.[1] The usual type of contract stipulates *communauté de biens*, according to which the husband and wife are joint owners of the property but the property is managed independently by the husband. Recklessness on his part would justify the wife in applying for *séparation de biens*. If the bride's parents feel that the dowry should be tied down very

---

[1] At one time army officers were only allowed to marry brides whose dowry reached a figure laid down by military law.

firmly, they insist on the *régime dotal*,[1] long favoured by the canny Normans.

Divorce is not recognized by the Roman Church, nor can the Church, strictly speaking, nullify a marriage, a decree of nullity implying the solemn declaration that no real marriage ever existed. The Church can, however, authorize *séparation de corps*, the equivalent of judicial separation, when the couple find life together intolerable. Neither party is free to marry again, since the original marriage is indissoluble. The State allows both divorce and judicial separation.

Minors whose parents are both dead may have a guardian appointed for them by a family council (*conseil de famille*), an institution conceived long ago in France to look after the interests of those members of a family incapable of looking after themselves. The *juge de paix* acts as chairman of the *conseil de famille* and six relatives or friends of the family serve as members. A minor without parents who wishes to marry must obtain this council's permission.

In France the *droit d'aînesse*, giving privileges to the eldest son in the inheritance of property, was abolished at the Revolution, and the present law aims at assuring equality. Estates and heritages must be divided, and the eldest son enjoys no privilege on the score of his seniority. When a man makes his will he has a limited measure of freedom, for he can dispose as he wishes of a certain proportion of his estate (*la quotité disponible*), a proportion which varies with the number of children who must be provided for. It was said, not so long ago, that many small farmers, in order that the farm should not be cut up into such small plots as to make it impossible to earn a living, used to limit the size of their family. Alternately, arrangements were carried out whereby the farm in its entirety was worked by the son most competent to manage it, while he 'bought out' the shares of his brothers and sisters.

[1] A settlement in trust that makes the dowry inalienable.

READING LIST

A. *Parliamentary*

Barthélemy, Joseph. *Le Gouvernement de la France.* Paris, 1939.

Bryce, Viscount. *Modern Democracies,* 2 vols. London, 1921.

Donnedieu de Vabres, H. *L'Etat* (Coll. Que Sais-je?). Paris, 1953.

Duverger, M. *Les Constitutions de la France* (Coll. Que Sais-je?). Paris, 1950.

Fauvet, J. *Les Forces politiques en France.* Paris, 1951.

Finer, H. *Foreign Governments at Work.* Oxford, 1921.

Goguel, F. *France Under the Fourth Republic.* New York, 1952.
Encyclopédie Politique, 2 vols. Paris, 1950.

Laferrière, J. *Manuel de droit constitutionnel.* Paris, 1947.

Lauderdale, D. W. S. *The Parliament of France.* London, 1951.

Malézieu, R., and Rousseau, J. *La Constitution de la IVᵉ République.* Paris, 1947.

Ogg, F. A. and Zink H. *Modern Foreign Governments.* New York, 1949.

Pickles, D. *French Politics. The First Years of the Fourth Republic.* London, 1953.

Poincaré, R. *Ce que demande la cité.* Paris, n.d.

Prélot, M. *Précis de droit constitutionnel.* Paris, 1948.

Siegfried, A., and others. *Aspects de la société française.* Paris, 1954.

Strong, C. F. *Modern Political Constitutions.* London, 1949.

Taylor, O. R. *The Fourth Republic of France.* London, 1951.

Williams, P. *Politics in Post-War France.* London, 1954.

Wright, G. *The Re-shaping of French Democracy.* London, 1950.

B. *Local Government*

Chapman, Brian. *Introduction to French Local Government.* London, 1953.

Delton, H. *L'Administration régionale et locale de la France* (Coll. Que Sais-je?). Paris, 1952.

C. *Justice*

Amos, Sir M. S., and Walton, F. P. *Introduction to French Law.* Oxford, 1935.

Donnedieu de Vabres, H. *Traité élémentaire de droit criminel.* Paris, 1935.
La Justice Pénale d'Aujourd'hui. Paris, 1953.

D. *Social Security*

Getting, R. *La Sécurité sociale* (Coll. Que Sais-je?). Paris, 1953.

CHAPTER VI

FRANCE BEYOND THE SEAS

ALTHOUGH some critics have averred that France has always lacked initiative in colonization, this view cannot well be maintained if one casts back one's mind over French history, with its nine centuries of colonizing tradition, and remembers that France built up two or three successive empires. In the colonial struggles waged between France and Britain, so many French possessions changed hands that the British Empire has sometimes been referred to, not without irony, as 'a present from France'. Although, in this colonial war, France lost and Britain took over the magnificent Indian and Canadian possessions, the French have since acquired such vast territories that these now cover an area twenty-one times as large as that of France herself and more extensive than the territory of the U.S.A. The population of the overseas territories considerably exceeds that of the homeland, making in all a nation of 102 million inhabitants. Nine-tenths of the Empire lies in Africa, stretching from the Mediterranean as far as the Equator. France beyond the seas ranks, in size and population, second among colonial empires.

France acquired her earliest empire—if it can be so termed—in the Middle Ages. One of the first—and perhaps the most successful—of French attempts at colonization was that of 1066, when the Normans, who had adopted the French language only half a century before and in whose veins still pulsed the blood of the restless Vikings, conquered England. The Norman colonization left its mark on English institutions and on the English language, and this affords no matter for surprise, since Norman-French became for four centuries the official language of England. The Norman Conquest spread to southern Scotland, and Scottish national heroes like Bruce and Wallace[1] could

---

[1] See R. L. G. Ritchie *The Normans in Scotland*, p. 224.

claim descent from the Norman knights who settled north of the Tweed.

Soon after the Normans landed at Pevensey, fellow-countrymen of theirs, a few hundred knights in glittering armour under the command of the twelve stalwart sons of Tancred de Hauteville (these Normans ran to large families), had wrested Sicily from the Moslems. They gradually extended their conquests along the shores of the Mediter-ranean, spreading from southern Italy towards the east. Palermo, set among flowers and orchards, became the rich, learned and luxurious capital of the central Mediterranean territories. The Crusades, in which French knights, intent on sustenance and booty though they had been promised the everlasting bliss of Heaven, played so extensive and brilliant a part, merit in some measure the name of colonial enterprises. When that saintly king, Louis IX, was taken prisoner at Man-sourah in 1250 during the seventh Crusade, this time directed against Egypt, French nobles were kings in Naples, Palermo and Acre, others were dukes of Athens, Thebes and Sparta, and yet another was the seventh Latin emperor in Constantinople. Capetian kings ruled Hungary in the fourteenth century. The family of Lusignan, as every student who has studied Voltaire's *Zaïre* will remember, once reigned in Jerusalem, and they also ruled over Cyprus and even Armenia.

The landscape at several points on the eastern Mediterranean (at Rhodes for instance) still reveals churches, fortresses and castles which, even in their ruins, bear witness to the skill of the mediaeval master-masons of France. The French language played so important a part in the Levant that through the centuries the synthetic language used for commercial transactions was called the *lingua franca*, all West Europeans being dubbed Franks. From the time Francis I signed the Capitulations with the Sultan of Constantinople in 1536, France obtained a preponderant position in the Levant and became the protector of all Christians in the eastern Mediterranean. She has always been recognized as enjoying a privileged position in that region.

As was to happen again and again in her chequered history,

France was constrained to relax her overseas efforts in empire-building because of threats to the home country, and the vast French dominion in the Mediterranean vanished like the unsubstantial shadow of a dream. This first 'colonial empire' owed its existence to the doughty deeds of ambitious knights and their retinues in search of military adventure and its attendant profits. Meanwhile a second French colonial empire was being sketched out tentatively by the explorations of enterprising, active merchants and bronzed, hard-bitten mariners. Many of these hardy seamen hailed from the Atlantic coast of France. Though in 1493 Pope Alexander VI had divided the New World between Spain and Portugal, these two countries did not possess an entire monopoly of daring explorers. It appears that French sailors, despite the papal bull, had ventured both into North and South America, but these were isolated efforts, and owing to the discretion observed by these bold men and the disappearance of certain documents, little is known of the achievements of these pioneers. It is known, however, that Francis I, when the Spanish ambassador complained of French ships in American waters, replied: 'Le soleil luit pour moi comme pour les autres, et je voudrais bien voir l'article du testament d'Adam qui m'exclut du partage.'

Naturally enough, the coast of West Africa, much more conveniently near at hand than the vast unknown regions on the other side of the Atlantic, offered greater attractions. Men from Dieppe founded, as early as the fourteenth century, two posts in Guinea, where the estuaries, overhung by a tangle of tropical vegetation, provided an opportunity of approach to the rich market in ivory, gold and other products for which European goods might be exchanged. Meanwhile, in the very opening years of the fifteenth century the Norman, Jean de Béthencourt, set out with fifty men, conquered and christianized the Canary Islands, and proclaimed himself sovereign (1402). Two centuries later the settlers in Guinea, displaced by the Spaniards, set up, in the reign of Louis XIII, an establishment in Senegal, a little further north.

The sixteenth century, which in England marked a period

of high and distant adventure by the Elizabethan seamen, saw
the first notable and lasting achievements in the New World
by the French. As early as 1516 men from Dieppe settled
in Canada. In 1535 Jacques Cartier sailed up the mighty
river, to which he gave the name of St. Lawrence, as far as the
point where it is overlooked by a high hill. On this eminence
he bestowed the name of Mont Royal and from it now shines
down nightly on the vast city of Montreal a huge illuminated
cross. In the following century another significant step in
French colonization was taken in Canada when, in 1607,
Samuel Champlain founded Quebec and reached the Great
Lakes. Champlain later became Governor, and by many
is regarded as the real founder of Canada. A journey
along the St. Lawrence to-day, with its hundreds of white
wooden churches with wooden spires, with its seminaries,
schools and several universities, carries back the mind of the
traveller to those pioneer days of Cartier and Champlain from
whose early settlements have sprung up the immense area
peopled by millions of French Canadians whose numbers
continue to grow and who by their religion and culture slow
down the Americanization of Canada.

We may just glance at the attempts France made during the
religious strife of the sixteenth century to find refuge for
Protestants under distant skies. The Admiral Gaspard de
Coligny dispatched Villegagnon, his Vice-Admiral, to Rio de
Janeiro, where he attempted a settlement of five hundred
very mixed individuals on an island off the coast in 1555.
Since religious disputes divided the colonists and zeal for hard
toil was lacking, the venture came to grief. So did another
attempt in 1562—nearly sixty years before the *Mayflower*
arrived with its cargo of Puritans seeking religious freedom in
America—the handful of Huguenots finding altogether too
grim the torrid and damp regions of Florida where they landed.

Kings and ministers took a keen interest in colonization and
in foreign trade in the seventeenth century. Henry IV founded
an India Company very soon after the East India Company
had been founded by Queen Elizabeth. Colonization and
foreign trade were at this period carried on by companies

holding a monopoly. In France, under Colbert as under Richelieu, these companies, unlike those of England, were directed, not always successfully, by the government. Colbert, that most energetic of ministers, fired with admiration and envy of the wealth of the Dutch and English enterprises, dreamed of a great maritime empire with a teeming population of colonists. Unwilling to leave the ordering of the lives of French colonials to the adventurers who undertook these hazardous tasks, Colbert regulated the lives of men living in exotic conditions, and whose problems were often remote from those faced by the citizens of a French home town, with a precision that all succeeding French governments—and even Napoleon—considered necessary. To Colbert, whose chief aim was to increase the wealth of the mother-country, France owed the development of her colonies in North America, her fisheries off Newfoundland, plantations in the West Indies and in Madagascar, and trading-posts in India. Colbert's mercantile system, known as the Colonial Pact or *Le régime de l'exclusif*, implied that the colonies, having been founded by the mother-country, existed for her benefit. No colonial enterprise, commercial or industrial, was to compete with the products of the homeland, and all foreign traders were to be excluded from the market of the colony. Colbert also speeded up the supply of negro slaves from Africa to toil on the West Indian plantations. When Louis XIV died in 1715, France possessed a considerable colonial domain: large parts of Canada and Louisiana,[1] about ten islands in the West Indies, the island of Cayenne and a part of Guiana in South America, West African trading-posts in Senegal, Gambia and Casamance, l'Ile Bourbon and the Ile de France off the east coast of Africa, and some half-dozen trading-posts in India and Ceylon.

In the course of the eighteenth century this flourishing empire was lost. France, obliged by her neighbours' hostility to keep her eyes fixed on the Rhine, or inclined by national tradition to put European land campaigns before far-off maritime

[1] 'Une délicieuse contrée que les habitants des Etats-Unis appellent le *Nouvel-Eden*, et à laquelle les Français ont donné le doux nom de Louisiane' (Chateaubriand, *René*).

adventure, had neglected her navy, and England had become mistress of the seas. The Treaty of Paris in 1763, which closed the Seven Years War, practically brought to an end France's second colonial empire. France was evicted from India, except for a few trading-posts; Canada, where she had found the fur trade very profitable, and Senegal, whence she drew the supply of labour for the sugar islands, passed to England. She was allowed, however, to retain her valuable fishing-rights off Newfoundland and in the St. Lawrence. When, thanks to help received from France, England's North American colonies were successful in breaking away and the English had to make peace in 1783, France showed no desire to have back Canada. Had not Voltaire some years earlier, in *Candide* (1757), referred to Canada as 'quelques arpents de neige' which he would have liked to see at the bottom of the ocean? At that period, the exotic produce of the West Indies—especially sugar and tobacco—which supplemented, and did not compete with, the products of the home country, interested France more than the broad acres of Canada. Though Suffren took back Pondicherry in 1782, France did not attempt to regain India. The spirit of initiative and adventure in France was, however, still vigorous, and between the treaties of 1763 and 1783 French explorers showed great activity. Bougainville made extensive discoveries in the Pacific, penetrating before Captain Cook as far as Australia; a new attempt on Madagascar was made, and Lauzun retook Senegal, while, shortly afterwards, La Pérouse discovered, in his Pacific wanderings, the Friendly and Norfolk Islands.

During the Revolutionary and Napoleonic periods, though Napoleon occupied Egypt and was tempted by glittering dreams of founding an Indian Empire, his defeat in the Eastern Mediterranean brought these projects to an end. In 1803 he sold Louisiana—whose population of 5,000 in 1717 had by then grown to 50,000—to the United States, thus doubling their territory, while the English gradually occupied or re-occupied the French colonies. At the 1814 Peace Treaty France lost even the Ile de France, re-named Mauritius. France kept her sugar islands in the West Indies, except Tobago and St. Lucia; she retained her trading-posts in India and also Ile Bourbon (La Réunion). If the vast but almost uninhabited territory of Guiana, far away on the other side of the South Atlantic, is left out, France's colonial possessions in 1814 had shrunk to the size of about two French Departments.

The Restoration government saw the beginning of new efforts to revive or reconstitute the colonial empire, particularly in Africa. In 1830, Charles X, remembering perhaps that his namesake Charles IX had negotiated with the Turks for a protectorate over Algiers in 1572, sent an expedition to Algiers, whence, since the fourteenth century, the Barbary pirates had waged war on Mediterranean shipping. This project of 1830 was undertaken against the will of both of the Chambers, of almost all the generals and of public opinion. The city of Algiers was captured after a brief engagement with practically no loss of life among the attackers, a notable feat of arms. The July Revolution of 1830, taking place shortly after the fall of Algiers, did not cause France to withdraw from this legitimist adventure. Even when the British government protested, France decided to maintain her authority there. The conquest of Algeria, a territory about the size of France, continued under Louis Philippe and Napoleon III.

The third colonial empire was built up mainly in Africa and Asia. Under the Third Republic the conquest of Algeria was rounded off by the establishment of a French protectorate first over Tunisia (1881-83) and then over Morocco (1911). The Italians kept a watchful eye on Tunisia, once Roman territory famous for its cornlands. To forestall Italian intervention the French moved an army into Tunisia and set up a French Resident to control foreign policy and to supervise the administration. The Bey of Tunis, nominally a vassal of Turkey, remained, nominally also, the ruler of his territory, and the personnel of his administration was Tunisian.

Though Germany, which after the 1870 war had encouraged the French in colonial adventure, in the hope that such enterprises would weaken the country and embroil France with Great Britain, attempted to cause trouble herself when France proposed to add Morocco to the protectorate in North Africa.

After an incident at Agadir which led her to the brink of war with Germany, France took over the government of Morocco and administered the territory in much the same way as that of Tunisia. The Sultan remained sovereign and religious leader and the native administration functioned under the control of the French Resident, who also handled foreign policy.

Meanwhile the scattered fragments of French possessions in Africa were gradually built up into a new empire: Senegal, Guinea, the Ivory Coast and Dahomey, to which were added the Nigerian territories inland. The conquest of the vast regions in Africa now administered by France was begun under Napoleon III in 1855 and took forty years to complete. For much of the conquest credit must be given to the Third Republic. In comparison with the extent of territory that came under the French flag, the military effort expended was small, much of the fighting being done by native troops under French command. The legendary city of Timbuctoo (Tombouctou), first visited by the Frenchman René Caillé in 1828, became French in 1894. During the second half of the nineteenth century France also gained control of the Sahara, a desert greater in extent than Europe, by occupying the oases. Off the coast of East Africa the island of Madagascar—larger than France—on which Richelieu (the first Minister to conceive a large colonial policy for France) had founded a post in the time of Louis XIII, was conquered in 1895 and declared a French colony.

In Asia, France sought a naval base and a commercial route leading into China and gradually acquired that part of the southern pensinula, known as Indo-China, which divides China (Yunnan province) from Siam: Cochin-China, Cambodia, Annam and Tonkin. These acquisitions brought France her richest colonies, for Indo-China was more than 400,000 square miles in area and had over 50 million inhabitants, but involved a war with China which terminated in 1885. Cochin-China, Annam and Tonkin formed the Republic of Viet Nam.

Such, in brief outline, is the chequered history of France's colonial expansion. To carry out this work, France produced many great colonial governors who were empire-

builders, inspired and sagacious leaders and far above mere
functionaries. Such were, among the military, Marshal
Lyautey (1854-1934), who did his finest work in Morocco,
and Marshal Gallieni (1849-1916), who organized Madagascar.
Among civilians Paul Doumer (1857-1932), who was once
Governor-General of Indo-China and afterwards was elected
President of the French Republic. Since the Second World
War the French Empire has become the French Overseas
Departments and Territories, which, with France, constitute
the French Union. As five categories of overseas territories
exist, the relations between France and the various ex-colonies
present a certain complexity. The Overseas Departments are
(a) Algeria constitutes a Government General and is divided
into three departments (Algiers, Oran, Constantine); (b) Martinique, Guadeloupe, Réunion, Guiana, all colonies of long
standing, have become overseas Departments of France, each
under a Prefect, as in France. The Overseas Territories
are (a) French West Africa—Senegal, Mauretania, Guinea, the
Sudan, the Ivory Coast, Dahomey and the Upper Volta,
(b) French Equatorial Africa—Gabon, Middle Congo, Ubangui
Chari and Chad, (c) Madagascar and its dependencies, the
French Settlement in India,[1] New Caledonia and its dependencies, the French Settlements in the South Sea Islands and
St. Pierre and Miquelon, islands off Newfoundland. Togoland
and the Cameroons (once German colonies, then mandated
territories under the League of Nations) are territories under
trusteeship; and the New Hebrides constitute an Anglo-French
Condominium.

To these categories must be added the French Associated
States, the Protectorates of Morocco, Tunisia and Indo-
China, this last now consisting of Viet Nam and the Kingdoms
of Cambodia and Laos. The position of these Associated
States within the French Union was defined by treaty for each
of them in 1949 and 1950. Since 1946, war has been going
on in Indo-China between France and the nationalists, who
are also Communists (the Viet Minh under Moscow-trained

[1] In the 1954 agreement with Nehru France ceded the territories to the Indian
Government.

President Ho Chi Minh). The French since 1949 recognize the Emperor Bao Dai, once Emperor of Annam, as ruler of Viet Nam. The Government established in N. Viet Nam under Ho Chi-minh is officially known as the Democratic Republic of Viet Nam, that of S. Viet Nam under Bao Dai, is officially designated as the State of Viet Nam. The situation is analogous to that of Korea. The estimated cost of the Indo-Chinese War, it has been stated, reached in 1953 twice the value of all American aid, and 50,000 Frenchmen, all regular soldiers, were fighting in the war.

The differences in political status of the various territories arise from historical causes (e.g. treaties, etc.) and reflect varieties in the general level of culture and civilization reached in each. The N. African territories, for instance, inhabited by Arabs and Berbers, are more developed than the African interior peopled by negroes.

The French Union differs widely from the British Commonwealth. The great empty regions of the French Union are not, like those that gave such scope to the British settlers in Australia and Canada, situated in climates suitable for European settlement, for they include vast deserts like the Sahara. Except for these, the territories of the French Union are already fully occupied by an indigenous population, and this population tends to increase rapidly owing, in a large measure, to the peaceful conditions and the better hygiene brought by the French administration. Lying under a tropical sun and already supporting a large population, the French colonies naturally became colonies of exploitation, not colonies of settlement. Even in Algeria, with its million European settlers—farmers, fruit-growers, wine-growers, traders, as well as administrators—the native African population outnumbers them by eight to one. In New Caledonia, which has a relatively large French settlement, the native population is twice as numerous. In the other overseas territories the French, mostly engaged in administering the country, constitute a small minority—42,000 in Indo-China, in normal times, among 51 million natives, 5,000 in Equatorial Africa among $3\frac{1}{2}$ million Africans.

Since nothing like the mass emigrations from Great Britain to Australia and Canada occurred in France—which had no such excess of population and whose overseas territories were less tempting and mostly unsuitable for settlement—the French Empire held an infinitely smaller place in the daily preoccupations of the ordinary family. Colonization, it might seem, would affect only a small section of the home population in France: families of colonial officials, of army officers, of colonial traders. Yet it must be remembered that a large number of conscripts have served in French overseas territories, and this adds greatly to public interest in what is happening in the French colonies. The French colonial empire of the nineteenth century was built up as the result of persistent government planning and by the efforts of a small number of 'men with a mission'. Little enthusiasm, scant interest even, greeted the far-ranging and significant conquests they made. The mass of the people and the politicians of both Left and Right frequently showed marked hostility to the acquisition of colonies, looking upon them as a burden rather than an asset. A Right Wing deputy stigmatized as 'the maddest and most criminal of enterprises' the conquest of Algeria, and Jules Ferry when Premier was bitterly attacked, first for having acquired Tunis, later for having conquered Tonkin. The wits of the Paris boulevards sneered at Ferry, calling him the Tonkinois. Yet Ferry was a great patriot. In his view the rapidly increasing population of France's aggressive neighbour made it imperative that France, in founding an Empire, should seek not only economic resources but manpower.

Colonial policy or empire-building may proceed along at least three different lines: (*a*) the colonizing power may seek merely to subjugate the territory and exploit its resources; (*b*) it may set out to assimilate the native peoples by instructing them—or the most promising among them—in Western culture and civilization, and admit to citizenship, as a reward, those who reach a satisfactory standard; (*c*) on the other hand, it may attempt to train the native peoples in Western democratic methods of government and administration, so that they may in due course fit themselves for self-government.

I

The policy of subjugation, though once supplying the real motive power of colonization, can hardly commend itself to countries who declare their adhesion to the Atlantic Pact and the United Nations Charter. In the seventeenth and eighteenth centuries French colonization, directed by the State, aimed at increasing the prosperity of the mother-country, for whose interests exclusively the colonies had been founded. The natives were the care of the missionaries, who in Canada and elsewhere displayed great zeal to convert them to Christianity. So zealous indeed were the Jesuit missionaries that Canada was closed to Protestants. The French colonists were governed from Paris; the institutions of their home country were transplanted overseas with them and maintained in the new exotic setting. France, as her own institutions have always shown, was imbued with the spirit of Roman jurisprudence and has always tended to prefer centralized rule for her colonies, as for herself. The colonists were ruled paternally by functionaries dispatched from the mother country.

For centuries France thought first, and sometimes exclusively, of her own citizens established in the colonies; she was inclined to cherish most the interests of her own sons representing France under tropical skies rather than those of the natives among whom they lived. When the native populations began to be considered, the French tended to apply to them the same policy of centralization and assimilation already applied to the colonists. The natives, black, brown or yellow, were to be gradually transformed into neo-Frenchmen. Teaching of native languages was long discouraged, and the boys and girls in the colonial schools filled their copy-books industriously with French words and phrases and the most promising of them passed on to cope with the niceties of the most academic of languages. The policy of assimilation was practised by the Third Republic, tempered to a certain extent during the period following the First World War.

The Second World War brought many of the French colonies into closer touch with the West, and particularly with the Americans, who, with their decided anti-colonial outlook, forgetting that when they broke away from Britain they were not *colonisés* but colonists, encouraged the indigenous peoples to become more insistent than ever on self-government. Moreover, many examples, in the Middle and Far East, of States once occupied by Western powers becoming self-governing (Egypt, Irak, etc.) increased the eagerness of the nationalists in some of the French possessions. Particularly in North Africa and Indo-China the nationalist groups demanding complete independence became more vocal. After all that happened during the war and afterwards, the Fourth Republic was bound to modify its policy in colonial matters. In some measure the idea of assimilation remained powerful. The fully Gallicized 'old colonies' like Martinique, Guadeloupe, Réunion and Guiana became departments of France, governed by Prefects just as is a department in the mother-country, and were proud of this promotion.

The new policy, that of replacing assimilation by the ideal of association and even ultimately granting a measure of self-government in the one-time colonies, reflects a new ideal both among Frenchmen in France and among the indigenous populations themselves. The new view is set forth in the Preamble of the French Constitution of 1946, which declares that: 'France and the overseas peoples constitute a Union founded on equal rights and duties without distinction of race or religion.' Another article of the Constitution (No. 80) states that: 'All nationals of the overseas territory shall have the status of citizens, in the same capacity as French nationals of Metropolitan France or the overseas territories.' And the article continues: 'Special laws shall determine the conditions under which they may exercise their rights as citizens.' The putting into force of such a principle requires a certain amount of time, and, as it is to be expected, some groups of the overseas native populations consider that the pace of reform is too slow.

Revolutionaries are always impatient, and the nationalist minorities in Algeria and Indo-China would in any case have been satisfied with nothing less than immediate autonomy. The mother-country, bearing in mind perhaps that little gratitude would be shown by autonomous ex-colonies for her remarkable achievements in her colonial empire, understand-

ably refused to accept the doctrine that members of the French
Union should have the right to secede from it as Eire had
seceded from the British Commonwealth of Nations. No
doubt France also considered that the vociferous nationalists,
generally town-bred, did not necessarily represent the views
of the less vocal masses, particularly of the vast agricultural
regions generally little known to urbanized agitators; nor did
the impatient agitators necessarily represent the best interests
of the indigenous populations.

Nothing, therefore, is said in the Constitution of 1946 about
the right of the members of the French Union to secede. The
Union was declared to be 'composed of nations and peoples
who pool or co-ordinate their resources and their efforts in
order to develop their respective civilizations, increase their
well-being and assure their security.' The Constitution says
nothing about the co-ordination being undertaken by 'free
consent' of each, as this would have implied the right to break
away. France has no intention of inviting the constituent parts
of the Union to go their own way. France intends to remain
the centre round which the territories revolve and which deter-
mines their course. The system is not centrifugal but centri-
petal. The Union may be far flung, but it is to remain closely
knit. The new colonial régime implies, not shedding each
territory as it reaches self-government, but giving fuller representation in Paris of the interests both of the colonists and of the
indigenous peoples. Thus many more colonies were given
representation by their own elected senators and deputies
in the Council of the Republic and the National Assembly, a
privilege enjoyed already by the old assimilated colonies, who
had long sent their delegates to sit in the Senate and the
Chamber of Deputies. Algeria, which it was once attempted
to assimilate entirely, was declared by statute to constitute
a group of departments, endowed with civil personality,
financial autonomy and a separate organization. In other
colonies and other associated territories local-elected assemblies were set up, not law-making but advisory.

Under the Constitution of 1946 a new body, the Assembly
of the French Union, was set up. It is a purely advisory body

representing, as one of its members said, not a federation but
the hope of a federation. It consists of an equal number of
delegates from France and from the overseas territories of the
Union. It meets in the semicircular hall, otherwise used only
every five years, by the Senators and Deputies combined, to elect
the President of the Republic, in the historic Palace of Versailles,
where the inaugural assembly was held in December 1947.
Its rôle is to advise, not to make laws. Its acting President is
to-day, 1955, an octogenarian administrator, M. Sarraut, and
the Vice-President is a tiny Cambodian princess. A High
Council of the French Union presided over, like the Assembly,
by the President of the Republic, and which met for the first
time in November 1951, is also an advisory body. The actual
government of the overseas territories is still carried out in
Paris by Parliament and by Presidential decrees. Let us not
forget that Overseas France is represented on the National
Parliament by 118 members, 53 in the assembly and 65 in
the Council of the Republic. Algeria, since her charter of
1947, is outside the scope of these decrees. In the case of other
territories the Assembly of the French Union must be consulted before these decrees can be enforced.

Though it has sometimes happened that the advice tendered
by the Assembly of the French Union has not been followed,
it should not be assumed too hastily that France has no intention of ever allowing her overseas territories to progress towards
a wider measure of self-government. But France intends to
maintain the links with the mother-country and to be the guide
and director of the Union. As the last paragraph of the
Preamble to the Constitution declares: 'Faithful to her traditional mission, France proposes to guide the people for whom
she has assumed responsibility towards freedom to govern
themselves and democratically to manage their own affairs;
putting aside any system of colonization based upon arbitrary
power, she guarantees to all equal access to public office and
the individual or collective exercise of the rights and liberties
proclaimed or confirmed above.'

France has done much and spent vast sums of money
on the territories which constitute the Union which she

administers. Her foresters have replanted the arid zones of
North Africa, using new techniques, and will attempt to make
the Sahara, once the granary of Rome, a land where figs and
almonds, olives and apricots ripen on the slopes and terraces.
She has developed their agricultural and mineral resources;
her engineers have built, with native labour, bridges and
dams, roads and railways; her officials and soldiers have
ensured the rule of law; her doctors have, in newly built and
up-to-date hospitals in the towns and by visits to the villages,
raised the standard of health in many regions once ravaged
by epidemics and reduced immensely the death-rate; her
teachers have laboured unceasingly to bring the elements
of education to the inhabitants in the villages as well as the
cities. In education, the French have a double purpose in
mind: 'Instruire la masse et dégager une élite.' Her celebrated *Ecoles rurales* set out to impart elementary education
without causing the natives to despise village life and to hanker
after life in the towns; agriculture and hygiene figure largely
in the syllabus as well as reading and writing in French. For
the masses, rural and urban, vocational training remains the
primary object. For the élite, higher education is provided,
fitting the natives for posts in the government service.

The schools illustrate the absence of that colour prejudice
which tends to be so marked in Anglo-Saxon communities.
In the French African territories black and white children
study together, and a coloured girl may share a desk with an
Admiral's daughter. It has been said that in French African
schools the only difference lies not between black and white
but between those who pass and those who fail their examinations! All learn the French way of life and French language
and something of French civilization. In recent years much
criticism has been directed against the disastrous effect of
European education on the natives, who are freed from tribal
discipline and morality, and often have acquired nothing to
replace duty to the tribe. The French have consequently
somewhat modified their view, and they now allow a place
to indigenous culture. France offers less opportunity to the
coloured population than do the British for training in self-

government, for she intends to remain as the leader and ruler of the diverse peoples who belong to the Union, and for whose benefit she has expended large sums (2,403 million francs for 1931).[1]

And what have the territories of the Union done for France? They have provided a home and a living for one and a half million Frenchmen. During the First World War they contributed no less than 27 million gold francs to the French cause, and large contingents of colonial troops, the most famous being the *tirailleurs sénégalais*, fought for France. Though France does not receive from her vast colonial empire all that she would require in order to be self-sufficient—she remains short of coal, rubber, petrol and cotton—her overseas territories supply a wide range of products to the mother-country more cheaply than she could procure them elsewhere. The French West Indies send rum and tobacco, West Africa coffee and cocoa, Indo-China rice and tea; North Africa sends meat and wine and cereals and olive oil, enormous quantities of ground-nuts are obtained from West and Equatorial Africa. Minerals, especially phosphate and iron, from North Africa and manganese from New Caledonia, reach France, to say nothing of the fisheries still active in St. Pierre and Miquelon, as they have been for centuries.

In times like these, when colonization has to face so many bitter attacks from East and West, wisdom and justice counsel us to remember that great benefits have been brought by France to her overseas territories, and many noble lives spent in improving the lot of distant populations. We may conclude in the words of one of the historians of France's colonial empire: 'La colonisation, pour un pays comme la France, est vraiment la plus noble des œuvres et le plus beau couronnement de son histoire.'

READING LIST

Blet, H.   *Histoire de la colonisation française*, 3 vols.   Paris, 1946-50.
A first-class work, fuller than the manual mentioned below. Numerous and excellent illustrations.

[1] An equivalent at the time of about 25 million pounds sterling.

Hardy, G. *Histoire de la colonisation française.* 5th ed. Paris, 1947. An excellent manual, with interesting illustrations.

Leblond, M. A. *Anthologie Coloniale.* Paris, 1929. Extracts from stories and descriptions of the various parts of the French Union.

Lyautey, Maréchal. *Paroles d'Action.* Paris, 1927. Expounds the ideals of one of the great French colonial administrators.

Revert, E. 'La Politique coloniale de la France. Etude rétrospective', in *Principles and Methods of Colonial Administration.* London, 1950.

Townsend, M. E. *European Colonial Expansion since* 1871. New York, 1941. A comparative study of colonization, designed as a text-book for American colleges. Careful, but with some anti-colonial bias.

Julien, C. A. *From the French Empire to the French Union.* *International Affairs.* Vol. XXVI, p. 487 (Oct. 1950). London.

Part Two

CHAPTER VII

EDUCATION

DURING the Middle Ages, in France as in all Western Europe, the Church controlled education. Even in the Dark Ages, particularly from the time of Charlemagne, the monastic and cathedral schools provided education, not only for future clerics but for young nobles and bourgeois. The mediaeval curriculum comprised the seven liberal arts: the *trivium*—grammar, logic and rhetoric—followed by the *quadrivium*—arithmetic, music, geometry and astronomy. The University of Paris, which received from the Pope its first written statutes in 1210, provided, in its Faculty of Arts, a 'secondary' education consisting of the *trivium* and *quadrivium*. Study in this Faculty was a necessary preliminary to that in the 'higher' Faculties of Divinity, Law and Medicine. In the reign of Henry II (1547-59) 20,000 students from all over Europe frequented the colleges which formed the University. All the Universities of Northern Europe were built up on the model of the University of Paris, and traces of that origin can be discerned in the older Scottish Universities to this day.

In 1530 Francis I, inspired by the new learning imported from Italy and in opposition to the scholastic tradition ruling in the Church establishments, founded the Collège Royal (later Collège de France), with the first Chair of Greek. When Henry IV reformed the University of Paris in 1600, Greek took its place beside Latin. The new learning was not confined to Paris, and in the same year as the Collège Royal the College of Guyenne, at Bordeaux, was established with several distinguished humanists as teachers, among them George Buchanan, the Scottish poet and historian. Montaigne, who as a small boy studied at this college, called it 'le meilleur de France', but he also averred that he and the other young nobles who were pupils there almost lost their taste for reading as a result of their experience. After that one learns without surprise that he protested against the dull, mechanical soulless teaching perpetrated in sixteenth-century schools, still scholastic and mediaeval in their outlook. Montaigne demanded that culture should be a personal acquirement, insisting that wisdom rather than knowledge, judgment rather than memory were what mattered. Educators should concern themselves with the development of body and soul, not confine themselves to filling heads with a useless lumber of knowledge and the pedantic technique of dialectics. Rabelais, equally a man of the new learning, showed equal dissatisfaction with scholasticism, for it developed only deductive reasoning by syllogisms. He, like Montaigne, declared that reform had become urgent. Rabelais, however, in his humanistic ardour, pleaded for a more encyclopaedic learning, in which not only the ancient tongues but the sciences and a practical knowledge of the concrete world should find a place.

In the seventeenth century, when the numerous colleges of the University of Paris were in decline, 'secondary' education, transferred in a great measure from the Faculty of Arts, became the preserve of religious orders specializing in teaching, particularly the Jesuits and the Oratorians. As the University of Paris had become secularized, the Church thus regained control over the education of the young. The Jesuit Collège de Clermont (afterwards Louis-le-Grand), founded in 1563, had nearly three thousand pupils twelve years later. The Jesuits, highly competent and zealous teachers, succeeded in making education more attractive to the young layman than it had been under the scholastic régime. Their aim was not only to produce Christians but to fit their pupils to take their place in society as cultivated men of the world. They taught Latin well, as a living language, and stressed literary style, breaking away from the unmitigated pedantry of the schoolmen. Condé, Bossuet, Corneille, Molière and Fontenelle owed their intellectual formation to the Jesuits, and Descartes, who attended their celebrated school at La Flèche, discusses the curriculum in his *Discours de la Méthode*. The anti-clerical Voltaire, though he affirmed they had only taught him 'des sottises et du latin', always showed some tenderness for the Jesuit fathers who had formed his literary taste.

The Jesuits dominated education in France until their expulsion in 1762. Their rivals, the Oratorians, continued to teach in French schools until the outbreak of the French Revolution. They were pioneers in using French instead of Latin as the medium of instruction and in teaching the history of France in addition to ancient history. The Little Schools of Port Royal, founded in the seventeenth century by the pious and austere Jansenists, though they existed only for a score of years before the hostile Jesuits had them suppressed, left a mark on French educational history by their curriculum and their methods. Greek figured prominently with Latin, and the mother tongue with modern languages (Italian and Spanish). The learned *solitaires*, who taught and meditated at Port Royal, based their methods of teaching on a more enlightened notion of child psychology than was current at the time, and they expounded their methods in excellent text-books. Racine, their most illustrious pupil, owed to his years at Port Royal that familiarity with Greek literature, so unusual in the Grand Siècle, which his works reflect.

Port Royal, as well as such religious orders as the Ursulines, gave some attention to the education of girls, but they all tended to put piety before intellectual achievement. Though a few exceptionally cultured ladies like Mme de Sévigné and Mme de Lafayette adorned the literary circles of the seventeenth century, the average young lady's official reading at school did not go beyond the catechism; needlework, singing, dancing and deportment completed her social armoury. Marriage, of course, with the alternative of the convent, offered the only career. Husbands, in those days, generally preferred to take as brides girls who, since their schools had not trained them to hold their own in argument, would look up to and meekly obey the better-educated head of the household. Even enlightened writers like Mlle de Scudéry, who favoured education for women, agreed with Guez de Balzac that the first duty of a lady who happened to be cultured was to conceal her intellectual prowess. The charming Fénelon, whose archiepiscopal dignity did not preclude a considerable insight into feminine psychology, realized that ignorance and idleness offered real dangers to young ladies. In his *Traité de l'éducation des filles* he puts forward sound and interesting views on how learning can be made attractive, how knowledge may be pleasantly insinuated into the child's mind instead of being forced upon it. He remembers, too, what most of his contemporaries tended to forget, that physical exercise should not be neglected as part of the education both of boys and girls.

Mme de Maintenon, in her institution at St. Cyr, founded, under Royal patronage, for the benefit of girls of noble birth but without fortune, attempted at first to adorn the minds as well as form the characters of her young charges. Unhappily, such overweening pride and vanity resulted that the noble lady came to regret having endeavoured to give the girls anything more ambitious than 'une éducation simple et chrétienne'. Teen-agers who thought it below them to handle a broom, and said so, were sternly admonished by Mme de Maintenon herself; she told them that, if visitors to St. Cyr found all the girls there wielding brooms, it would be no surprise to them and no dishonour to the young ladies.

The idea that manual labour brought no degradation was taken up by Jean-Jacques Rousseau in the following century. His novel *Emile*, one of France's outstanding contributions to educational theory, appeared in 1762, the very year in which the Jesuits, then dominant in secondary education, were expelled from France. Rousseau holds that education should be progressive, natural and negative. Attention will be given entirely to health and the education of the senses until the age of twelve; from then until fifteen the child will learn, by applying himself to practical science, to calculate and reflect; after the fifteenth year begins (rather late) the moral training of the child. In opposition to the Church's doctrine of original sin, Rousseau affirms that the child is by nature good. Society on the contrary, is evil. Education will therefore be mainly negative, will merely make sure that the child's nature develops spontaneously and ward off the influence of society. Books—except *Robinson Crusoe*—will have no place in this education, for in this literary man's view literature, like society, complicates and spoils life. The best method, according to

Rousseau, of forming a vigorous mind is to cultivate a healthy body. Ideas, if they are to have any value, must come not from books but from personal experience and personal reflection.

Rousseau's book set forth some Utopian conceptions and not a few paradoxes. It revolutionized educational thinking at the time, though many of his views had been put forward previously, by Montaigne and Locke among others. *Emile* exerted its world-wide influence less by the novelty of the ideas than by the magic Rousseau put into his prose, a persuasive magic arising from intense conviction. Like his *Nouvelle Héloïse* it expressed the author's yearning for what life had failed to give him, his ardent dreams of the might-have-been. If *Emile* appears as a 'set book' in most education courses, it owes its place there, not to its value as a text-book to be learned and to be taken literally, but to its power of inspiration.

In the decades immediately preceding the Revolution, many treatises on education declared that the State and not the Church should undertake the training of the future citizen. Certain of them maintained that every citizen had the right to obtain the education most suitable for him. The chaotic opening years of the Revolutionary period were studded with ambitious schemes for universal education. Once equality had been declared to be the corner stone of the State, and once the age of the common man had come, the *ancien régime*'s educational system, administered by the Church for the few, became an obvious anachronism. The people, now the source of power in the State, must be educated to become conscious citizens. No longer could education have salvation as its chief aim, it would be essentially secular. The Constitution of 1791 guaranteed universal public education, of which the lower grades would be free. Ambitious projects of great theoretical interest were put forward by Talleyrand and Condorcet in the Constituent and Legislative Assemblies respectively, but only with the coming of Napoleon did a national system pass from theory to reality. The Napoleonic system, uniform, centralized, hierarchical, proved lasting and, with some modifications, remains in force to-day. Let us examine this system which for nearly a century and a half, while régimes and dynasties have come into power and passed away, has provided the intellectual formation of the majority of Frenchmen and Frenchwomen.

In every country the system of education is an expression of the national ideal, and this is true of France in a very marked degree. France is, one might say, an all-round country and has achieved results of equal importance in the divergent branches of artistic and intellectual activity. Most of the great nations of Europe excel in some special branch of art or of thought; Italy in the plastic arts, Germany in philosophy and music, England in poetry and the sciences. Each of these nations has, unconsciously, because of its national genius, specialized. France, on the contrary, has produced philosophers, musicians, painters, scientists, without any noticeable specialization of her effort. The French ideal has always been that of a perfect balance of the faculties—the ideal of *l'honnête homme*, the man who has a good all-round knowledge, better still, an all-round understanding: it is the ideal of general culture as opposed to specialization.

This is the ideal reflected in the education France provides for her children. By studying this education we may learn a few things useful to ourselves even though, perhaps indeed because, our own character and tradition have evolved a system very different in its aims, its organization and its results. The French child, the raw material of this education, is different too, and differences in the raw material may account for diversity in the processes employed.

The French child, boy or girl, gives one the impression of being intellectually more precocious than the product of our chillier northern climate. This precocity is encouraged by his upbringing among adults, not in a nursery. Moreover, English parents readily adapt their conversation to the child's point of view and interest themselves more in his games and childish preoccupations. The English are, as regards national character, younger than the French, or, as Taine put it, there is in England no deep division between the life of the child and that of the grown man. The art of talking to children in

The Souk at Fez

The Port of Algiers

the language they understand is so much an English art that most of the French children's favourite books are translations from the English. French parents do their best to develop the child's intelligence as rapidly as possible. They have little patience with childish ideas even if they do not go so far as to look upon childhood as an unfortunate but necessary prelude to adult life. Not that they need to force the child, for he usually lends himself willingly to the process, and enjoys the effect of his unexpectedly clever remarks and quaint sayings and of his piquant judgment of men and things. It is not without significance that the French mother, instead of appealing to the child's heart by saying 'be good', appeals to his reason when she says 'Sois sage' or 'Sois raisonnable'. Reasonableness is looked for early in France, and the age of reason is fixed at seven years.

What are the educational machines waiting to swallow up these young innocents? The principal one—the State educational system, the University of France—which includes primary, secondary and University education. Until 1932 the State Department dealing with education was called the Ministry of Public Instruction, now it has become the Ministry of National Education. Nor was this merely a matter of a name. The French system, until 1932, aimed at giving instruction of the mind. Education, in the sense of physical education, or character building, or inculcating principles that are other than intellectual in their appeal, was the business of the parent rather than of the schoolmaster, and, indeed, many French parents of secondary pupils would resent State interference in what they regard as their own domain. Parents who have sufficient leisure for it jealously guard their family prerogative of training despite all their confidence in State institutions.

Often French parents do not leave the State to do all the work of intellectual development. They are frequently so eager for the intellectual progress of their offspring that they personally supervise the children's homework, and even give them supplementary coaching. Mothers have at times gone to the length of learning Latin in order to be able to keep in touch with their sons' studies. This zeal is, of course, partly due to the prestige

K

attributed to scholastic success in France, for France is an examination-ridden country. French parents are, as a rule, keenly interested in their son's place in class and usually do not care about his success in sports. A French father would more likely than not look rather grim if his boy, to excuse failure at the *baccalauréat* examination, pointed out that he was in the first fifteen at rugby. Sport is, however, making progress in French schools. A *brevet sportif* has been instituted and widely publicized. The presence of British and American troops in France is credibly reported to have been the occasion for adopting a more virile ideal. In one *lycée* of 1,000 boys, 15 boys played rugby in 1923. Now there are nearly 100 players.

Like other branches of administration in France, the educational system was conceived on a logical and uniform basis. So uniform, indeed, that one Minister under the First Empire (it was Fontanes) is said to have looked at his watch one day with the remark: 'At this moment in such and such a form, every schoolboy in the Empire is construing such and such a page of Virgil.' The present system dates from the Revolutionary and Napoleonic period, before which education was in the hands of the Church. Napoleon made education a State monopoly and unified the system. The monopoly lasted until 1850, from which time the Church has been allowed to open schools of its own, the *écoles libres*.

Attendance at the elementary school is compulsory between the ages of 6 and (since 1936) 14. Before 1936 most of the children obtained their elementary leaving certificate (*Certificat de fin d'études primaires élémentaires*) at about the age of 12. Moreover, regular attendance, especially in country districts, was not always strictly enforced for a variety of reasons, including the need for labour in the fields and for looking after the family cow.

French elementary schools are, in many respects, very like those in Great Britain, though the aspect of the class is altered by the black or coloured overalls worn by the boys and girls. The school day lasts from 8 till 11.30 and from 1.30 to 4 in the afternoon, but the children may stay on in school an hour or two longer to do their homework under the supervision of the teacher. (The teacher is paid extra for this, of course.) There is a canteen in most schools where the midday meal can be had very inexpensively.

Two or three points in the curriculum call for special mention. The first is the extreme care with which the national language is taught. Almost every district in France has its own dialect, and the elementary school—with conscription— plays a major part, by its teaching of French, in unifying the nation. French boys and girls, even in remote villages where their parents address them in dialect, generally speak the national language with marked correctness. In France there is certainly a standard language. Is there a standard English? Or are we to believe G. B. Shaw, who said that there was none, but that there were 40 million dialects, each person speaking English according to his own standard?

No religious teaching is given in the French State elementary schools. Its place is taken by a class of 'moral and civic instruction'. The teaching of this subject in the junior classes is, of course, very largely practical—instilling habits of neatness, order, honesty and the like—though inspectors have now and again reported cases where the teacher gave a neat and formal lesson on neatness without observing that his classroom was ill-kept and untidy. The best teachers get their moral training done by example and by using concrete instances of lapses from virtue by the class or by individuals. Only the inexperienced would be capable of quoting Nietzsche and Schopenhauer or of brandishing over the heads of the 11-year-olds the categorical imperative of Kant.

The essential principle, laid down by M. Raymond Poincaré in 1911, is this: 'In ethics, it is practice alone which interests small children. Let us point out to them the current truths which are valid on both sides of the Pyrénées. Let us take from the masterpieces of classical antiquity, from the Ten Commandments, from the Gospel, from the works of the moralists of all periods, the few essential precepts accepted by all religious creeds, consecrated by tradition and confirmed by human reason.'

Does the moral teaching have any effect? That, of course, depends on the teacher. In general, it may be said that there

is full justification for putting before a reflective child—and
the French child is fairly reflective—an ideal to live for. The
difficulty arises in deciding what ideal, and on what to base
the teaching. When the religious element was abandoned,
appeal was made to patriotism. In the years between the two
wars this ideal was not palatable to many schoolmasters, left-
wing or pacifist, and they preferred to stress international
solidarity. In the last resort the ideal put before the children
depends, just as the value of the moral lesson does, on the
conscience of the teacher. This moral teaching must have been
particularly difficult in the period of disorganization and moral
chaos through which France passed for several years after the
end of the war.

Civic instruction, into which the moral training develops
as the child goes further up the school, may comprise abstract
disquisitions on the mechanism of French administration. The
more thoughtful teacher turns it into a concrete study first of
all of the community in which the children live. Then the
pupils pass on, gradually, to the larger units and learn exactly
what their *arrondissement* and *département* mean, and finally
learn about the working of the national administrative machine
in Paris and the political institutions—all this taught, of course,
in the simplest terms, and illustrated by concrete examples.

A last point which calls for mention about French elementary schools is the teaching of arithmetic. The metric
system makes this so simple that whereas the English boy is
obliged to devote many hours to mastering the intricacies of
our curious and complex system of weights and measures, the
French boy can be getting further ahead with other studies.
Not all the advantage lies on the side of the metric system, however, for the French boy never becomes so much at home in
mental arithmetic as the English boy does. Every English
visitor to France must have noticed how the shopkeeper puts
down on paper the simplest addition or subtraction . . . and
then gets it wrong! One French visitor to this country declared that what impressed him most was the uncanny skill
of barmaids in lightning additions.

The State secondary schools furnish the most characteristic

example of the French system. The *lycées* and *collèges* are very similar—the *lycées*, maintained by the State, are found in the largest towns, the staff has higher qualifications, in general, than in the municipal *collèges*, and the highest forms in the big *lycées* have no parallel in the *collèges*. The boarders in the *lycée* still wear uniform—peaked cap, tunic with brass buttons, hooded cape—and meal-times and class change-over are announced by the rolling of the kettle-drum. These are all reminders of the military character Napoleon I impressed on these schools, founded to provide the officers and administrators of his Empire. Something of this stern atmosphere persists—in the bare, barrack-like buildings with an entry through a barred entrance-gate guarded by a *concierge*—in the organization, too, with the ceaseless supervision at play-time, during meals, every hour of the day and night, with the rigid time-table, the long hours of work—the boarder's day has as much as eleven hours' study and classwork and two hours' play. In practice, things are not always quite so bad. Boys will be boys and they react instinctively against overwork. Not all hours spent in the study rooms are entirely devoted to school work. In the *lycée* time-table it is noticeable that six or seven hours' preparation are allocated for four or five hours' classwork. This is in accordance with the general principle that boys attend school not merely to obtain knowledge but 'to learn how to learn'. They have many essays and compositions to write, enough to ensure that they leave school able to use their pens with ease, sometimes with distinction.

The syllabus covering what is now called 'second degree' instead of secondary, that is the period from 10 years to 17-18 years of age, is an encyclopaedic one. Latin used to be compulsory for the first three years of the period—it was the key-subject in the traditional secondary education. Under the highly centralized administration a great measure of correlation can be achieved between the subjects taught. The aim is general culture; classics or modern languages—the humanities ancient or modern—furnish the basis of this culture.

The same master teaches Latin and French. To a Frenchman Latin is the language of his intellectual ancestors and the primitive form of his own language—and it is studied as such. In Great Britain we incline to lay stress on skill in grammar and philology, and we devote a great deal of our attention to translation into Latin. No doubt the average French schoolboy could not compete in Latin prose with an English one of the same age. But when the English schoolboy tried his hand at the art of translation from Latin as practised in French school examinations, he would be less happy. He would be given a short passage, a dictionary would be supplied, and three hours would be allowed for the translation. Used to a more or less rough-and-ready style of oral translation in class, the English boy would finish long before the three hours . . . and would be surprised when he saw his mark. The French boy would spend most of his time polishing and re-polishing his version and attempt to achieve in it something of the finish, and of the manner, of the original. The exercise is thus as much a training in French as in Latin, more so even, and is meant so to be. In the higher classes, literary commentary, the *explication de texte*, so generally used in the study of French literature, is applied to Latin. An ode of Horace, a page of Tacitus, a play of Terence are studied as poetry. as historical prose or as drama, and are analysed as such—with comparisons with French lyric poetry, French historians and with Molière. The French schoolboy has, of course, to learn his Latin grammar, but he runs no risk of regarding Latin texts as so many quarrying-grounds for syntactical examples. Even if he never becomes a professed Latinist, he will have obtained from his Latin studies something more than that disciplinary training which the older-fashioned teachers used to assure us was good for us.

Perhaps the highest tribute paid to the classics is that implied by the absence of moral instruction from the *lycée* syllabus until after the first part of the *baccalauréat*. It is assumed that a thorough classical training—and that was traditionally the basis of secondary education—would suffice without any other kind of moral instruction. Let us observe, however, that to Latin and Greek was added the intensive study of French seventeenth-century texts and that Corneille, Descartes,

Pascal, Bossuet, Fénelon and La Bruyère were so impregnated with Christian morality that the seemingly 'neutral' instruction really inculcated an elevated form of morality—in fact, practically religious teaching.[1]

The teaching of French literature in the *lycée* is based on the principle that literature must be studied *in the texts* and not learned by rote from manuals. An intensive study of typical passages of the great writers achieves more than does a careful conning of what the critics have said. La Bruyère, two and a half centuries ago, expressed the French view on the matter: 'L'étude des textes ne peut jamais être assez recommandée; c'est le chemin le plus court, le plus sûr et le plus agréable pour tout genre d'érudition.'

The study of French literature, like that of Latin texts, aims at forming the pupil's taste and judgment by the practice of *explication de textes*. From his study of history—not only French history but world history—the schoolboy learns something about the history of civilization and also acquires some notions of the development of the pictorial arts. The history text-books contain many reproductions of the masterpieces of painting in the countries studied, and in addition there are reproductions of works which throw light on the social history of the different countries. Naturally French art is more fully studied than that of other countries.

The syllabus of studies leading to the *baccalauréat*, the first part of which is taken at the age of 16, is a heavy one, and success at the examination (between 50 and 60 per cent. of the candidates fail) constitutes a considerable achievement. Memory alone will not see one safely through, and the written examination calls for a serious effort of composition, interpretation and reasoning.

Let us take an example from the syllabus of Latin-Modern Languages option. There are in Part I four written papers of three hours each in French composition, Latin unseen, one modern language and mathematics. If and only if he obtains 50 per cent. average marks on these papers is the candidate allowed

---

[1] Chaplains, Roman Catholic, Protestant, and Jewish, attend once a week to give religious teaching to those pupils whose parents so desire.

to attempt the oral examinations, which consist of an *explication* of a passage in French, a passage in Latin, one in the foreign language and an interrogation in history and geography and in physical science. In the following year the survivors of Part I take Part II, either Philosophical or Mathematical. On the Philosophical side there is a four-hour philosophical essay, a two-and-a-half-hour paper on science, and the oral tests cover philosophy, history and geography, a modern language, mathematics and science. Though these oral tests occupy each only fifteen minutes, these fifteen minutes can be very decidedly 'un mauvais quart d'heure.'

It is not surprising that an examination so exacting, and so largely devoted to what may be called 'disinterested' study, carries with it important privileges, unobtainable through other difficult examinations like the *brevet supérieur*, lately abolished, which used to be taken at the same age by those coming from the primary school system. The young *bachelier*, who has received what is, from the intellectual point of view, the finest secondary education in Europe, has not been prepared for any profession when he leaves the *classe de philosophie*, though he has passed the barrier admitting to the liberal professions and the University. He may stay on at the *lycée* and prepare for the special schools like St. Cyr and Polytechnique. The most interesting of these special post-*baccalauréat* classes, is, perhaps, that which prepares its members for competitive entry to the *Ecole Normale Supérieure*. This class, officially called *première supérieure* but known to schoolboys as '*khagne*', provides the best literary training in France.[1] The twenty or thirty bright young men who compose *première supérieure* are taught by particularly distinguished teachers. Their syllabus, purely literary, covers Latin, Greek or a modern language, French literature, with some history and philosophy. The lesson period is two hours, and the standard is high. The boys take an active part in the classwork. The master will interrupt his lecture, and call upon a pupil: 'Monsieur X, in twenty minutes you will explain the poem on page so-and-so of the Anthology'.

---

[1] There is a parallel class called *mathématiques spéciales* for those scientifically inclined.

He resumes his lecture while Monsieur X prepares his lesson. When called upon, Monsieur X proceeds to give a fifteen minutes' lesson on the poem, carefully planned, with an introduction, the main points set forth in logical order, and a conclusion. The best pupils find new and interesting remarks to make on their texts. When one listens to the pupils' lessons in *première supérieure*, one understands why little pedagogical training is needed by these young men before they can teach a class in a *lycée*.

The seventeen French Universities, most of them successors of the twenty-two foundations created by the Popes in the Middle Ages, date their resurrection from the end of the nineteenth century. (Law of 10 July 1896). The number of students is about 100,000 (of whom roughly 55,000 are in Paris)—that is one student for every 390 people approximately. Like the *lycées* and *collèges*, the Universities are under the direct control of the Ministry of National Education. The functionary who directs each University is the Rector, nominated by the Minister in Paris. He supervises also secondary and elementary education in his *académie*.[1] The Minister appoints the professors, and the University finances are largely under his control. Each University has, however, a budget of its own, with which it can found chairs and lectureships and thus it gradually acquires an individuality, often linked with the interests of the region in which it stands. From the staff point of view the main advantage of the centralized control is that, except for the Dean, the professors have little administrative work and more time for research. The very limited number of hours' teaching—generally three hours per week—also helps to assure more leisure for research. In the British Universities to-day teaching takes up more hours, and the professors pay the price of the democratic system of University government by serving on innumerable committees.

Moreover, the professors in French Faculties of Arts do not undertake to lecture on all the set books. Sometimes a whole year is spent on one book out of the dozen or so prescribed,

---

[1] The Rector corresponds to the Vice-Chancellor in a British University, but he also is responsible for all State education in the area (*académie*).

and the first few lectures are consecrated to bibliography.
The student thus learns how to deal with prescribed books—
and once he has learnt the method he can prepare the rest
of the syllabus himself. To give him practice it is customary
in the Faculties of Arts for the students during the second
and third terms to take, in turn, their place beside the pro-
fessorial chair and to give a lesson of twenty minutes on some
aspect of the set book or the subject being studied. The
professor then analyses and criticises the lesson, pointing out
the good and the less good points in method and matter.

There is no strict division into first, second and third years
in the Faculty of Arts. There are classes for candidates for
the *Licence* and for candidates preparing the *Agrégation*. The
Licence ès Lettres (*Licence d'enseignement*) calls for a minimum of
two years' University preparation and the winning of five
certificates, of which one must be a test in translation from
Latin and a French essay. Each certificate entails an oral
examination. There is no Honours degree, but distinction
(*mention*) is awarded for outstanding merit on any certificate.

When he has obtained his *Licence*, the student who intends
to become a secondary school teacher spends the following
year in preparing his *Diplôme d'Etudes Supérieures*, for which a
short original thesis (*un mémoire*) on some theme within the scope
of his subject must be written. The *diplômé* then begins to get
ready for the *Agrégation*, a difficult competitive examination. If
he passes—and in some subjects four hundred candidates contend
for a dozen places—he has the right to a Chair in a *lycée*. All
agrégés are specialists. There are a dozen types of *Agrégation* in the
Faculty of Arts besides those in Science: *Lettres* (classical languages and French), *Grammaire* (the same subjects but with stress
on language instead of literature), English, German, Italian,
Spanish, Philosophy, History and Geography. Before the
Second World War geography and history, now separated,
formed a single group for the *Agrégation*. This linking of the
subjects probably accounts very largely for the high place
France holds in human geography; all French geographers
had a thorough historical culture, while all her historians
were excellent geographers.

Many *agrégés* leave the profession and take highly paid posts in administration, in commerce and in industry. This has happened to such an extent in the post-war years that at present two-fifths of the chairs in *lycées* are occupied by non-*agrégés*. *Agrégés* who desire to enter University teaching spend five or six years writing two theses for the degree of *Docteur ès Lettres*.

Nobody who has been to a French secondary school or to a French University would deny that when the human material is suitable the education given does produce *l'honnête homme*, and this education has achieved a deservedly high reputation. Why then, may we ask, have there been such urgent calls for reform in the last twenty years or so? And why was it necessary to produce a revolutionary document like the report of the Langevin Commission published in 1946?

The reason is that France, in common with her neighbours, has seen her national life transformed by the growth of new political ideas, by scientific inventions and psychological discoveries. In spite of the revolutionary changes in political and social life brought about by the events of 1789, the national ideal, in secondary education at any rate, remained aristocratic. It continued to aim at developing the seventeenth-century ideal of *l'honnête homme*, and, in the case of the girls, the ideal may be said to have been Mme de Sévigné, that highly cultured lady who carried her learning with so much grace and so unobtrusively. French secondary education set out to develop and adorn the mind while respecting its individuality, so that boy or girl could eventually take a conscious part in and be an asset to a cultured social group. To many of our contemporaries in France this ideal appears antiquated and bourgeois. The reform tends to attach more importance to the practical contribution of the future citizen to the life of the community. As M. Jean Guéhenno puts it, 'Il faut faire des hommes d'aujourd'hui.'

The reformers want changes in the French educational system for pedagogical and practical reasons. They complain that the traditional system of education fails in flexibility, that the whole of the teaching is too collective, and that there is no individual approach. The teacher fires his daily broadside of information on to a long-suffering class. It is not the *individuals* who are aimed at but the class, a fictive collective being. This method of education, say the reformers, is like offering standard suits to a large group in which there are tall and small, stout and slim—few will be fitted. The first reform must be smaller classes. Then the pupils, instead of being passive targets for the broadside, must be aimed at individually; also they must be active. Appeal must no longer be made mainly to their memory, and books must no longer be the sole instruments of teaching and learning. Under the present system, it is averred, too much insistence is laid on the examination yield of knowledge required—and this knowledge is the kind of knowledge that lends itself most easily to evaluation by written or oral examination. In a word, French education is accused of being a distribution of encyclopaedic learning appealing only to very intellectual children. It is said to turn out pupils fit only for literary activity or for employment as functionaries and lawyers. Modern education, the reformers maintain, should be a process of acquiring skills—especially practical skills.

French education, State-governed, uniform, centrally organized, has been less open to new ideas than has education in England, with its flexible and independent diversity, and some of the reforms proposed cover ground which has already been worked over in Great Britain. The idea of active learning instead of learning from the book or from a set lesson is largely an application to older children (11+) of methods which have been familiar for years in the kindergartens of France as well as in our own.

The new conception of active work (proposed in 1937 by M. Jean Zay, Minister of Education) has recently been tried out in many of the *lycées* in France. The classes in which the new method was first tried out were those for the beginners in secondary education, the 11-year-olds, the *sixièmes*.[1] The *sixièmes nouvelles*, as these experimental classes were called, were organized as small classes—maximum

[1] The numbering of classes is the opposite order to that used in British schools.

twenty-five. The number of specialized teachers was reduced to give each teacher the opportunity of getting to know the pupil more fully. Instead of eight or ten specialists there were only three teachers. The syllabus remained the traditional one, but whereas in the old *sixièmes* the intellectual subjects occupied all day, in the *sixièmes nouvelles* these were relegated to the morning, and the afternoon could be devoted to subjects in which the children might be actively employed instead of sitting down and listening. They sang, they modelled in plastics, they learned to use tools, to construct. Once a week the teacher took the children out and they learned by actual contact the aspects of the town or district they lived in. Under this new dispensation the children could react to their teaching—under the old, there was too often no reaction. The teachers in the *sixièmes nouvelles* had a much freer hand in method of teaching. They had fuller opportunity of judging the capacities, temperament and interests of the children. Two periods of *orientation*—at age 11-13 in the *sixième* or *cinquième nouvelle*, and again at age 13-15 when all kinds of optional subjects, intellectual, artistic, manual and rural, would be available—were expected to reveal the attitude of the children for some particular career.

These reforms in the method and spirit of school teaching were being tried out gradually. By 1948 the *troisièmes nouvelles* were in being. The measure of success possible was, naturally, limited by lack of apparatus, workshops and tools, for French secondary schools were strictly academic and had no provision for such things. As one might expect, many of the older teachers found it hard to break with their bookish tradition for these new-fangled work-by-play methods. They held that with the old methods you knew where you were and could be sure exactly what had been learned. It is easy to understand how revolutionary these new methods appeared to those who had spent their lives teaching in the conservative and traditional atmosphere of a French *lycée* or *collège*, although to us these methods do not even appear novel. Complaints were heard about the cost of the new methods—material, class excursions and increased number of teachers owing to small classes—and it was on the grounds of cost that, though the experiment was carried out successfully as far as the *bacca-lauréat*, the project was shelved.

Much more sweeping changes than these were envisaged by many reformers; they proposed to alter the structure of the traditional French system. This system—though when looked at from a short distance away, it strikes us as being constructed with rigorous logic, centralized and uniform—did not appear to the reformers to be sufficiently logical or uniform. They pointed out that the three degrees—primary, secondary and higher—were not in fact established as part of a co-ordinated scheme, but that they really grew up one after the other, the secondary under Napoleon I, the primary after 1882, the new Universities later still.

What, from the political point of view, appeared more serious still is the duality of the system, its division as it were into an aristocratic or bourgeois section and a democratic section—like the French clergy under the *ancien régime*. Up one stairway came the sons and daughters of the bourgeoisie, who could afford to pay the fees in the *lycée* and *collège* and who alone could enter the University, since the *baccalauréat*, for which *lycée* and *collège* alone gave the preparation, was the key to the Faculties. Up the humbler stairway, from elementary primary school, through higher primary school, and thence, if he wished to be a teacher, to the Training College (*Ecole normale*) came the boy who had to be content with free education. If he were very ambitious, he passed from *Ecole normale* to the Higher Normal College, and became a Training College instructor. The primary school system was self-contained, without relation to the secondary and University system. It was difficult, if not impossible, for a bright boy to be transferred from the primary school to the *lycée*, because the syllabus in the lower forms of the *lycée* was not the same. The primary school child, with no Latin, was handicapped if he won a scholarship to the *lycée*. Maintenance grants would have been necessary, and these were not forthcoming. The disinterested studies in the *lycée* were also a luxury which the working people felt they could not afford for their children.

The reformers might have taken as their text the words of the Revolutionary Roger Ducos, who, in a speech made on 18 December 1792, proclaimed the necessity of the same education for all citizens, if equality was to be attained: 'Car citoyens, tant que vous n'aurez pas rapproché le pauvre et le riche, le faible et le puissant: tant que, pour me servir des expressions de Plutarque, vous n'aurez pas acheminé à une même trace, et moulé sur une même forme de vertu tous les enfants de la patrie, c'est en vain que vos lois proclameront la sainte égalité, la République sera toujours divisée en deux classes: les *citoyens* et les messieurs.'

Much was said in 1940 and before about '*les deux jeunesses*', the two rival nations into which the French population had split. On the one side was envy and some jealousy, on the other scorn of *le primaire* and *l'esprit primaire*. The ill-will arising from the existence of the double system appeared to many to be injurious to French unity. During the occupation, the Vichy Government, which had heard a great deal about Communist fermentation in the Training Centres, decided that the isolation of the *instituteurs* from the secondary and University grades was a mistake. They declared their intention of bringing the primary and secondary systems into closer connection. As a first measure, they decreed that henceforward holders of the *baccalauréat* would be eligible to teach in primary schools.

Teaching in the *lycée* is now free; moreover, the primary classes in the *lycée* have been assimilated to the classes in the primary schools so that all start their secondary education (now called *second degré*) without handicap. Entry to the second degree is now by examination for all; the idea was that *all* fit for secondary education should be accepted. In practice, owing to the enormous number of candidates for secondary education, this examination has become a competitive one and many children who could certainly have benefited have had to be excluded from the *lycées*. The classrooms in the *lycées* are already overcrowded. The former *écoles primaires supérieures* (Higher Elementary Schools) have now been transferred into the secondary school category under the name of *collèges modernes*.

The linking up of the primary and secondary systems of State education will still leave a duality between the State schools and the Church schools (*les écoles libres*). The Church schools have developed and multiplied since the *loi Falloux* of 1850 gave them their opportunity. During the occupation period the Church schools received government subsidies, and though these were stopped after the liberation in 1945, there were more pupils attending the Church secondary schools than the State secondary schools.[1] This increase is all the more striking because the Church schools are not, like the State schools, free. The explanation is no doubt in part a desire on the parents' part for a more definite moral training than is given in the State schools, in part the difficulty of getting children into the *lycées*. Many parents believe that the only hope of recovery from the moral crisis which affected the young people in the war years lies in religious teaching. This is the particular contribution made by these *écoles libres*. Their syllabus of study is perforce modelled on that of the State schools, so that the children of the *écoles libres* may pass the *baccalauréat* which alone admits to the professions and the University.

The parties of the Left, traditionally anti-clerical and professedly democratic, express alarm at the success of the Church schools which, they affirm, do not foster democratic thought. Many would like to see the State monopoly of education re-established, on the grounds that it is the duty of the State (as Langevin said) to provide the fullest education for *all* its citizens. There is, of course, no question of re-imposing the Church monopoly of education, such as existed under the *ancien régime*. Why then does not the Fourth Republic re-impose the State monopoly? It is because the non-Communist elements on the Left are afraid that the monopoly, once established, may fall into Communist hands. It has been affirmed that a bill for State monopoly of education would inevitably cause the fall of the government sponsoring it, or might even be the signal for civil war. The violent feeling about Church schools was evident in 1948, when a government crisis suddenly

[1] The figures for the Paris district, which are typical, are 88,000 in Church schools, 63,000 in State schools.

Louis XIV and Colbert on a visit to the Academy of Sciences

Scene from Gluck's *Armide* (27 September, 1777)

sprang up on the question of the State taking over some Church schools or subsidizing them while allowing them to retain religious teaching. A second crisis arose out of the question of the grants in aid of poor parents who sent children to Church schools.

Another compelling reason makes State monopoly unthinkable. The cost of taking over the education of the whole youth of France and of building new schools, of training and paying all schoolmasters would be colossal. Though more than half the secondary school population is provided for by the Church schools, the State schools cannot cope with the multitude knocking at their doors. Forty *lycées* and *collèges* were destroyed during the war, 136 damaged and no new ones have been built. Were the Langevin plan to be adopted fully, and State education provided for every child up to the age of 18, it would be necessary not only to build or take over an enormous number of schools but to provide maintenance grants for the young people who would otherwise be earning money. France cannot afford the Langevin plan at present. Her losses in men and production in the two world wars have not been made good; the real income of the average Frenchman in the post-war period was one-third that of the average American, one-half that of the Englishman. The destruction of buildings in France in the First World War was equivalent to the total destruction of the city and port of London; the destruction in the Second World War has been calculated by some as the equivalent of the entire destruction of London, Liverpool, Manchester, Glasgow and Birmingham.

Is it surprising, in view of the impoverishment of France and the need for reconstruction, that the Langevin plan, while demanding education *for all* until the age of 18, stresses the importance of technical training rather than, as tradition in France always did hitherto, the disinterested pursuit of culture, the ideal of *l'honnête homme*? What France needs most, declared Langevin and his colleague Wallon, is this: sufficient educated peasants to make the most of the soil, artisans capable of dealing with modern techniques, bridge-builders and industrial chemists. Technical education, which since 1918 had made

L

great progress in France though scorned by those who had had the privilege of an education directed towards disinterested culture, will loom large if the new reforms develop. The aim is to reduce proportionately to a third the present secondary population (now belonging to the *l'enseignement théorique du second degré* and to treble the proportion of the population undergoing technical education.

Under the new scheme the young men of 14 to 18 will not, except those destined for academic pursuits, be kept sitting learning in schools. They are to be systematically trained on model farms or in model workshops. Their teachers will be skilled workmen or progressive farmers, and only the supervisors and consultants will be recruited from the technical college staffs.

Everybody is to 'start fair'. Only those who have shown clear evidence during the orientation period (10-15 years age-group) that they possess real aptitude for academic studies will attend the higher classes at the *lycées* (now called *l'enseignement théorique du second degré*), where they will specialize either in classics or in modern languages or in science for three years (15-18). They will then sit for their *baccalauréat*. But the young bachelors will not, as at present, be entitled to proceed direct to a University degree. They will undergo a period of one or two years of further intensive preparation called the propaedeutic period, and will be admitted to the University classes only if they are successful in a competitive examination at the end of this probation. The Sorbonne introduced in 1948 the system of a year's pre-University study. Other Universities did so later. The French Universities aim at reducing, by perhaps as much as 50 per cent., their intake. It is considered that many of the students who attend at present might be better employed elsewhere.

It is not intended that the products of this academic education shall be allowed to consider themselves, as heretofore, an aristocracy. The technicians, like the academics, must have their *baccalauréat*, a new-type philosophy-sciences. This new *baccalauréat* (without Latin) has already been established. In years to come, if the scheme of reform is completed, every teacher will have three years at a secondary school, before preparing to become a *licencié.* Every teacher, moreover, will have been trained in teaching at an *Ecole normale*— re-named *Institut de Formation Professionnelle.* The distinction in name between secondary school teachers (*professeurs*) and elementary school teachers (*instituteurs*) will be obliterated. Teachers will be of two kinds— teachers of general subjects and specialists. Even the *agrégé*, the flower of the academics, will be liable to be sent to teach in a technical college. The difficulty will be to recruit the lower ranks. Already in 1947 there was an acute shortage of candidates for Elementary Training Colleges, and the authorities were considerably exercised about what they considered to be not a mere passing difficulty but a new and grave situation. The shortage of men teachers for primary schools is even greater than the shortage of women. Since the *baccalauréat* can now be obtained without Latin, there has been a large influx into the Faculties of Arts of students from the primary school system who hope to be appointed to secondary school posts. This appears likely to aggravate the crisis in recruiting for primary schools. One wonders whether the answer to this problem will not have to be direction of labour.

The new policy of education in France will, it is estimated, require twenty-five years of peace before the reforms can be completed. If such a revolutionary change has become necessary, may it not be because, in France, the State system of education so dominated the field that little opportunity was offered for experiments in new methods of teaching? In any case, few such experiments were made in comparison with the number made in this country, the results of which, if successful, gradually filtered through into general practice. French educationalists consequently came to the conclusion that the State system had become hide-bound, rigid and antiquated and that nothing except a root-and-branch upheaval could bring about the necessary rejuvenation. No doubt the reformers realized that only by proposing a revolutionary programme of changes could they shake conservative opinion out of its comfortable traditionalism. They were probably well aware, also, that the present, after the upheavals of recent years, was the opportune moment for attempting to carry out a reform designed to obliterate the class barriers already in some measure crumbling.

It may be suggested, in conclusion, that France does not intend simply to replace one rigid system by another. The doors and windows of the old structure are being thrown open. Fresh air and fresh ideas can now enter more freely. France, with its highly individualistic spirit, its highly individual achievement, is unlikely to set up a system for mass production of citizens all upon the same model and trained exclusively to fit into the new social pattern. However logical and uniform the system may appear, however much it may seem to cater for the common needs of the common man, France is no more likely than we to forget that each man is unique. She will also remember that, for the sake of producing useful citizens, education must not sacrifice the uniqueness of the individual in the modern world, so hypnotized by mass production.

READING LIST

Boyd, W. *The History of Western Education*. London, 1921.

Compayré, A. *Histoire critique des doctrines de l'éducation en France depuis le seizième siècle*, 2 vols. Paris, 1879.

Kandel, J. L. *Studies in Comparative Education*. London, 1933.

Meyer, A. E. *The Development of Education in the Nineteenth Century*. New York, 1949.

Ministère de l'Education Nationale. *Instruction du 30 septembre 1938 relatives à l'application . . . des programmes de l'enseignement du second degré*. Paris, n.d.

Les Sixièmes nouvelles. Paris, 1948.

Nouveaux Horaires de l'enseignement du second degré, 1948-49. Paris, 1948.

Piobetta, J. B. *Les Institutions universitaires de France* (Coll. Que Sais-je?). Paris, 1951.

THE PROJECTED EDUCATIONAL REFORM

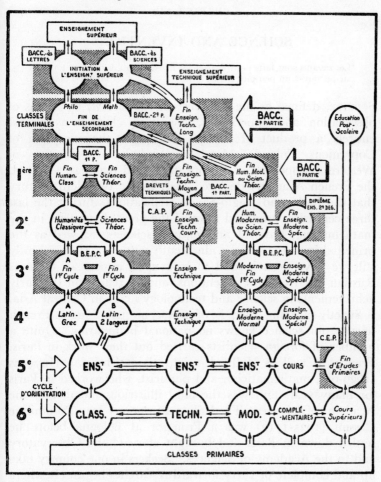

The Ministerial Project of Reform was announced in December 1953. The above diagram (from *Le Monde* of 20 December 1953) illustrates the new organization as proposed. The arrows show the possible transfer from one branch of education to another. The shaded portions indicate the classes in which the examinations are prepared.

(Reproduced by permission from *Le Monde* 20 December 1953)

CHAPTER VIII

SCIENCE AND INVENTIONS

'Les savants sont faits pour écarter les mystères, qu'ils finissent toujours
par retrouver un peu plus loin.'   HENRI POINCARÉ.

SCIENCE, defined as the discovery of causal laws by means of observation and experiment, has been claimed as almost entirely a product of Europe and—with the exception of Copernicus (Poland), Mendeleev and Pavlov (Russia)—of Western Europe and of Europeans settled overseas. Indeed, the French Academy declared early in the twentieth century that the Latin and Anglo-Saxon civilizations, during the last three centuries, produced most of the great discoveries in the mathematical, physical and natural sciences, as well as the principal inventions of the nineteenth century. More recently still we have been invited to look upon almost all these as Russian discoveries or inventions, and to reflect on the early achievements in science and technology made in Central Asia.

Strictly speaking, there is, of course, no such thing as French science, for science knows no national boundaries. Quite a number of foreign scientists carried out their work in Paris. France, as well as Holland, might claim Christian Huygens (1629-95), mathematician and physicist, who worked in Paris for many years and was the most illustrious member of the Academy of Sciences. The Italian astronomer Jean Dominique Cassini (1625-1712) was a Professor at Bologna before he settled down in Paris and brought glory to the Observatory and to the Academy of Sciences. Seekers in one country take up and complete or carry forward researches begun elsewhere by other savants, while at any given moment the same line of inquiry may be pursued in more than one country. Before the age of scientific journals, men of science corresponded with one another throughout Europe, and disputes occurred about priority of discovery. Mariotte (1620-84) was working in France on the same problem as Robert Boyle (1627-91) in

Ireland, and the 'Boyle's Law' of the simple quantitative relationship between pressure and volume of gas is known on the Continent as 'la loi de Mariotte'. Isaac Newton (1642-1727) and Leibniz (1646-1716) were simultaneously engaged upon the differential calculus, and though Newton acknowledged a debt to Leibniz, the Royal Society claimed all credit for Newton.

It is not always easy to determine which nation should be credited with the glory of some invention or discovery, and in any country readers are usually more familiar with the names and works of their compatriots than with what is being done abroad. An English schoolboy, when asked who invented the steam-engine, will probably reply that it was James Watt. He has perhaps never heard the name of Denis Papin (1647-1714). Every French schoolboy has learnt that Papin—born nearly a century before Watt—was the first to discover the expansive power of steam, that he invented the piston, built a steam chariot and a steamboat, and died in poverty.

Though the Renaissance stirred men's minds to speculation, modern science began only in the seventeenth century and France then made a brilliant start. She has maintained a high place ever since, rising to an undisputed pre-eminence in the late eighteenth century and the earlier part of the nineteenth. She can exhibit with pride a long roll of illustrious names: original thinkers, inventors and discoverers of new methods—of new sciences even. If her achievements did not always get the credit and reap the reward that they deserved, it may be because France, satisfied with the glory of making the discovery or invention, often apparently lost interest in it, and left others to work out its practical application, and push forward its commercial or industrial exploitation. If photography (Daguerre and Niepce), the use of fingerprints for identification (Bertillon), the sewing-machine (Thimonnier), the petrol motor (Forest and Belmont), wireless (Branly), cold storage (Tellier), and the cinematograph (Lumière and Pathé) were for the most part developed and applied elsewhere and in some cases great industries built up, the earliest discoveries and inventions are attributed to those Frenchmen whose names are bracketed with them above. The manufacture of glass and of soap was transformed by the cheap and abundant supply of soda, due to the discovery, in 1791, by Nicolas Leblanc (1742-1806), that carbonate of soda could be made from salt; aeronautical developments of the present day owe something to the Montgolfier brothers, Joseph (1740-1810) and Etienne (1745-99) who invented the balloon. French achievements in the pioneering days of the aircraft industry (Farman made the first real air journey in 1908 and Louis Blériot crossed the Channel in 1909) left its mark in the English vocabulary with such terms as 'fuselage' and 'aileron'. Nor does this list by any means exhaust the debt of the modern world to French inventive genius.

Disinterested satisfaction with the invention itself does not perhaps go far enough as an explanation of why so many French inventions and discoveries came to be exploited elsewhere than in France. It may be remembered, too, that France remained predominantly agricultural for much longer than the Anglo-Saxon countries and Germany; farming communities are essentially conservative. Her industrial revolution came very late—until 1870, when England already counted a century of industrial development, exports were of minor interest to France—and no such urgent calls were made for the adoption of mechanical inventions to multiply manpower as in the case of Britain or America. Often the French inventor was much too far ahead of the felt needs of the community to have any chance of seeing his discovery eagerly taken up by manufacturers.

French industry, most of it organized in small enterprises, has been reproached for its indifference to science during the present century; only now are central research laboratories for each industry being set up, the cost of which is to be borne by all the firms in each industrial group—textiles, fuels, etc.

Scientific research, as distinct from mechanical invention, was encouraged by the State as early as the seventeenth century. Colbert, a penetrating and far-seeing genius, founded the Academy of Sciences in 1666, a few years after the beginnings of the Royal Society of London. Both these bodies originated as unofficial meetings of private citizens curious about scientific matters. It is typical of the centralizing and co-ordinating tendency of French administration that the Academy was endowed by the State, and within a few months of its founding the members were working in concert on natural history in accordance with a general plan laid down by Claude Perrault. It is typical of private initiative that the Royal Society required no grant from the Treasury, depended on entrance fees, members' subscriptions and private donations, and, in its earlier years, adopted no coherent plan. Colbert also created the Paris Observatory—of which the architect was the versatile Claude Perrault—which early won for France a high place in astronomical science. France was the first country to publish a scientific periodical—the *Journal des Savants* dates from January 1665, while the first number of the Philosophical Transactions, published by the Royal Society, appeared on 6 March of the same year. In the mid-eighteenth century the monarchy founded the Engineering School at Mézières, among whose pupils were many distinguished scientists: Monge the mathematician, Coulomb, who formulated electrostatics and magnetism, and Lazare Carnot, mathematician and 'Organizer of Victory' during the Revolutionary Wars.

Around the Revolutionary period there was a blossoming of inventions, and a group of scientific institutions was founded by the Convention: Ecole Polytechnique, Conservatoire des Arts et Métiers, Ecole Normale Supérieure; and the Jardin du Roi was reorganized as the Musée d'Histoire Naturelle (1794). These special schools, and not the Universities, produced many discoverers and inventors—as well as technicians. Nor must the ancient foundation of Francis I, the Collège Royal, re-named the Collège de France, be forgotten, for it later became an outstanding centre of research, and many of France's great scientists taught there. The Faculties of Science, mere examining bodies in Napoleon's University of France, did little or nothing for research until they were reorganized at the end of the nineteenth century; they have always lacked the necessary funds for their scientific research. Ampère, working in his flat with home-made apparatus, Claude Bernard, whose laboratory was an unhealthy cellar in the Collège de France, and Pasteur, who obtained only at the end of his scientific career the sort of laboratory he wanted, all carried out epoch-making investigations under conditions of great material difficulty. Research was done by men who were paid as teachers and professors, and only on the eve of the Second World War was research, as a profession, recognized and furnished with proper remuneration, when the Centre National de la Recherche Scientifique was founded.

It is understandable that French scientists still suffer from lack of adequate financial provision for their work; the two world wars have taken a heavy toll of wealth as well as of lives. Scarcity of funds may be more of a handicap, now that much expensive apparatus and large teams of research workers are needed, than when research could be carried out by inspired and enthusiastic individual savants. A certain diminution of the brilliance of French research has been diagnosed from the incidence of Nobel prizes for the sciences. From 1901 to 1913 France won 10 as against Germany's 13 and Great Britain's 5. During the period 1914-47, France won 7, Germany 25, Great Britain 20, and U.S.A. 21. Among the latest French scientists to be rewarded were M. and Mme Joliot-Curie, in 1935.

Under the educational reform now being put into effect, large provision appears to be made for the scientific and technical education of the future and a special fund (*Caisse autonome*) allocated to scientific research. It is remarkable that, working under conditions often difficult, French scientists have, through the centuries, achieved so many triumphs. When one remembers the work done in co-operation, particularly just after the founding of the Academy of Sciences or during the Revolutionary wars, it seems perhaps a little unkind to apply to the scientists the dictum that the French, a nation of individualists, do not work well in teams. If any particularly national feature can be discovered in the scientific work published by the French, it is style.

In no other country has science been so closely linked with literature, and in none has so much attention been paid to

the manner of saying as well as to what is said. French prose
expresses ideas with unrivalled clarity. When a French thinker
of the last century maintained the view that France's rôle in the
world of thought was primarily to put into clear, logical and
intelligible language the complex conceptions of the modern
world, he had in mind her philosophers; he might have said
the same of her scientists. Rivarol's maxim, 'Ce qui n'est
pas clair n'est pas français', is valid for the savant no less than
for the literary man. French scientists have almost invariably
set forth the results of their discoveries with admirable lucidity;
the reader has the impression—or is it the illusion?—of understanding their demonstrations with ease. True to French
literary tradition, French scientists realize that writing should
give pleasure to the reader as well as information. They aim
at eliminating what is superfluous and setting down only the
essential, less anxious to give 'toujours plus de faits' than to
achieve 'toujours plus de lumière'. Obscurity, in their view, is
rarely essential to the expression of profound thought. Nor
do they forget Pascal's luminous observation in his sixteenth
Provincial Letter: 'Je n'ai fait celle-cy plus longue que parce que
je n'ai pas eu le loisir de la faire plus courte.'

Mathematics and Physics

Let us now briefly examine the record of achievement in
French science, leaving aside all but the greatest names and
all but the most outstanding discoveries of each scientist. The
seventeenth century, which produced Newton, was a great
mathematical age, and astronomical and mathematical discoveries were being made all over Europe. The mathematical
and physical sciences, enriched by the recent work of Galileo
and Kepler, developed first. In France the two towering
geniuses were undoubtedly Descartes and Pascal, who left
their mark on science as well as on literature and philosophy.
René Descartes (1596-1650) wrote the first manual in French
of modern scientific method.[1] In his *Discours de la Méthode*

---

[1] Francis Bacon's *Novum Organum*, which is also a *Discourse on Method*, had
appeared in 1620.

(1637), Descartes rejected the appeal to authority, ecclesiastical or Aristotelian, that had sterilized scientific thought in the Middle Ages and even in the sixteenth century, and prescribed the method of free examination. The rules he proposed were: (1) never to accept anything as true until one clearly knew that it was; (2) to divide each difficulty into as many parts as possible and requisite to solve it best; (3) to conduct one's thoughts in an orderly manner, beginning with the objects that were the simplest and the easiest to know and moving on gradually to the knowledge of the more complex; (4) to review and revise until one was certain that nothing had been omitted.

To this method, declared by modern philosophers to have little value outside mathematics, Descartes attributed his remarkable discoveries in optics, which included the first theory of the rainbow. By the discovery of the 'Cartesian co-ordinates' he laid the foundations of analytical geometry, being the first to apply algebraic equations to represent lines and curves, a method of which the 'graph' is a development and which proved of the highest importance in scientific calculations. Modern algebra had already been invented in the previous century by another Frenchman, François Viète (1540-1603). The application of algebraic methods to the geometric field, declares an expert, is probably the greatest step ever made in the progress of the exact sciences. Descartes also evolved a theory of the material universe in which he pictures the heavenly bodies spinning round in vortices (*tourbillons*) in the invisible ether, a subtle fluid which fills all space, leaving no vacuum. He held that the material universe consisted of an infinite number of these vortices. The whole mass of celestial matter comprised between the sun and the fixed stars whirled round in a circle and, carrying the planets with it, made them rotate round the sun. This was a *grand tourbillon*. At the same time each individual planet comprised a *tourbillon*, and, as it turned round the sun, it also turned on its own axis. With it whirled round a certain quantity of celestial matter, always ready to follow any movement given to it. This constituted the particular *tourbillon* of the planet.

This brilliant conception was very fashionable in the succeeding decades, as Molière's *Femmes Savantes* (1672) bears witness, and in 1686 Fontenelle, discoursing gracefully and charmingly in his *Entretiens sur la Pluralité des Mondes* on the Copernican system and the *tourbillons* of Descartes, brought science for the first time into the literature read by society. Descartes' cosmology was rendered obsolete by the simple and all-embracing theory of gravitation put forward by Newton, born seven years before Descartes' death.

Though his physiological theories, like his idea that animals are unfeeling and unthinking automata, have long been abandoned, Descartes remains as the founder of modern philosophy as well as of co-ordinate geometry.

'There was a man who at the age of twelve,' wrote Chateaubriand, 'with lines and circles had created mathematics; who at sixteen had written the most learned treatise on conic sections known since antiquity; who at nineteen mechanized a science which exists entirely in the understanding; who at twenty-three demonstrated the phenomena of the weight of air and demolished one of the greatest errors of old-fashioned physics; who, having completed the circle of the human sciences, at an age when other men are hardly conscious of their existence, perceived their emptiness, and turned all his thoughts to religion; who, from that moment until his death in his thirty-ninth year, always frail and ill, fixed the language spoken by Bossuet and Racine and provided a model of the most perfect wit as of the most vigorous reasoning; who, lastly, in the short intervals between his illnesses, solved by abstraction one of the most abstruse problems of geometry and jotted down thoughts which are as much divine as human: this terrifying genius was called Blaise Pascal.'

Pascal (1623-62), when a boy of twelve, had been forbidden by his father to learn mathematics until he had mastered Latin more fully, and, working by himself, discovered the first thirty-two propositions of Euclid. He invented the calculating machine (*machine arithmétique*) to help his father, an official in the government finance department, to do his accounting more rapidly. In 1648 he carried out experiments which proved for the first time without doubt that the pressure of the air diminishes as we go upwards, thus confirming that air has weight and demolishing the Aristotelian theory, still current at that time, that Nature abhors a vacuum.[1] Pascal was also the author of extensive writings on the equilibrium of liquids, and he invented the hydraulic press. He may thus be considered as the founder of the science of hydrostatics.

Pascal and Descartes were the initiators of the modern period in geometry, and Pascal is looked upon as the man above all others responsible for the advances in synthetic geometry made in his century. Modern analysis was created by another Frenchman, Pierre de Fermat (1601-65), by profession a judge, who seems never to have left Toulouse and whose mathematical genius so impressed Pascal, with whom he corresponded on mathematical subjects, that Pascal called him *le premier homme du monde*. Working independently of Descartes and not publishing his discoveries, he is credited with having laid the foundation for the differential calculus. Besides his work on the theory of numbers, his so-called 'last theorem', never yet proved or disproved, keeps his memory green among mathematicians.

Newton read Descartes' mathematical writings in his youth, and Leibniz, a German wholly trained in the French school, developed Descartes' work on differential calculus. Newton's revolutionary theory of the material universe furnished the basis of the deductive work done by the mathematical physicists of the eighteenth century, most of them French. France was again at that period the main centre of scientific activity, after having known a less productive period during the ascendancy of Newton. In the earlier years of that century the scientist best known in French society, Pierre-Louis Moreau de Maupertuis (1698-1759), worked with Alexis Clairaut on problems of Newton's *Principia*. With Clairaut and other astronomers he went to Lapland in 1735 to measure an arc of meridian, the object being to determine the exact shape of the

[1] Descartes claimed that he suggested the experiment to Pascal. On the question of priority see J. G. Andison, 'Pascal and the Great Experiment', *Univ. of Toronto Quarterly*, XVIII, No. 1, 1948.

earth. Voltaire, who had quarrelled with Maupertuis at Potsdam, where the French mathematician was President of the Berlin Academy, alludes to the Lapland expedition in *Micromégas*, written in 1752 for the delectation of Frederick II of Prussia.

Though not usually best known as a scientist, Voltaire did more than contribute the story of the apple to the Newton legend. In his *Lettres Philosophiques* or *Lettres sur les Anglais* (1734)—burnt by order of the Paris *Parlement*—he was the first to popularize Newtonian physics.[1] This he did with that matchless clarity and elegance which were his outstanding qualities. Voltaire's friend Madame du Châtelet, *la belle Émilie*, a competent mathematician coached by Clairaut, translated Newton's *Principia* into French, while another friend, Algarotti, published in dialogue form *Le Newtonianisme pour les dames*. The title of this last work (translated from the Italian) reminds us that Newton enjoyed in fashionable circles a vogue comparable to that of Einstein in Paris during the nineteen-twenties. But Voltaire was a philosopher more than a man of science: the God-fearing Newton, like Locke, came out of his hands somewhat transformed, and the views of both were used to forward the mechanical and materialist outlook favoured by the Encyclopaedists.

The publication of the *Encyclopédie* (1751-72), which set out to expound the order and the interdependence of human knowledge and to be at the same time a *Dictionnaire raisonné des sciences, des arts et des métiers*, affords both an indication of the interest taken in science and in the practical arts and an example of team work. The chief burden fell upon Denis Diderot, but his co-editor, Jean-Baptiste le Rond d'Alembert (1717-83), was in charge of the mathematical and scientific articles. D'Alembert was not only a writer and a philosopher, he was a mathematician of genius and discovered one of the central laws of dynamics, known by his name.

Lagrange, Laplace and Monge are the greatest names among the mathematicians of the later eighteenth century.

---

[1] It was not Voltaire but Lévesque de Pouilly, one of the editors of *L'Europe savante*, who first grasped Newton's idea.

Joseph Louis Lagrange (1736-1813) was the author of *Analytical Mechanics*, a work of which A. N. Whitehead, himself a philosopher and a mathematician, wrote this striking appreciation: 'The beauty and almost divine simplicity of these equations is such that these formulae are worthy to rank with those mysterious symbols which in ancient times were held directly to indicate the Supreme Reason at the base of all things.'

Pierre Simon, who became Marquis de Laplace (1749-1827), was the son of a poor Norman peasant. He set out for Paris, after some years as a mathematics teacher, to meet the influential D'Alembert, for whom he had a letter of introduction. D'Alembert would not see him, so the young man wrote a letter of his own in which he expounded the general principles of mechanics. D'Alembert, much impressed, sent for him at once, and a few days later he was appointed to a chair at the Paris Military School. It was Laplace who examined the cadet Napoleon Bonaparte for the artillery. By his *Essai philosophique sur les probabilités*, Laplace raised to a new level the theory of probability which he defined as common sense put into figures. This theory, on which French mathematicians have been particularly engaged, arose out of the correspondence between Pascal and Fermat on a problem concerning a game of chance. Its importance lies in its use in statistics; it allows dispassionate analysis of social problems and can be applied not merely to mortality rates—as is done by actuaries—but to problems like the effectiveness of medical remedies, the results of elections, the influence of punishment in checking crime, in fact, to any matter in which 'average' behaviour is important.

Of Laplace's *Essai* and his *Exposition du système du monde*, the astronomer Sir John Herschel declared that, were all the literature of Europe to perish, these essays excepted, they would suffice to convey to the latest posterity an impression of the intellectual greatness of the age which could produce them, surpassing that afforded by all the monuments antiquity has left us. Laplace formulated at the end of the *Exposition* a nebular theory, according to which the sun and the planets were formed from a rotating mass of incandescent gas. His

Traité de mécanique céleste, the first comprehensive elaboration of Newton's ideas, led to his being referred to at times as the French Newton. It was Laplace who, to Napoleon's question about the place of God in the scheme of nature, replied, 'I have no need of that hypothesis.'

Gaspard Monge (1746-1818), when a pupil at the military engineering school at Mézières, created descriptive geometry. On his own initiative he used geometrical methods in making plans of fortifications instead of the old, tedious, slow arithmetical processes. He generalized and put on a scientific basis the craft, empirically employed, of the stone-mason and the carpenter. Though of very humble birth—one of his fellow-Academicians stated that Monge's father was an itinerant knife-grinder—he became, even under the *ancien régime*, an instructor in the school of officers, most of whom were nobles, and afterwards taught at the Ecole Polytechnique— of which he was one of the founders—and the Ecole Normale Supérieure. Tradition has it that the authorities, regarding the nature of his discoveries as 'top-secret', discouraged him from early publication. In any case his *Géométrie descriptive* was first given to the world in a transcription of shorthand notes taken at his lectures.

Augustin Fresnel (1788-1827) confirmed Huygens' wave theory of light as against Newton's corpuscular theory, and with inexpensive home-made apparatus carried out experiments which made possible the estimation of the length of light-waves. Devoting his later years unremittingly to the improvement of lighthouses, he invented the parabolic reflector, thus immensely increasing the power and range of the light. André-Marie Ampère (1775-1836), whose highest ambition as a young man was to teach in a Lyons *lycée*—the *lycée* now bears his name—is known to-day in every physics laboratory by the ampere, the practical unit of electric current, and by 'Ampère's Rule' for determining the deflection of a magnet by an electric current. He created electrodynamics, having in a short space of time worked out all the laws implicit in the experiments of the Danish physicist Oersted; he clarified the ideas put forward by the Italian Volta and his work led the

M

way to the formulation of Ohm's Law. His contemporary
Auguste-Louis Cauchy (1789-1857), one of the outstanding
mathematicians of the nineteenth century, achieved fame by
his theory of the functions of an imaginary variable, a discovery so fertile that it has occupied mathematicians ever since.
Sadi Carnot (1796-1832) founded the science of thermo-
dynamics, enunciated the second law on the subject and, as
was later revealed, had already formulated the first law twenty
years before anyone else did so.

Evariste Galois (1811-32), a precocious genius who linked
up the theory of algebraic equations with the theory of substitution groups, is held in the highest repute by mathematicians
of to-day. His brief tragic career began by a failure at the
entrance examination of the Ecole Polytechnique. At the
age of seventeen he presented two mathematical papers to the
Academy of Sciences. The papers were lost. Re-written, they
were allotted for examination to an Academician who completely failed to understand them. Galois was expelled from
the Ecole Normale Supérieure for denouncing the professors
as reactionaries. A short and stormy spell of political agitation
landed him in prison, and in his twenty-first year he was killed
(so it is said) in a duel for a girl about whom he had no illusions.
The night before the encounter he wrote a sort of mathematical last will and statement ending with the words 'Je n'ai
pas le temps.'

The outstanding name among more recent mathematicians
is that of Henri Poincaré (1854-1912), whose *magnum opus* was
Les Méthodes nouvelles de la mécanique céleste and whom mathematicians revere as the discoverer of the Fuchsian functions.

When Henri Becquerel (1852-1908) discovered, in 1896, the
property of radioactivity, he little suspected what grim significance it was to have, half a century later, for the layman
haunted by the possibilities of the atomic bomb. Becquerel
found that the compounds of uranium emit continuously rays
having the power of passing through wood, paper and other
opaque materials. He noted that these rays affect a photo-
graphic plate, like the X-rays, just previously discovered by
Röntgen. The discovery of radium in 1898, a much more

highly radioactive element, was the work of Professor Pierre Curie (1859-1906) and of his Polish wife, Marie Sklodovska Curie (1867-1934). After a long series of researches, Mme Curie prepared radium chloride, the form in which radium is usually employed. She isolated the pure metal in 1910. On the death of her husband she succeeded him in the Chair of Physics at the Sorbonne, making history as the first woman to be a University Professor in France. She and her husband received a Nobel prize.

So did the physicist Louis de Broglie (b. 1892), whose work helped to elucidate the problem of atomic structure and who shared in the establishment of the present theory of light. In the seventeenth century Huyghens held that light consists of waves. Newton rejected this theory, in favour of the corpuscular theory, according to which light consists of a stream of particles. Fresnel in the eighteenth century declared, as a result of his experiments, that the wave theory was the right one. Both views triumphed at various times and, in the early decades of the present century, physicists, one finds, were seeking for a combination of the two. Present-day physicists favour the theory of 'wave mechanics' and credit Louis de Broglie and J. J. Thomson of Cambridge with the establishment of proof that Newton was wrong and the wave theory right. Among recent physicists in France stand out Gabriel Lippmann (1845-1921), who discovered electrical capillarity and the first process of colour photography, and Jean Perrin (1870-1942), who measured molecules.

Chemistry

In France, as elsewhere in Europe, chemistry grew up out of the quest for the philosopher's stone, and many weird and wonderful hypotheses, not all of them a legacy from the alchemists, cumbered the path of the new science. At the time when Antoine-Laurent Lavoisier (1743-94) was carrying out his experiments on combustion, chemists firmly believed that when a substance burns, the 'principle of combustibility', called phlogiston, escapes, leaving behind, as in the case of metals, the calx or ash. To any objection that the products of a combustion sometimes proved heavier than the original substance they retorted that phlogiston, the 'principle of levity', had negative weight and therefore left the substance which had been burned heavier. Even the great Priestley, who discovered oxygen, called it 'dephlogisticated air' and was a lifelong believer in the quaint phlogiston theory, evolved a hundred years before by the German chemist Stahl. Lavoisier was the first man to realize that chemical science must be based on weighing and measuring, and from his work dates modern chemistry. 'That we owe to France the existence of chemistry,' wrote Buckle, the historian of civilization, 'will be admitted by everyone who uses the word science in the sense in which alone it ought to be understood. Until Lavoisier entered the field there were no generalizations wide enough to entitle chemistry to be called a science.' Lavoisier's work illustrated the maxim that 'Science is measurement'.

He started quantitative chemistry on its fruitful career by his proof that mass remains constant during all changes of form, that is to say, however much chemical change alters the form and properties of a substance, the total weight is unchanged. This is the fundamental law of physical science, the principle known as the 'conservation of mass' or the indestructibility of matter, concisely expressed by Lavoisier himself as 'Rien ne se perd, rien ne se crée.'

Lavoisier also established the principle that respiration is slow combustion in the body and discovered the calorific rôle of perspiration and of digestion. He thus laid the foundations of general physiology. He was secretary and treasurer of the commission which established the metric system of weights and measures, now adopted throughout the world for scientific work. The basic unit of measure, the metre, represents the ten-millionth part of the arc of the meridian comprised between the Equator and the North Pole. It is piquant to remember, when the metric system is denigrated as artificial, that the basic measurement was chosen as being 'natural' in opposition to the arbitrary traditional measures.

The funds needed for his experiments Lavoisier furnished

from his private fortune, for he was a rich man. He was in fact a tax-farmer, and during the Revolution a trumped-up charge was made against him on this account and he was guillotined. A brother chemist, who dared to plead that Lavoisier should be spared on account of his great services to science, was sternly informed by the president of the 'people's court' that the Republic did not need scientists. Under the stress of war the Republic was soon to discover that it needed them urgently. When its arsenals were empty, its steel and saltpetre supplies cut off by the British navy, France was saved by the practical genius of its savants. Fourcroy taught the methods of extracting and refining saltpetre, Guyton de Morveau and Berthollet made known a new method of manufacturing gunpowder, Monge expounded the theory of casting and boring brass and cast-iron cannon. Meanwhile, in England, a young man called Humphry Davy was stirred to an interest in chemistry by reading, in 1798, a translation of Lavoisier's *Traité élémentaire de chimie*.

The new science inherited, with the odd notions of the old alchemy, a nomenclature quite unsuited to the new age. Lavoisier set about the creation of a new terminology—which is in great measure the one used to-day—and with him worked Guyton de Morveau, Fourcroy, author of *La Philosophie Chimique* (1792), and Claude-Louis Berthollet (1748-1822). In those happy days the war between France and England did not rule out fraternization between the scientists, and Berthollet in his country retreat was visited by many British travellers, including Watt and Humphry Davy, the latter of whom said very charmingly of Berthollet that he had 'no airs but many graces'. By demonstrating the use of chlorine, in the solution now known as *eau de javelle*, Berthollet created the bleaching industry. All Europe admired this discovery and fortunes were made by the industrialists. Berthollet was so disinterested that all he deigned to accept from those whom his discovery had enriched was a bale of linen bleached by his process.

Joseph-Louis Gay-Lussac (1778-1850), both physicist and chemist, held the Chair of Physics at the Sorbonne and the Chair of Chemistry at the Ecole Normale Supérieure. He observed that gases combine in simple proportions by volume, and the experiments by which he established this law laid the foundation for the further development of all knowledge of atoms and molecules and hence of all investigations into the structure of matter. Gay-Lussac's Law has still to be learned by every schoolboy, and so has Charles's Law as to the equal expansion by heat of all gases, of which the modern version runs, 'At constant pressure, the volume of a given mass of gas is proportional to the absolute temperature.' Alexandre Charles (1746-1823), a physicist, first suggested the use of hydrogen for inflating balloons. He has a place in literary history as the husband of Lamartine's Elvire, immortalized in the *Méditations*.

Marcelin Berthelot (1827-1907) played an important part in the development of organic synthesis (the alcohols), and discovered in 1885 that microbes fix nitrogen in the soil; he also obtained ozone by electricity. His researches led him to the creation of thermochemistry and chemical mechanics. In the course of a long life Berthelot, one of the greatest chemists of the second half of the nineteenth century, contrived, in addition, to serve his country as Senator, Minister of Education and Foreign Minister. His son Daniel (1865-1927) won renown for his work on ultra-violet rays.

Much better known to the layman, however, is Louis Pasteur (1822-95). He has the advantage of having a biographer, Vallery-Radot, whose *Life of Pasteur* ranks as a classic, and of having had his life-story dramatized for the films. Moreover, his work favourably affected the welfare of mankind to a degree that no other chemist's discoveries can rival. His first researches concerned the forms of crystals, and initiated a revolution in the current ideas regarding the molecular structure of organic compounds. These experiments led him on to the exploration of ferments. Investigating milk, beer, etc. (some of his experiments were made in Barclay's Brewery in London), he discovered that fermentation was due to living organisms. He showed that these micro-organisms could be destroyed by heat-treatment. This process, now widely applied to milk, is called *pasteurization*.

Pasteur found that the presence of air was necessary for fermentation to take place. Air therefore must contain the micro-organisms. By a series of experiments Pasteur exploded the old notion of spontaneous generation. Further study and experiment brought the discovery that a number of animal and human diseases are due to particular microbes or bacteria. Pasteur's crowning achievement was the discovery that, by inoculation with a culture of these microbes, the diseases may be prevented, or their virulence decreased. He began these experiments on animals, finding means first of preventing anthrax, rabies or hydrophobia, then a silk-worm disease called *pébrine*. By this last achievement he saved from extinction the silk cultivation of France, Spain and Italy. His discoveries of the part played in disease and in putrefaction by micro-organisms have brought about revolutionary changes in methods of food-preservation, have been of immense service to the farmer (plant diseases and soil science) and have transformed the outlook and practice of doctor and surgeon. Lister's antiseptic technique was based on the work of Pasteur, creator of the new science of bacteriology. T. H. Huxley said that the monetary value of Pasteur's discoveries was sufficient to have paid off the whole of the heavy indemnity demanded by Germany from France after the 1870 war. So world-wide was the renown of his discoveries that, as a tribute to his genius and in gratitude for his services to mankind, the Pasteur Institute was founded by international subscription.

Natural History

In natural history France made considerable contributions to knowledge in the eighteenth century, which was less purely mathematical than the seventeenth. The natural sciences were not only pursued by many specialists, they had an extraordinary vogue in society, for Jean-Jacques Rousseau had made botany popular among society people. Fashionable ladies collected flowers and plants and consigned them to a herbarium. Linnaeus's classification, which had just appeared, gave these

amateurs a method of arrangement. Drawing-room lectures
by savants, visits to 'cabinets' of natural history, manuals of
science 'à l'usage des jeunes demoiselles' provided not merely
a pleasant antidote to idleness and boredom but edification
and a mental tonic. As a contemporary poet phrased it:

> Nature! oui, je le sens, c'est cette heureuse étude
> Qui seule nourrit l'âme, affranchit la raison
> Des fers, des préjugés, et de l'opinion.

One great lady was so enamoured of anatomy that when she
travelled she had a corpse packed into the boot of her carriage
so that she might do some dissection whenever, during visits
to distant friends, she had an hour to spare.

René-Antoine de Réaumur (1683-1757) was a pioneer in
natural history as well as a physicist, and is sometimes called
the Pliny of the eighteenth century. He experimented on
iron, porcelain clays and cobwebs, carried out a most ingenious
series of experiments on the digestion of birds, devised a method
of tinning iron that is still employed, and made an inquiry
into turquoise-mines and auriferous rivers. His outstanding
work is the six-volume *Mémoires pour servir à l'histoire des insectes*,
still looked upon with respect by zoologists. He is best remembered for his thermometer—80 degrees between the freezing
and boiling points of water—used in Central Europe though
replaced in France by the centigrade instrument.

The man who did most to interest his generation—and
many succeeding generations—in natural history was Georges-
Louis Leclerc, Comte de Buffon (1707-88). While still in his
twenties, he translated the classical English work on plant
physiology, Hales' *Vegetable Statics*, and, a few years later,
Newton's *Method of Fluxions*—a work on differential calculus.
He immensely improved the Jardin du Roi—botanic and
zoological gardens—of which he was Keeper, adding to its
resources and its popularity. His *Histoire Naturelle*, in thirty-
six quarto volumes in the original edition, looms largest on
the library shelves among French scientific books of this period.
Most modern biologists willingly leave them there. Buffon's
descriptive method brings a bored frown to the modern scientific

brow, and an ironical smile condemns his constant preoccupation
with the strictly human point of view and his tendency to adopt
towards the animals he is describing an attitude of hostility or
sympathy. Why does he speak of this animal's 'vices' and that
animal's 'virtues'? Why praise this animal for its fidelity and
blame the other for its laziness? Buffon disliked the tiger, the vul-
ture and the cat—these were, as Nisard put it, his *bêtes noires*.
Some of his contemporaries, qualified or not, treated themselves
to the luxury of pungent comment. 'Cette *Histoire Naturelle* ... pas
si naturelle' was Voltaire's devastating epigram, and D'Alembert dismissed this stylist (Buffon was the author of a celebrated
Discours sur le Style) as 'le plus grand des phrasiers.' Though
as a scientific treatise the *Natural History* has become in some
measure obsolete, sharing the common fate of scientific
manuals, present-day biologists admit that by the variety of
questions he raised concerning the distribution and changeful-
ness of species, Buffon laid the foundations of modern evolution
theory in zoology and botany. He especially stressed the
significance of environment, upholding the theory of the
mutability of species against the Linnaean view of absolute
fixity of species. On the foundation laid by this speculative
genius arose the remarkable and lasting structures of Lamarck
and Geoffroy Saint-Hilaire. Buffon, moreover, by pointing
out that all the animal species in South America were different
from those of the Old World, has a claim to have founded
'zoological geography'.

Buffon is eminently readable, and the elegant style of the
early volumes had a prejudicial effect on the popularity of
Réaumur's writings. The general reader of his time delighted
in the variety of the descriptions and in the weighty philosophical reflexions on the general laws of nature. The stately
rhythm of the sentences and a harmonious turn of phrase give
Buffon's work a certain majestic and poetic charm. His
descriptions of animals were too successful, and he early
became a nursery favourite. Even in his own century the
Histoire Naturelle was proposed as a substitute for La Fontaine's
Fables, to be read by children aged two to four—after which,
one presumes, these precocious toddlers would begin to study

real science! For many generations Buffon was one of the
authors in which French boys—like Fritzel, the youthful hero
of Erckmann-Chatrian's *Madame Thérèse*—learned to read,
and he certainly provided them with an admirable model of
academic French. G. B. Shaw, in his Preface to *Back to
Methuselah*, avers that in the 1860s every literate child in this
country knew the *Natural History* of the 'celebrated Buffoon'! as
well as he knew Aesop's *Fables*.

Though not a stylist like Buffon, whose protégé he was, Jean-
Baptiste Lamarck (1744-1829) is treated to-day with greater
respect by zoologists. He began his career as a professional
soldier, made a name as a botanist, and then, at fifty, was
appointed a professor of zoology at the Museum, which had
once been the Jardin du Roi. Long before Charles Darwin,
whose *Origin of Species* appeared in 1859, he was an evolutionary
transformist, refusing to believe with Linnaeus that species
are fixed and unalterable. As a result of painstaking systematic work on living and on extinct invertebrate forms (e.g.
mollusca) he evolved the view that species change slowly under
changing environmental influences. He also brought out
clearly the principle of unity of type as the basis of classification and reached the conception of the interrelation of the
differing groups of animals as branches of a single tree. In
his *Philosophie zoologique* (1809), called by the German biologist
Haeckel 'the first connected and thoroughly logical exposition
of the theory of descent', Lamarck brought together and co-
ordinated all his ideas on the phenomena presented by the
whole of animated nature. The glory of Lamarck was eclipsed
by that of Darwin. His work was misunderstood during his
lifetime and for long afterwards. He lived in studious retirement, without ambition, entirely absorbed in his studies and
meditations, and died in poverty, having used up all his means
for his researches. In England Samuel Butler, the author of
Erewhon, stoutly defended Lamarckism in a series of books of
which the first, *Life and Habit*, appeared in 1877, proclaiming
that Buffon and Lamarck were nearer the truth than Darwin,
though no doubt convinced that Butler was nearer still.

Georges Cuvier (1769-1832) owed his interest in natural

history to copying out and colouring, in his boyhood, the illustrations gracing Buffon's unwieldy tomes, which provided his staple reading for several years. He carried forward the subject by refining and extending the Aristotelian idea of correlation: certain characteristics in animals necessarily occur together, whereas others are mutually exclusive. His solid experimental work laid a sound basis for inferences as to the nature of fragmentary remains, e.g. fossils. His studies on fossil bones found in the neighbourhood of Paris were set forth in his *Recherches sur les ossements fossiles*, still looked upon as a model of clarity, precision, scientific method and style. This book aided in the establishment of the new science of palaeontology. Science had travelled far since Voltaire had dismissed the fossils found in the Alps with the flippant comment that they were cockle shells fallen from pilgrims' cloaks and the petrified fish were the remains of the pilgrims' meals!

Fundamentally averse to speculation, Cuvier, having at first followed Buffon's views about the influence of environment on the mutability of species, reverted to the conservative Linnaean view of the fixity of species and his ideas of geology and embryology were likewise conservative. This firm attitude is credited with having spared French natural history the excessive evolutionary theorizing which handicapped British and Germans alike in the nineteenth century. His own work in descriptive zoology —especially marine zoology—set a standard well maintained subsequently by his countrymen.

In attributing mutation of species to direct, not indirect, influence or environment, Etienne Geoffroy Saint-Hilaire (1772-1844) adhered to Buffon's view rather than to Lamarck's. He also differed from Lamarck, who was his colleague at the Museum, in believing that such change need not be slow and gradual but may on occasion be sudden. In his *Principes de philosophie anatomique* he reaffirmed very strongly the principle of unity of type, for he saw all animal species as so many modifications of a single pattern. All vertebrates have a similar skeleton, the underlying unity is only hidden by the various modifications.

The zoological theories of the early nineteenth century in

France enjoyed such great vogue that they attracted the attention of literary men. Saint-Hilaire's hypothesis of the unity of organic composition in the animal world appealed very strongly to Balzac. In the preface to his *Comédie Humaine* he summarizes Saint-Hilaire's doctrine and adds that, just as in the case of animal species, so the variations of man in society are brought about by his environment. The different social classes really correspond to the different species in the animal world: 'the differences between a soldier, a workman, an administrator, a barrister, an idler, a scientist, a statesman, a tradesman, a sailor, a poet, a pauper, a priest are, although more difficult to perceive, as great as those which distinguish the wolf, the lion, the monkey, etc.' In each case you see an example of what diversity of environment can make of the universal pattern. Balzac uses the theory to justify those copious descriptions of streets, houses and furniture to which he was very prone. He liked to think that his method was scientific, the method of the zoologist who regards his description of species as incomplete unless supplemented by a detailed study of the environment that moulded them.

The methods of science had brought such a rich reward in new knowledge that literary men were tempted to try scientific methods in their own sphere. Novels needed no longer to be mere works of pure imagination, stories told for man's delight, but might achieve value as *documents humains*—documents to be treated with the respect due to scientific pronouncements. Criticism tried to become scientific too, instead of depending on personal impressions and individual taste.

The critic Taine, a great admirer of Balzac, quotes the zoologists to justify his own method in history and literary criticism. His famous formula, *race, milieu, moment,* recalls one of Lamarck's fundamental laws, and the theory of the *faculté maîtresse* reminds one of Cuvier's law of the subordination of organs.

Claude Bernard (1813-78), the outstanding French physiologist, wrote an *Introduction à l'étude de la médicine expérimentale* in which he set forth, in the light of his own experience, general rules of experiment and research, much as Descartes did in his

Discours de la méthode—but Bernard was more a man of the laboratory than Descartes. This book inspired the novelist Emile Zola and was the starting-point for his attempt, in the Rougon-Macquart series, at writing the experimental novel, in which the hero was to be studied scientifically, from the point of view of heredity and environment. More important than his influence on Zola was the influence of Claude Bernard on medicine. He made many important discoveries: the building up and distribution to the body of glycogen by the liver, a discovery that threw light on the cause and possible treatment of diabetes; the rôle of the nervous system in digestion and secretion. He also made known the existence and the function of the vaso-motor nerves that control the blood-vessels. His outstanding achievement was to demonstrate that the body is no mere conglomeration of separate organs but a close and complex system of vital mechanisms whose object is to keep constant the conditions of life in the internal environment. A pioneer in what was to become the science of biochemistry, he is still to-day, by his method, his ingenuity in experiment, and by his spirit, an inspiration to medical men engaged in research, not only in France but in the whole world.

Scientists have been defined as men who observe facts and describe them; philosophers explain facts and link them together. The earliest scientists—like the alchemists before them —called themselves philosophers. The sciences were, indeed, at one time part of philosophy, as we are reminded by the use, still current in the Scottish Universities, of the term 'natural philosophy' for physics. Each new science, once it was organized into a body of definite knowledge, broke away from philosophy and set up on its own account. One of the tasks left for philosophy—its main task according to Auguste Comte's Positivist doctrine—is to endeavour to reach some rational unification of the knowledge derived from the various sciences. Philosophy also undertakes to examine afresh the validity of the assumptions on which each science is built up. This is all the more necessary since each science tends, not unnaturally, to apply to the universe in general those hypotheses that have served it so well in its own domain and that it has come to look upon as 'laws' too valuable to be restricted to that limited field in which they were verified.

French scientists, though never accused of the alleged Germanic propensity towards cloudy metaphysics or the building of 'an inverted pyramid of theory on a pin point of reality', have felt, perhaps more than other scientists, the urge towards a unitary explanation of the universe. They have been tempted to cross the boundary which separates science from philosophy, in a sense that they wished not only to observe and describe, but to explain and link together their facts. 'L'âme française,' wrote Bergson 'va tout droit à ce qui est général.' Descartes and Pascal, both profound philosophers as well as great scientists, set the example of the dual rôle. In the following century D'Alembert, La Mettrie and Cabanis, in the nineteenth Auguste Comte, Renouvier and Henri Poincaré, with others, went from science (mathematics or medicine) to philosophy. More striking still is the number of French scientific works whose titles suggest a philosophical outlook, among them Lamarck's *Philosophie zoologique*, Geoffroy Saint-Hilaire's *Philosophie anatomique*, Ampère's *Philosophie des sciences* and M. Berthelot's *Science et philosophie*. As used here by Lamarck and Saint-Hilaire, *philosophie* implies merely the system of general ideas belonging to a particular science. It may not be entirely fanciful to suggest that the French scientist when, by a unifying generalization, he has consolidated a limited group of phenomena in his special field, may feel impelled to attempt to relate this group to the whole picture. He wishes to carry into the widest possible sphere that order and unity which he has achieved in his particular science. A certain eagerness to generalize has its value, for the hypotheses evolved may suggest new lines of research to future workers in the field. Buffon's philosophizing certainly inspired later zoologists, and even geologists, and Lamarck's hypotheses, after many years, stimulated the biologists.

A tendency to love general ideas and to regard facts as uninteresting unless they can be used in formulating a hypothesis did not always meet with the approval of more cautious and fact-loving scientists; these preferred to concentrate attention on

details, to distrust broad generalizations, and to accept only
working hypotheses dealing with the particular task in hand.
Like the thorough-going scholar, they resented any speculation
tending to connect their own particular patch of knowledge
with knowledge in general. This cautious, positivist attitude,
sometimes inspired by the philosophy of Auguste Comte, is
alleged to have clipped the wings of French scientific speculation during the middle years of the nineteenth century and to
have handicapped French science at a moment when the need
of the time was bold hypothesis that might lead to the solution
of problems like the atomic theory. A century earlier Réaumur
had feared the opposite defect. 'On cède trop volontiers,' he
writes in 1752, 'au penchant qui porte à généraliser ses idées;
il est commode de s'épargner des discussions: d'ailleurs on
s'y croit autorisé par des analogies qu'on étend souvent trop
loin en regardant les loix de la Nature comme plus uniformes
qu'elles ne le sont généralement.'

The attitude of the best French scientists is no doubt that
expressed by Claude Bernard. 'Comme expérimentateur
j'évite donc les systèmes philosophiques, mais je ne saurais
pour cela repousser cet esprit philosophique qui, sans être
nulle part, est partout, et qui, sans appartenir à aucun système,
doit régner non seulement sur toutes les sciences, mais sur
toutes les connaissances humaines.'

It is evident that both tendencies—to generalize and to
abstain as far as possible from other than working hypotheses—
have had their adherents in France, as elsewhere. It would
be unwarranted, therefore, to assume that a taste for general
ideas, *un esprit philosophique*, so widespread in France, has
harmed French science. Careless observation, neglect of
details, or vagueness of presentation, are defects not to be laid
at the door of France's great savants. On the contrary, French
scientists, however philosophically inclined, have produced
an imposing amount of new, well-tested material, harmoni-
ously proportioned, precisely chiselled and neatly arranged,
to be built into the temple of Science.

READING LIST

There are readable accounts of French science in:

La Science française, edited by H. Poincaré and published in 1915 by the Ministère de l'Instruction Publique et des Beaux Arts. Each science is treated separately by a French expert. 2 vols. Paris, New Edition, 1933.

La Science, 2 vols., edited by G. Urbain and M. Bell. Larousse, Paris (1933). Some forty collaborators treat separately the history of each science from antiquity to the present day. Volume II deals with contemporary discoveries, new inventions and theoretical problems. 1160 illustrations.

Hanotaux, G. *Histoire de la nation française.* Paris, 1924-25. Volumes XIV and XV are entirely devoted to the history of French science. Mathematics, Physics, Chemistry, Biology, and the philosophy of the sciences are treated by experts in each group.

Discovery, Vol. VIII, Nos. 9-10 (September and October 1947).

French Science, Past and Present, by E. M. Friedwald. Also by the same writer, *La Science française* in *La France Libre*, Vol. XIII, p. 75.

French science finds a place in the following manuals, all very readable:

Rousseau, P. *Histoire de la Science.* Paris, 1947.

Singer, A. *A Short History of Science to the Nineteenth Century.* Oxford, 1946.

Whetham, W. C. D. *A Shorter History of Science.* Cambridge, 1944.

FOR FURTHER READING

Broglie, L. de. *Savants et découvertes.* Paris, 1951.

Caullery, M. *La Science française depuis le* xviie *siècle.* Paris, 1933.

Lenard, P. *Great Men of Science.* English translation, London, 1933.

Merz, J. T. *European Thought in the Nineteenth Century*, 4 vols. London, 1896-1914. The first volume (pp. 89-156) contains an interesting chapter on *The Scientific Spirit in France*, with very informative notes.

Mornet, D. *Les Sciences de la nature en France au* xviiie *siècle.* Paris, 1917.

Whetham, W. C. D. *Science and the Human Mind.* London, 1912.

A History of Science. Cambridge, 1929.

Whitehead, A. N. *Science and the Modern World.* Cambridge, 1926.

Wolf, A. *A History of Science, Technology and Philosophy in the Sixteenth and Seventeenth Centuries.* London, 1935.

CHAPTER IX

MUSIC

FOR many people, perhaps for most, Germany and Italy are the lands of music. The Germanic musicians have scaled the highest peaks, and the land of the cypress and myrtle has for centuries charmed men's ears by the voluptuous beauty of its vocal melodies. France, though no towering genius like J. S. Bach or Beethoven looms in her musical history, has a tradition of musical achievement stretching back into the Middle Ages. Before Germany, with Bach and Handel in the early eighteenth century, had produced her first world-figures in music, France had formed Lully, who, with Couperin and Rameau, laid down the lines along which a distinctively French musical tradition was to develop. French music of this tradition belongs to the middle way, the realm of precise and clearly defined forms. In music, as in the other arts, France has shown a certain distrust of the unleashed imagination; reticence and tact have put a brake on the untrammelled surge of violent emotion. Lyrical effusion and philosophic meditation are not outstanding qualities of her traditional music. Not passionate lyricism, but measured and controlled emotion, is its dominant note. It spurns what André Gide referred to somewhere as the *épanouissement vague* that the Germans find in music.

The traditional music of France, like her painting, her architecture, and her sculpture appeals primarily to the rational element in man. It prides itself on being intellectual and descriptive. D'Alembert wrote 'Toute musique qui ne peint rien n'est que du bruit' and Marmontel averred 'La musique qui ne peint rien est insipide.' Rameau himself declared that 'L'expression de la pensée, du sentiment, des passions, doit être le vrai but de la musique.' Not particularly prone to dream-like qualities, or to imperious rhetoric, French music prefers to have a subject which it translates and comments

N

upon; it is music which, as an American critic wrote, 'would charm, entertain and perhaps move, but without tears and violent passions'. French critics point out that even in the first quarter of the eighteenth century the nation showed its distaste for 'la musique pure'. Even at a concert, the public yearned for something resembling the music of the theatre: 'ils réclameront des effets surtout dramatiques; ils exigeront tout au moins que, dans leur plaisir, on fasse la plus grande part à l'esprit et que les compositions qu'on leur offre aient un intérêt surtout littéraire ou pittoresque.'

This linking of music with literary expression, whether the explanation lies in the preferences of the composers themselves or in their acceptance of the desires of those for whom they wrote, occurs frequently in the history of French music. In the Middle Ages music was linked with the lyric poetry of Troubadour or Trouvère. Much Renaissance music was written to accompany poems such as those of the Pléiade, and Ronsard, though deaf, believed that 'sans la Musique la Poésie était presque sans grâce' At Louis XIV's Court, music adorned the *comédies-ballets*. In the eighteenth and nineteenth centuries it blossomed in opera. The French love for ballet and dance rhythms must have often drawn their composers towards these forms of music, in which they have excelled.

Parallels between the arts at a given period may be perilous, for some music critics are confident that their art, untouched by the world, pursues its way indifferent to all other activities of society at any given time. It is tempting to suggest that in France the literary ideals and movements are to some extent reflected in the music of each period: classical tragedy, in the dignified compositions of Lully; the graces of the literature of Enlightenment, in the works of Rameau; Romantic poetry and drama, in the flowering of opera and of Berlioz; the poetry of Mallarmé and the Symbolists, in the music of Debussy. Nor would it be far-fetched to discover, in the development of music during those periods, parallels with Poussin, Watteau, Delacroix, and the impressionists. In any case the arts express the thoughts, feelings and emotions of any given period, and though some novel form of expression may appear in one art before another is ready for it, currents run from one to the other. The arts are not pursued in isolation.

Nations do not live in water-tight compartments either, and a glance through the names of French composers reveals that Paris exerted a strong attraction on foreign musicians. The French spirit imbues the music of those who settled down in Paris or merely sojourned there; the Florentine Lully, the Germans Gluck, Meyerbeer and Offenbach, the Belgians Grétry and César Franck, to say nothing of Chopin, born in Poland of a French father. The French themselves often borrowed from foreign sources but, as in the other arts, they created, with what they took from abroad, works distinctively French.

'La France,' wrote a French musical critic, 'est née une chanson aux lèvres.' A vast treasure of folk-melodies for dances and songs, in addition to those that had already found their way into the current musical tradition of the country, was unearthed in the nineteenth century.[1] The traditional dances of the country folk were the joy of the villages in Brittany and in Auvergne in Louis XIV's time, as must have been noticed by every reader of Madame de Sévigné's *Lettres* or Fléchier's *Les Grands Jours d'Auvergne*. The *bourrées* from Auvergne, the *gavottes* from Provence, the minuets from Poitou, formed, with the stately Spanish saraband, the *allemande* from Germany, with the *courante* and the *gigue*, the very texture of music that delighted the aristocratic audiences of Lully's *comédies-ballets* in the age of Louis XIV, and, in the century of enlightenment, charmed the leisure of the *beau monde* which listened to the *suites* of Couperin and Rameau.

In addition to the development of secular music, popular and homophonic, the Middle Ages had seen the development of Church music, learned and polyphonic. Polyphonic music, in which several melodies are superposed, originated at Notre-Dame in Paris at the end of the twelfth century and its greatest

[1] See the eight series of *Mélodies populaires* published by Julian Tiersot (Heugel et Cie, Paris).

masters were Okingham and Josquin des Prés. It was France, with Flanders, that gave Italy, from the fourteenth century onwards, her first musical education. During their stay in Avignon, the Popes learned the art of descant, and during the fourteenth and fifteenth centuries French musicians performed in the chapels of the Vatican. France may also claim to have trained the Tuscan monk, Guido d'Arezzo, who had some share in the invention of the four-line stave.

Mediaeval Europe owed much to the aristocratic Troubadours of Provence and to the Trouvères, whose home was in Northern France, for they were musicians as well as poets. Music was so closely allied with poetry that verse was always sung, not recited. The 'Cours d'Amour' of the Troubadours not only instructed Europe in a new conception of the Art of Love, they taught the Minnesingers in Germany, and the Italians, something about the art of music. The Trouvère Adam le Bossu or Adam de la Halle, besides composing motets and rondos, wrote two dramatic pieces. One of them, 'Le Jeu de Robin et de Marion', a pastoral play in which dances and songs diversify the dialogue, has been called the first French *opéra comique*, though opera properly so called was still to be invented by the Italians. The music of the play, probably composed between 1282 and 1288, though simple, is regarded as perfect of its kind. While the Italians, at the end of the sixteenth century, were developing instrumental music and moving from polyphony to harmony, France specialized in elaborate *ballets de cour*, in which dances, dignified or comic, were produced in a sumptuous decorative setting with elaborate stage effects. Out of these spectacular *suites* of dances grew the *comédies-ballets*, and even the operas, which Lully composed for Louis XIV.

The first French tune most of us ever learned was 'Au clair de la lune'. Lully, we were told, composed that simple melody, but modern critics throw doubt on that assertion. Jean Baptiste Lully (1632-87) was brought to France from his native Italy when a small boy and, before becoming one of the King's violinists, for a time (so legend assures us) served as a page to the Duchesse de Montpensier, la Grande Mademoiselle.

He became a Frenchman in 1661, when appointed to super-intend the royal musicians just as Le Brun supervised the King's painters. Lully's name is for ever linked with that of Molière, for he wrote the music for the *comédies-ballets*: 'Le Mariage Forcé', 'M. de Pourceaugnac', 'La Princesse d'Elide' and 'Le Bourgeois Gentilhomme'; in this last the versatile musician scored a further success by his performance as the Mufti. The dances composed for 'Le Bourgeois Gentilhomme', particu-larly the delightful *menuet*, are tuneful enough to justify Louis XIV's partiality for this form of entertainment. Lully also wrote the dance music for mythological ballets and other Court *divertissements*, including 'Psyché' (1671), a tragi-comedy in which Corneille and Molière collaborated and which is sometimes referred to as the first real French opera. On occasions Lully had the honour of dancing side by side with the King, who, with members of the Royal Family and others of the highest nobility, deigned to perform in these spectacular entertainments, while thousands of guests looked on, amazed and delighted.

These ballets were sumptuous and dignified. So were the operas which the amiable and docile poet Quinault wrote to the order of Lully and to the glory of Louis XIV. For a score of these Lully composed the music—'putting the gardens of Ver-sailles into music', as a French critic phrased it—in other words, putting into music the same French qualities of logic, clarity and symmetry which had found expression in the palace gardens. The most famous of his operas was 'Armide et Renaud' (1686), the dramatization of an incident from Tasso's *Jerusalem Delivered*. Into this he put his finest music. Though Lully may be looked upon as the founder of French opera, it is just to remember that a native-born Frenchman, Robert Cam-bert, had preceded him, having written the music to 'Pomone', a pastoral play by the Abbé Perrin, in 1659, which became the first French opera ever publicly performed in Paris. Lully, an unscrupulous intriguer, a *coquin ténébreux*, as Boileau calls him, contrived to oust Cambert and Perrin, who had been granted the monopoly of the production of operas in French. A consummate courtier, he bowed to the taste of his French public by including recitatives and shortening arias. By using a style of unaccompanied recitative he made the declamatory portions of his operas more attractive, and he developed the overture into a much fuller and more perfect musical introduction than the meagre preludes which had satisfied Italian audiences. These operas were so popular in 1677 that, as La Fontaine bears witness, everybody who was anybody was singing or humming the tunes:

> 'On ne va plus au bal, on ne va plus au Cours:
> Hiver, été, printemps, bref opéra toujours.
> Et quiconque n'en chante, ou bien plutôt n'en gronde
> Quelque récitatif n'a pas l'air du beau monde.' [1]

Lully's music is noble and symmetrical, less sensuous and sentimental than that of Italian opera. The symmetrical movements of the ballet, and its rhythms, influenced his style of composition. He was an intellectual artist, a writer of descriptive music, music whose aesthetic value results from its sense of proportion and its appropriateness.[2] His religious music was much admired by Madame de Sévigné, and of his 'Miserere', for solo voices, chorus, organ and strings, she wrote 'Je ne crois point qu'il y ait une autre musique dans le ciel.' Lully met his end in a manner which his enemies must have looked upon as a 'judgment'. Conducting a *Te Deum* to celebrate the recovery of Louis XIV from a dangerous illness, he slipped and struck his foot with the long heavy baton, then used by the *chef d'orchestre* to beat the time. Gangrene set in and Lully expired after much suffering.

Charles II, at whose Court Cambert took refuge when Lully ousted him from the Court of Louis XIV, was so enthralled by French music that when he returned to England in 1660 he replaced the graver music of Tallis, Byrd and Gibbons in the Chapels Royal by music in the French taste.[3]

---

[1] Epître à M. Niert.

[2] Lully also composed military music for the Prussians and the Dutch.

[3] Marc-Antoine Charpentier (1634-1704), like his adversary Lully, worked with Molière on Court performances, e.g. 'Le Mariage Forcé'. Charpentier wrote the music to Thomas Corneille's opera 'Médée', 1693, and showed dramatic insight and enterprise.

In the succeeding generation the outstanding name is François Couperin (1668-1733), called Couperin le Grand to distinguish him from the other members of a family of illustrious musicians. At the age of seventeen he took his father's place as organist at the church of St. Gervais in Paris. Much esteemed at Louis XIV's Court, he taught the harpsichord and composition to the young princes of the Royal Household. He brought to perfection the art of playing the harpsichord, a branch of music in which the French were pre-eminent, and in 1717 published *L'Art de toucher le clavecin*, which influenced J. S. Bach's method of keyboard practice. His *suites* inspired Bach's six *suites françaises*, sometimes flippantly referred to as his lightest and brightest. Couperin attached descriptive titles to his pieces: 'La Tendre Nanette', 'La Laborieuse', 'Sœur Monique', 'Le Moucheron', 'Les Idées heureuses', etc. delightful character-pieces, psychological studies expressed in musical form, with delicacy, tact and entire absence of rhetorical display. These were the qualities most appreciated by the *honnête homme*, the social ideal of the French classical age. Many of these pieces are in the form of dances, but were written to be listened to and not for the ballroom. Couperin was the forerunner of the composers of 'programme music'. His compositions have for the modern listener a quaint old-world charm, evoking the atmosphere of the courtly society of the most elegant period in French history. They recall the paintings of Watteau, equally delicate, poetic and evocative; both possess the same easy grace, the same mysterious tenderness.

Jean-Philippe Rameau (1683-1764) contemporary of Handel and J. S. Bach, continues the golden age of French dramatic and chamber music that Lully inaugurated. Like Lully he wrote for a courtly society—*gentilshommes et capitaines en dentelles*. He made a rather unfortunate start to a long life by getting himself taken away from school in Dijon, where his father was organist, because he scribbled music all over his exercise books instead of learning his Latin. At eighteen he was sent off to study music in Italy, where he found the vocal flourishes of the opera singers intolerable and is said to have worked his way home as a fiddler to a band of strolling musicians. After

holding various posts as church organist in the provinces, he
settled down in Paris, where the farmer-general, Le Riche de
la Pouplinière,[1] engaged him for his private concerts. This
wealthy patron used his influence to have Rameau's first opera
performed at the Opéra, in the composer's fifty-first year. The
first of thirty-six, it was based on a poor libretto taken from
Racine's 'Phèdre' and entitled 'Hippolyte et Aricie'. In the
gilded salons of La Pouplinière, Rameau was made much of
by the literary men, artists and society people whom the tax-
farmer gathered round him. Voltaire invited Rameau to
compose the music for his opera 'Samson'. Rameau's best-
known opera is 'Castor et Pollux' (1737), which owed its success to its emotional appeal, its feeling for dramatic effect.
The overtures to Rameau's operas were of a new type—descriptive overtures (*ouvertures-programme*) pre-figuring the events
of the drama—and this type was later brilliantly used by
Berlioz and the Romantics. Some of the arias and choruses
of 'Castor et Pollux' still figure on the programmes of British
concerts. Rameau also wrote a number of suites for the
harpsichord—'Pièces pour clavecin'—some of them picture-
tunes like those of Couperin. Of Rameau's music a French
specialist has written that nothing in it is left to the hazards
of inspiration, everything has its *raison d'être*, everything is
linked together with implacable logic. 'Reason has been
turned into music.' Rameau's qualities of clarity, concision
and expressiveness led to his being sometimes called the
Voltaire of music.

Rameau is looked upon as one of the greatest French
musicians not only because of his suites and operas but because
of his writings on the theory of music. The *Traité de l'harmonie
réduite à ses principes naturels* (1722) was the first and best known
of his score of works on this subject. Grimm, the philosopher,
observed sardonically that Rameau had made the study so
easy that the world was inundated with bad musicians! In
fact, this 'scientific method' of harmony was so revolutionary
that experts declare that it found its full expression only at the

[1] Often called, incorrectly, La Popelinière. His position was that of principal
tax-collector.

end of the nineteenth century in the musicians who adopted the modern doctrine of functional harmony. A group of musicians of that period, including Debussy, Dukas and Vincent d'Indy, under the direction of Saint-Saëns, marked their admiration for this master of French music by publishing an edition of his works.

Rameau's later years were disturbed by the 'Buffoon War'. In 1752 a company of Italians, actors of *opera-buffa*—opera with bourgeois or peasant subjects—gave, at the Paris Opéra, performances of Pergolesi's 'La Serva Padrona'. A bitter quarrel ensued between the partisans of the French tradition and those who favoured the music imported from Italy. In this dispute, which lasted two years, much ink was shed, no less than sixty-three pamphlets being published. The heavy artillery was on the side of the invaders: J.-J. Rousseau— whose *Lettre sur la musique française* was followed by his ironical *Lettre d'un symphoniste* [1]—Grimm, Diderot and d'Holbach, the whole battery of *Encyclopédistes*. The French champions were Rameau, Fréron (Voltaire's *bête noire*) and minor personages. The dispute only died down when the Italians left the Opera. This *guerre des bouffons* (the *bouffons* were the Italians) illustrates the lively interest of the French in music—at any rate in music associated with the theatre—and it provided Rousseau with an opportunity of carrying out his 'back to nature' plans by his production of 'Le Devin du Village'—a one-act opera with a rural setting. Napoleon Bonaparte, during the Consular period, used to hum tunes from 'Le Devin du Village' whenever he felt particularly cheerful. [2]

Twenty years after the Buffoon War, hostilities broke out again. Christoph Willibald Gluck, having tried out a new form of opera in Vienna, came to Paris in 1774, Paris being then the artistic capital of Europe. Its Opera would furnish him with first-rate actors, well-trained choirs, peerless dancers, Europe's finest orchestra and a public whose favour was worth winning. Gluck first carried out what would now be called a publicity campaign for a new, simpler and more

[1] J.-J. Rousseau published a *Dictionnaire de musique* in 1767.
[2] Méneval, *Mémoires*, p. 425.

poetic style of opera, in which wit would be replaced by
sentiment, gallantry by passion. He endeavoured 'to reduce
music to its proper function, that of seconding poetry by
enforcing the expression of the sentiment'. The 'chevalier
Glouk' was able to launch his 'Iphigénie en Aulide', thanks
to the influence of his former pupil, Queen Marie Antoinette.
It enjoyed immense success and was performed 170 times in
the course of two seasons. His masterpiece, 'Orphée', making
a stronger appeal to the emotions of the public than the style
of opera then in vogue, thrilled and harrowed the hearts of society
ladies as Rousseau's ardent novel, *La Nouvelle Héloïse* had thrilled
them a few years earlier. 'Cette musique me rend folle,' wrote
Mlle de Lespinasse, a woman of feeling, 'elle m'entraîne; je n'y
puis plus manquer un jour; mon âme est avide de cette espèce
de douleur.' 'Orphée' is the most ancient opera that remains
in the repertory to-day and the pathos and charm that Gluck
put into it still haunt the arias, the ballet music and the tune
played on Orpheus's flute.

Against Gluck the upholders of tradition adopted the Italian
composer Piccinni as their standard-bearer in Paris, Gluckists
and Piccinnists facing each other in hostile array. After a
period of fairly equally balanced success, Gluck and the
Gluckists were acknowledged to be victors.

The last three decades of the eighteenth century witnessed
a period of comparative decline. Most of the composers of
opera, who continued their activity under the First Empire,
were disciples of Gluck, putting his methods into formulas and
trying to realize his ideal. The best known are Grétry, Méhul
and Lesueur. Grétry (1741-1813), a musician whose tunes,
still played, have a natural spontaneous gracefulness and whose
'Richard Cœur de Lion' is still performed, furnished the
Opéra Comique with a whole series of perfect models of comic
opera. Méhul (1763-1817), whose operatic masterpiece, the
biblical 'Joseph' (1807), brought more colour into the orches-
tration of his operas, was like Grétry a pre-Romantic. J. F.
Lesueur (1760-1837) was the Emperor's official musician, now
remembered chiefly because he taught Berlioz. His 'Ossian,
ou les Bardes' (1804), charged with primitive 'Caledonian'

music, delighted Napoleon, already an enthusiastic admirer of Macpherson's 'Ossian'.

Lesueur's gruesome opera, 'La Caverne', had a tremendous success in 1793 in the period of the Terror, and memories of this grim period brought a melodramatic note into the music and libretto of operas produced during the succeeding years. To the Revolutionary period belong also the many hymns and songs destined to be performed by monster popular gatherings. Among the survivals of this stormy, excited period are 'Le Chant du Départ' (music by Méhul), 'Le Chant du Retour', and 'Le Chant de Guerre de l'Armée du Rhin', written by Rouget de l'Isle (1760-1836) at Strasbourg in the full exuberance of Revolutionary ardour. This last became the Hymn of the Republic in 1792 and later, as 'La Marseillaise', the stirring National Anthem of Republican France. The only other name of note among the Revolutionary musicians is that of Francis-Joseph Gossec (1734-1829), composer of the first French symphonies, for whom Rameau obtained the post of conductor of La Pouplinière's orchestra. Some of his minor pieces are still played, though his symphonies were eclipsed by those of Haydn. He was the outstanding figure in the musical life of France at a time of stress and change.

In some measure, Romanticism was a sequel of the Revolution. The most original composer of the French Romantic period was Hector Berlioz (1803-69), who, having escaped a musical education of the conventional kind, sought his inspiration in suggestions from poetic and historical art. A man of feverish and unequal genius, he wrote on the heroic scale. His work is dynamic, it is also descriptive, for it paints a picture and tells a story. His pictorial music, with its streak of demonic wildness, its intensely poetic expression, calls to mind Delacroix's canvases and the dramas of Hugo. His greatest period —1830-40—was also the peak period of French Romantic drama. His 'Roméo et Juliette', a dramatic symphony with choruses, shows him sharing the Shakespearian cult advocated by the Romantic dramatists. The 'Symphonie Fantastique', which he called an 'instrumental drama', depicts in a series of music-pictures the life of a Romantic artist, his love, his am-

bitions, his dreams, his disappointment and march to the scaffold
—a story not without a certain likeness to that of Hugo's Didier,
or of Ruy Blas. This work, like others of Berlioz, is marked by
audacious colouring, personal emotion and a certain melodramatic tinge equally reminiscent of Hugo's dramas. The
'Carnaval Romain', a favourite concert piece from the opera
'Benvenuto Cellini', is no less colourful and spectacular. The
'Damnation de Faust', with its famous 'Rakoczy March' or
'Marche Hongroise', attempts to extract the musical essence
from Goethe's poem, and some critics regard it as his masterpiece, perhaps because of the 'sulphurous eloquence' of much
of the music. 'Les Troyens' (1863), inspired by Virgil's
Aeneid II and IV, but written on the Shakespearian model, is,
with its Royal Hunt and Trojan March, a spectacular opera,
full of pageantry and movement. The 'Requiem' ('La Grande
Messe des Morts'), an astoundingly impressive work, requires
an enormous orchestra, including four separate brass bands.
Berlioz was a man who felt violently and who put into all his
works an intensity of emotion which grips the listener.

The period of Berlioz's compositions from 1825 till the Franco-
German War of 1870-71 was almost entirely given over in
France to operatic music, mostly *opéra comique*, that is, opera with
spoken dialogue not necessarily comic, a specifically French
art. Music was almost synonymous with the lyric stage;
orchestral and chamber music was under an eclipse. Time has
dimmed the glory of Boieldieu, Auber, Hérold and Meyerbeer,
once all-powerful, now reproached as mere purveyors of
bourgeois love-stories, bourgeois picturesque, bourgeois poetry
and bourgeois fun. Boieldieu (1775-1834) is remembered as
the composer of 'La Dame Blanche' (1825); his masterpiece,
inspired by the Waverley novels, has melodies of almost
Mozartian sweetness. Auber (1782-1871) opened, with 'Masa-
niello, ou la Muette de Portici', the era of grand opera, that
is, with no spoken dialogue—a spectacular genre very much
akin to Romantic drama. This particular opera achieved a
sort of historical importance because a couplet from it—
'Amour sacré de la patrie'—was the signal for the 1830 revolution in Brussels, when the Belgians freed themselves from

Dutch domination. The same year Auber produced his most popular comic opera, 'Fra Diavolo', an Italian bandit story. Of Auber it was said that of all musicians he is the one who has most successfully made music tolerable to those who do not like it!

In 1831 Hérold (1791-1833) gave 'Zampa, ou la Fiancée de Marbre' at the Opéra Comique, a pirate story of which the highly coloured overture is still a very popular item at concerts. Giacomo Meyerbeer (1791-1864)—'German for harmony, Italian for melody and French for rhythm'—gave 'Robert le Diable' in 1811 during his Paris period, with a success that echoes, with the world-famous aria 'Robert, toi que j'aime', through the opening chapter of Daudet's *Tartarin de Tarascon*. Meyerbeer's best-known operas are 'Les Huguenots', inspired by Mérimée's *Chronique de Charles IX*, a vivid picture of a period beloved by the Romantics, and 'Le Prophète', of which the story, curiously enough, came from an anecdote in Voltaire's *Essai sur les Mœurs*. The gorgeous settings of these operas are a reminder that they belong to the period of Romantic drama.

Bizet's opera 'Carmen' has worn better than others and must be the best-known dramatic piece in the world. Yet when 'Carmen', with libretto by Meilhac and Halévy, was first performed in 1875 its success hung in the balance. Georges Bizet (1838-75) had a good story—Mérimée's—with a well-knit plot, stark drama with a suggestion of fatality and a picturesque Spanish setting. The music, with its unforgettable melodies, its rich harmonies, recreates the atmosphere of the warm and temperamental south, and its brilliant orchestral effects help to make it the perfect lyrical drama. Bizet also wrote the incidental music for Daudet's 'L'Arlésienne', a piece now remembered for its 'choruses and symphonies', that is, for Bizet's tuneful airs, rustic and southern.

Edouard Lalo (1823-92), a great admirer of Wagner, was, like Bizet, happily inspired by Spain in his 'Symphonie Espagnole' for violin and orchestra and, as a composer of opera, made his name with his 'Roi d'Ys' (1888), melodies from which are frequently heard to-day. Léo Delibes (1836-91)

is very popular still on account of the delicious tunes from
his ballets 'Coppélia' and 'Sylvia', while his opera 'Lakmé'
has not ceased to charm the audiences of the Opéra Comique.
The same is true of the 'Mignon' of A. Thomas (1811-96), a
piece freely adapted from Goethe's 'Wilhelm Meister' and full
of charming melodies. Thomas also composed a grand opera,
'Hamlet', thought to be his best work.

The major work of dramatic music in the nineteenth century
is without doubt the 'Faust' of Charles Francis Gounod (1818-
1893), revealing, as all his operas do, a very effective combination of mysticism and voluptuousness. 'Faust' is the most
popular of operas even to-day, and can always be counted
upon to fill the theatre, as every touring opera company well
knows. Gounod's other popular success is 'Roméo et Juliette',
inspired by Berlioz's dramatic symphony. Massenet (1842-
1912) still provides lusciously sentimental music for young
dreamers, creating an enchanted world where sighs, tears and
caresses are the very stuff of life. His achievements in this
sense are best appreciated in 'Manon' (1884) and 'Werther',
which, with 'Thaïs', are the works most often performed.
Massenet was, however, something more than a composer of
music for the 'average sensual man'; his instrumental and
keyboard music influenced, it is averred, the Debussy generation.

It would be unkind to leave out of this list Offenbach, a very
Parisian German Jew whose sparkling operettas 'Orphée aux
Enfers' and 'La Belle Hélène' delighted boulevardier Paris
during the Second Empire. Thanks to him, that sophisticated
public had a chance of laughing at parodies of the mythological
operas that had enchanted their fathers, grandfathers and even
great-grandfathers. His 'Tales of Hoffman', with its seductive
barcarolle, hints that behind scenes of revelry there may be
sadness. But as Robert de Flers said of operettas in general,
'les larmes n'étaient point défendues pourvu que ce fussent
de toutes petites larmes.' Offenbach certainly added to the
gaiety of nations. On the other hand, a new and more realistic
note was brought to the Opéra Comique by Gustave Charpentier
(b. 1860), whose choice of a working-class family in a contemporary Montmartre setting for his 'Louise' (1900) shows how

far from classical mythology opera had progressed—or strayed.

Though the lyrical drama was so dominant in the musical life of nineteenth-century France, other music was not entirely neglected. Frédéric Chopin (1810-49) showed no signs of reflecting in his music, as Berlioz did, the highly coloured dramatic and even melodramatic features which marked so many works of the artists and writers among the Romantic generation. His life was concentrated on the study of the piano when that instrument was a comparatively new discovery; besides being a virtuoso, he composed entirely for the piano. His warlike polonaises, his stately mazurkas with their characteristic rhythm, his languorous waltzes, his dreamlike nocturnes, evoking the mystery, the sadness and the beauty of night, his preludes and sonatas, brought a new style into piano music. His Romanticism is revealed, if anywhere, in the passionate movement of his compositions, in his sadness and in his exaltation. He makes no attempt at the 'architectural' composition of the classics.

When Chopin died in 1849 César Franck (1822-90) was making a living in obscurity as a church organist and music teacher in Paris, far from the fret and fever of life on the boulevards, He was fifty when he wrote his great oratorio, 'Les Béatitudes', inspired by the Sermon on the Mount, a composition admired for its religious rapture, its unclouded bliss arising from faith in the midst of uncertainty. Some critics praise Franck's modern personal technique, others look upon his work as vitiated by being derived from other music, not from life. Franck wrote symphonic music, music for piano, for orchestra and organ. The piece most frequently heard, though not the most admired by the critics, is 'Le Chasseur maudit', a symphonic poem, as is 'Les Djinns', the brilliant musical picture inspired by Hugo's poem from *Les Orientales*. In a Paris mostly given over to facile and conventional music, Franck, steeped in the works of Beethoven, Wagner and also J. S. Bach, created anew a musical tradition and inspired a new school of composers of whom the best known is Vincent d'Indy

The year after the 'Chasseur maudit' came 'España', a

sonorous rhapsody by Emmanuel Chabrier (1841-94), a friend of the Franckist group. A very original, imaginative and lively composer, Chabrier is looked upon as in some respects preparing the discoveries of Claude Debussy and the coming of musical Impressionism. Paul Dukas (1865-1935) won world-wide fame by his highly dramatic and pictorial symphonic scherzo, 'L'Apprenti-Sorcier' (1897), founded on one of Goethe's ballads. The French classical tradition is represented by Camille Saint-Saëns (1835-1921), a virtuoso, a prolific composer whose variety of range can be indicated by the mention of his opera 'Samson et Dalila', his Third Symphony, his symphonic poems, 'Le Rouet d'Omphale', 'Phaéton', 'La Jeunesse d'Hercule' and his 'Danse Macabre'—a gruesome (or is it grimly humorous?) evocation of spectral horrors, with its parody of the Dies Irae—and his humorous 'Carnaval des Animaux' with its frisking parodies and its universally loved melody 'Le Cygne'. He also wrote a delicately beautiful violin concerto. The dignity of his compositions has always made him acceptable to the British concert-goer and the humour of his posthumous animal piece may also have helped to make him a favourite. In France he suffers from the reputation of being the artist of form whose wonderfully clever compositions, proofs of astounding versatility, leave the listener cold.

Gabriel Fauré (1845-1924), like Debussy, was inspired by contemporary poets, particularly Verlaine and Samain. He is a classical composer, of the lineage of Couperin and Rameau, restrained, exquisite, without vehemence or exaggeration of expression, and innocent of the flights of wild imagination that distinguished the Romantics. His chamber music, and the incomparable songs that won for him the name of 'the French Schumann', delight connoisseurs by their apparent simplicity concealing a subtle play of nuances, though the profane, and some non-French critics, tend to regard his music as monotonous and monochromic. His Requiem is a noble and moving work.

Claude Debussy (1862-1918) is looked upon as the first great master of twentieth-century 'modern' music. Proud of being a 'French musician', he expressed his approval of the French classical tradition of 'clearness, elegance, simple and natural

declamation' as exemplified by Couperin and Rameau. He
did not, however, seek inspiration simply in the past. Far
from doing so, he frequented the most revolutionary poets and
painters of his time, the Symbolists and Impressionists, and
contrived to create in music a style similar to the impressionist
technique of the painters. Just as the painters and poets turned
aside from the dramatic and the narrative and concentrated
on light effects or on the suggestive value of words, so Debussy
concentrated on tone. His first symphonic poem, 'Prélude à
l'Après-midi d'un Faune' (1892), was inspired by a poem of
Stéphane Mallarmé. He created an entirely new form of
operatic music by his composition for Maeterlinck's 'Pelléas
et Mélisande', a triumph of impressionism in which the music,
with typical French reticence, suggests rather than says, in
much the same way as the impressionist painters endeavoured
to do. His piano music, 'Pagodes', 'Reflets dans l'Eau',
'Poissons d'Or', and his orchestral pieces, 'Nuages', 'Fêtes',
'Sirènes', have been linked with the names of the painters
Monet and Cézanne. He put to music many of Verlaine's
'Fêtes Galantes'. Debussy enriched the resources of the piano
as none had done since Chopin, transforming into music what
made the essence of the poetry of Mallarmé and his group.
He replaced subject, development and formal composition by
a new harmony, a new and apparently capricious art that
attains its effects by nuances and implications. Debussy's
music, with its noble rhythms, its magic power of evoking
atmosphere, of reproducing the almost intangible fluttering of
light and shadow, is the music of a poet. Together with Fauré,
he re-created a French musical tradition.

Maurice Ravel (1875-1937), an Impressionist less atmo-
spheric than Debussy, like him represents a return to the
example of the classical masters of the eighteenth century, to
clarity, refinement and delicacy. Much of the driving force
of this renaissance of French tradition arose from the revolt
against the influence of Richard Wagner, whose dynamic
sonorities had at one time appeared to be on the point of
submerging all that French music stood for. Some of the
titles of Ravel's pieces are poetry in themselves: 'Pavane pour

o

une Infante Défunte', 'Jeux d'Eau', evoked by H. de Régnier's line: 'Dieu fluvial riant de l'eau qui le chatouille', 'Valses nobles et sentimentales', 'Le Tombeau de Couperin' (a suite in eighteenth-century form), 'Rapsodie Espagnole'. His 'Bolero', with its insistent, unforgettable rhythm, won an immediate world-wide success. Among his many other works may be mentioned the orchestral suite, 'Ma Mère l'Oye' and, as an example of literary inspiration, the 'Histoires naturelles', a set of songs interpreting some of Jules Renard's prose poems.

In this later French music it is noteworthy that inspiration has so often been sought in exotic subjects, particularly, as in Lalo, Chabrier, Debussy and Ravel, in Spanish and Spanish-American themes. French musicians have usually been happily inspired in their Iberian borrowings, and it might be piquant to find this once literary Romantic trait in the new exponents of the French classical tradition, were it not that the literary classics, including the great Corneille, had made fortunate borrowings from that same southern neighbour.

The history of French music does not end with the national revival achieved during the period following 1880 by Vincent d'Indy, Fauré, Dukas, Debussy and Ravel. On the contrary, France, as in the beginnings, has 'une chanson aux lèvres'. The newest school to become in a sense historic is the Groupe des Six dating from the First World War and influenced by Stravinsky. Among its best-known members are Arthur Honnegger (b. 1892), of 'Pacific 231' fame; Darius Milhaud (b. 1892), whose 'Alissa', a cycle of melodies on Gide's 'La Porte Étroite', is regarded as a masterpiece, and Francis Poulenc (b. 1899), who wrote piano and choral works, among the most important of the latter being 'Litanies à la vierge noire' and 'Figure humaine'. Among recent names frequently figuring on concert programmes are those of Albert Roussel (1867-1937), whose ballet 'Le Festin de l'araignée' still brings delight to audiences at the Paris Opéra, Jean Françaix, accounted one of the most brilliant of the younger composers, Jacques Ibert (b. 1890), composer of music to poetry of Ver-

laine, and the enigmatic Olivier Messiaen (b. 1908), chief of
the 'Jeune France' group, whose music is at times as disconcerting as some of the manifestations of contemporary painting.
France's contribution to music continues, still frequently linked
with literary works, undimmed in quality and rich in variety
of inspiration.

READING LIST

Short Histories of French Music

Brook, D. *Five Great French Composers*. London, 1946. Largely
   biographical, but gives useful notes on and lists of the works
   of Berlioz, Franck, Saint-Saëns, Debussy and Ravel. Very
   readable. For general readers and musicians.
Gillet, L. *La Musique*. Chapter XV in Vol. XI of *Histoire de la
   nation française*, edited by G. Hanotaux. Paris, 1922.
Landormy, P. *Histoire de la musique*. Paris, 1946. An excellent,
   well-written manual, dealing with French music and with
   music in general up to 1946.
Lavoix, H. *La Musique française*. Paris, 1890. A short and readable account of the history of French music from the beginnings.
   Illustrated.
Prunières, H. *Nouvelle Histoire de la musique*, 2 vols. Paris, 1936.
   Excellently written. A standard work.

For Further Reading

Champigneulle, B. *L'Age classique de la musique française*. Paris, 1946.
Dumesnil, R. *La Musique romantique française*. Paris, 1944.
Grenier, H. *La Musique symphonique de Monteverdi à Beethoven*.
   Montreal, 1947.
   See also *Encyclopédie de la musique et dictionnaire du Conservatoire*.
   Paris, 1918.
Grove, G. *Dictionary of Music and Musicians*. New edition, London,
   1954.
Hervey, A. *French Music in the Nineteenth Century*. London, 1903.
Hill, E. B. *Modern French Music*. Cambridge, Mass., 1924.
Láng, P. H. *Music in Western Civilization*. New York, 1941.
Lasserre, P. *L'Esprit de la musique française*. Paris, 1917.
Rolland, Romain. *Musiciens d'autrefois*. Paris, 1908.
   Musiciens d'aujourd'hui. Paris, 1908.

Tiersot, J. *Un Demi-siècle de musique française*. Paris, 1918 (deals
with Debussy and his school).

For separate composers see the series *Les Maîtres de la Musique*
(Presses Universitaires) and *Les Musiciens Célèbres* (Laurens). For
individual works see *Les Chefs-d'œuvre de la musique expliqués*. This
last under the general editorship of P. Landormy.

CHAPTER X

PAINTING

'To many people who take a gloomy view of life, studies of art and
beauty seem to be but trifling.'   SIR GEORGE SITWELL

FRENCH pictorial art, as everyone knows who has examined
the miniatures in mediaeval manuscripts or gazed at the
stained-glass windows in Chartres Cathedral, goes far back
into the Middle Ages. At the Renaissance, Italy flowered
more sumptuously than any other country, and Italian painters,
including Leonardo da Vinci, who were invited to France by
Charles VIII and Francis I, dominated for a time the art of
that country. From the Italians French painters learnt the
decorative possibilities of their art. The outstanding name of
the sixteenth century is that of François Clouet (1522-72),
King's Painter like his father, Jean Clouet, before him. To
the father is attributed a portrait of François I as Dauphin,
the son painted him as King and also portrayed Elizabeth of
Austria, Charles IX and many of the noble ladies and gentlemen of that time. The portrait of Mary Queen of Scots in
the Wallace Collection is also attributed to François.

The seventeenth century not only marks the beginning of
modern French painting, it is also one of the capital periods
in French art. Painters were numerous and active in Paris
and in the provinces; Burgundy, Toulouse and Lorraine had
their own schools. From Laon came the brothers Le Nain,
who painted with sincerity touching scenes of rustic life, quite
unlike anything in France or in Flanders at that time: 'Le
Retour du baptême', 'Les Joueurs de tric-trac', and household
scenes like the 'Intérieur dans une famille'. Many also painted
portraits (there is a 'Portrait Group' in the National Gallery),
but the great portraitist of the time was Philippe de Champaigne
(1602-74), who fixed for posterity the grave ascetic faces of the
Port Royal nuns and that of Cardinal Richelieu, impressive
in his red robes.

201

The greatest artists of the period are undoubtedly Poussin and Claude Gelée, otherwise known as Claude Lorraine and le Lorrain. Nicholas Poussin (1594-1665), who went off to Rome at the age of thirty, was called home to work for Louis XIII in 1640; disliking the rivalries and jealousies of the Court, he went back the following year to Rome, where he remained. Like the other Court artists he was a classical painter, both in the sense that he preferred mythological subjects and in the sense that he was more interested in the composition of his paintings than in the expression of his own personality. Cultured men of his time were steeped in the lore of Greece and Rome, and the 'learned Poussin' was no exception. His object in painting was to give a series of pictures of life in the world of classical antiquity; he not only studied the statues which were still being dug up everywhere in Italy but used the literary texts discovered by Renaissance scholars.

For Poussin the important thing about a picture was the composition, the perfection in design, harmonious attitudes and a certain dignity and nobility, not the colour—he was not a colourist—though there is much more colour in his works than the dark-toned examples of his unrestored pictures of the 'Quatre Saisons' in the Louvre would suggest. He has been called, like Raphael, an architect among painters. The human figures in his paintings have the graceful perfection of antique statues and, in the historical and mythological pieces, these figures often stand out like bas-reliefs against a background of trees. His instinct for grandeur, his reticence in the expression of emotion, and the conscientiousness, extending to every detail, that he brings to his task, suggest an intellectual kinship with the dramatic poets of his time such as Pierre Corneille. The most famous of his pictures is the 'Bergers d'Arcadie'. In a serene Arcadian landscape three shepherds, picturesquely garbed *à l'antique*, form a harmonious group around an ancient tomb and try to decipher the worn inscription while a gracefully robed lady stands near. The scene, a symbol of the meeting of life and death, has no dramatic or moving appeal, no obvious intensity of feeling. Poussin, like so many classical writers, 'exprime son âme à mi-voix'. The impression made is one of balance and discipline, restraint and austerity, intellectual qualities, rather than verve and vigour, passion or exaltation. This Arcadian scene, with the 'Moïse sauvé des eaux' and his other masterpieces, illustrates what he himself wrote of his work: 'My nature constrains me to seek after things well-ordered, eschewing confusion, which to me is as contrary and hostile as is light to gloomy darkness.'

Other well-known works are 'Orphée et Eurydice', 'L'Enfance de Bacchus', 'Orphée amoureux de Daphné', the joyous 'Triomphe de Pan', the 'Paysage au serpent'. [1] Among his paintings inspired by the Bible is 'Le Déluge', one of the 'Quatre Saisons', a magnificent landscape greatly admired by Hazlitt, who wrote of Poussin: 'This great and learned man might be said to see nature through the glass of time; he alone has a right to be considered as the painter of classical antiquity.' All French painters, and not they alone, are more or less the debtors of Poussin.

Claude Lorraine (1600-82), six years younger than Poussin, from whom he is reported to have learned something about composition—the two were in Italy at the same time—was not a classical scholar and has indeed been called almost illiterate—an eye, not a brain. He was a northerner—from Lorraine—who fell under the spell of the limpid Mediterranean light, the radiance of the Italian sky, and his lasting glory is that he was a painter of light. He studied the shifting of light and its infinite gradations, more interested in illumination than in any other aspect of landscape. Like Poussin, he introduced human figures into his landscapes, the Classical Age being persuaded that the proper study of mankind is man and that nature in itself does not provide a suitable subject for a picture any more than for a poem. With Claude, however, the figures serve as a pretext, the picture is really a study of trees, buildings in the classical style, water, and the reflection of the light on these. In many of the pictures a vision of graceful foliage, with buildings massed at each side, opens the magic door through the centre of the picture into vast, light-filled distances. These delicate aerial effects are to be found in the 'Mariage d'Isaac et de

[1] Musée Magnin, Dijon.

Rébecca',[1] the 'Campo Vaccino' and his seaport pictures with their 'gentle ripple of waveless seas'. Constable and Turner, a couple of centuries later, appear to have learned about light from Claude. Most contemporary art critics look with the greatest respect upon 'Whate'er Lorraine light-touch'd with softening hue'. and consider him as very modern. He was early a favourite in England, which in 1644 ordered no less than nineteen pictures from him. The National Gallery possesses eight of his works.

Poussin and Claude did not belong to the brigade of painters mobilized by Louis XIV and his minister Colbert and placed under the command of the energetic Charles Le Brun (1619-1690), the King's Painter, who directed the Royal Academy of Painting and Sculpture founded half-way through the century. To this brigade was entrusted the embellishment of the Louvre and the decoration of the new Palace of Versailles. Under Le Brun's guidance the splendid gallery of Apollo in the Louvre and the Gallery of Mirrors in Versailles were orna-mented with magnificent painted ceilings, the subjects being provided by the history and mythology of Greece and Rome. Le Brun directed not only the painters, architects and sculp-tors, but the goldsmiths, gilders and bronze-workers as well, finding time, in a long and well-filled life, to manage the Royal manufactory of Gobelins tapestry and to be a very distinguished portrait-painter. Other portrait-painters of the time who deserve mention are Pierre Mignard, also a decorator, who succeeded Le Brun late in life as director of the Academy, Rigaud, whose dignified noble portraits of 'Bossuet' and 'Louis XIV' are reproduced in French history manuals, and Largillière, whose masterpiece is 'La Belle Strasbourgeoise' [2] and whose imposing portrait of himself, his wife and daughter, hangs in the Louvre.

The Academy, at that time open to all artists and not, as in its present form, limited to a set number, gave standing to painters hitherto regarded as being artisans, who now became members of a great profession. It also marked the direct interest of the State in art; in no modern country has State

---

[1] National Gallery. [2] Meyer Sassoon Collection, London.

patronage of the arts been more continuous than in France. From the seventeenth century France took the place of Italy as the art centre of Europe. To Colbert France owes the foundation of the French school in Rome (Villa de' Medici) which still to-day provides five years' residence and study in Italy for young French artists of promise. After Colbert's death in 1683, painters were no longer so closely associated with the Court. More independent, having won greater prestige, artists in the following age worked for private individuals—nobles, tax-farmers, etc.—and were freer to choose their manner, to give rein to their own personality and imagination, less constrained to dignity and nobility, than when they were working for the Court.

The first in time and no doubt the greatest painter of the eighteenth century was Jean-Antoine Watteau (1684-1721), whose work was done during the gloomy closing years of Louis XIV and the gay, frivolous reaction of the Regency. He spent a period, which left its mark on his later art, as assistant painter of scenery for the Opera, and then for a master engaged on scenes and characters from the *commedia dell'arte*, the improvised Italian comedy with fixed dramatis personae; pierrots, harlequins and columbines. Watteau's short life, not an easy one in his youthful years and overclouded by the threat of death from consumption, was extraordinarily fertile in production. Among his outstanding works are his 'Gilles' (a sort of Pierrot), 'La Finette', 'L'Indifférent', 'L'Assemblée dans un parc', 'L'Enseigne de Gersaint',[1] 'Le Concert' and 'Plaisirs champêtres'. Edinburgh possesses, among other Watteau pictures, an exquisite 'Fête champêtre', a theme suggested by a passage in one of Dancourt's comedies.

Among his contemporaries Watteau stands out as a colourist —his range includes exquisite silvery blues, golden reds and amber yellows—as a draughtsman and as a master of composition. The painter of the most elegant, refined and polished society that Europe had ever seen, he delights to portray graceful, artificial ladies in sumptuous silks and satins and the gorgeously attired gallants who pay them court. For these

[1] Charlottenburg, Berlin.

Dresden-china figures he creates a park-like landscape, in which they perform their evolutions in a dream-world of his own, far away from the world of gross reality—operatic parks if one will, but elegant and graceful in the poetic twilight and not without relation to nature in her happier moods.

To this evocation of a gay, dainty, dancing care-free life he introduces a note of wistfulness; no doubt his frail health warned him of the rapid passage of earthly delights, and this awareness of the transient existence of these 'lords and ladies gay' brings the note of sadness into these Utopian harmonies. For this reason Watteau has been compared to Mozart, whose graceful melodic line and formal, elegant pattern of sound half conceal his emotion. No better commentary could be found on the painter of the 'fêtes galantes' than Verlaine's 'Fêtes Galantes', inspired by eighteenth-century engravings, conjuring up before our eyes

> Les donneurs de sérénades
> Et les belles écouteuses
> Échangent des propos fades
> Sous les ramures chanteuses . . .
>
> Leurs courtes vestes de soie,
> Leurs longues robes à queue,
> Leur élégance, leur joie
> Et leur molles ombres bleues
>
> Tourbillonnent dans l'extase
> D'une lune rose et grise,
> Et la mandoline jase
> Parmi les frissons de brise.

The best-known of the eighteenth-century painters belonging to the school of Watteau were Lancret, Fragonard and Boucher. Lancret was a fashionable painter of gallantry and his 'Acteurs de la Comédie Italienne' reminds one of a favourite theme of Watteau. The brilliant, versatile but superficial Fragonard's 'Chiffre d'Amour', 'Hasards heureux de l'escarpolette', 'Leçon de musique' and portrait of 'Diderot' are popular favourites. François Boucher (1703-70) was the protégé and favourite painter of Madame de Pompadour, whose dominant influence at the Court of Louis XV was more happily exercised in the arts than in politics. Boucher's most characteristic paintings deal with the love affairs of the Olympians, buxom white-skinned goddesses, especially Venus, in gallant conversation with some bronzed god, while chubby Cupids frolic round as in the picture of 'Venus dans la forge de Vulcain'. Boucher also painted pastoral scenes in which Arcadian shepherds pay court to Arcadian shepherdesses. Of one of these pastorals Diderot, who admired Boucher's colours, his variety and his incomparable skill as a painter, wrote: 'Cet homme a tout, sauf la vérité.' Boucher certainly had all the qualities that appealed to fashionable society in his day: grace and elegance, a remarkable facility, prettiness of style and wonderful skill in rendering the flesh-tints of his sophisticated goddesses, together with a technique unmistakable among the productions of his contemporaries. Like most of the fashionable artists of his time, he was a decorator, whose work was meant to take its place in an ensemble—as panels, for instance—rather than to be examined minutely like an easel picture.

A delightful portrait painter of the period is La Tour (1704-1788), the pastellist who depicted, with an uncanny insight into their psychology, many pretty ladies and distinguished gentlemen, e.g. D'Alembert. Nattier (1685-1766), without that insight, painted fashionable beauties with perfect complexions, exquisite smiles, daintily powdered wigs and soft rounded lines—all delicious and all alike. Many of the portraits can be seen at Versailles.

Jean-Baptiste Chardin (1699-1779), taught by the example of Dutch painters of indoor scenes, stands out in marked contrast to the painters of tenderly coloured panels for ladies' boudoirs. He is the artist of simple, 'petit bourgeois' existence, his themes are the everyday happenings in households that appear to shut off the outer world (no landscapes figure among his works): the servant in the kitchen ('La Pourvoyeuse'), the mother teaching her little girl to say grace ('Le Bénédicité'), or helping her to choose wool for her tapestry ('La Mère laborieuse'), a boy building a house of cards ('Le Château de cartes'), or engrossed in the act of spinning his top and lost to the world ('L'Enfant au toton'). All these are painted with simplicity and dignity, with no posing, no self-consciousness, no search for studied elegance, no dramatization. It is a world far sundered from that fleeting, graceful, languorous, sophisticated world that society painters were depicting, and it is painted in quite another manner. With loving exactness of detail, reminiscent of the Flemish painters, with infinite attention, as in the still-life pictures, 'Le Gobelet d'argent', 'La Fontaine de cuivre', Chardin renders the precise appearance, the very colour of some homely and worn utensil or some unpretentious garment.

'On se sert de couleurs,' said Chardin, 'on peint avec le sentiment.' It is the poetry of the everyday existence of God-fearing, honest people, the common, hard-working, thrifty folk who for centuries have formed the very web of French life, while the more brilliant, more artificial social groups have come and gone. Chardin might be regarded as the painter of workaday France, particularly of the toiling capital, since he is reported never to have left Paris except to work at Fontainebleau; it is the Paris home that he depicts. There is poetry in the homely objects as in the household scenes.

Jean-Baptiste Greuze (1725-1805), though art critics say hard things of him, is so much loved by the general public and illustrates so well certain features of the eighteenth century that he must find a place even in a summary account of French painting. He is the painter after Diderot's own heart, a painter of moral lessons who managed to give his pictures a melodramatic atmosphere. Diderot had tried to write moralizing dramas about ordinary people instead of the heroes of classical tragedy; the result, in 'Le Père de famille' and 'L'Enfant naturel', was melodrama. He highly approved of Greuze's choice of subjects, a choice, said the critic, indicating the artist's sensibility and his amiable character. Greuze, for example, takes a peasant family and shows 'le mauvais fils' cursed by his father, with the whole family in consternation around him ('La Malédiction paternelle'); then he shows 'Le Retour de l'enfant maudit' or 'Le Mauvais Fils puni', the son returning, punished by the sight of his father lying on his

death-bed, surrounded by the family, vociferous in its grief.
Greuze is a 'man of feeling', as he shows in 'L'Accordée du
village' and 'Le Paralytique soigné par ses enfants', and painted
at a time when sentimentality, imported from England, was
fashionable. Nothing could be more striking than a comparison between family life as depicted by Chardin and the
literary, unconvincing and melodramatic peasant scenes of
Greuze.

To-day Greuze charms not by his *genre* painting—pictures
which tell a story and tell it rather too obviously—but by the
delightful paintings of the lovely girls who figure in 'La
Laitière', 'La Cruche cassée', 'L'Oiseau mort', or 'Prière du
matin'.[1] Much of the charm of these somewhat theatrical
portraits arises no doubt from the loveliness of the models, but
Greuze adds a note of voluptuousness which gives a certain
piquancy to the youthful and ingenuous figures.

The gracious, artificial, decorative art of the eighteenth
century was distasteful to the earnest revolutionaries of 1789,
for it recalled the domination of the aristocracy, *les ci-devant*.
Life, for revolutionaries who are thorough-going, is serious,
and should be austere. Inspiration, they considered, might
more safely and suitably be sought among the city-states of
Greece and in republican Rome than in the decadent art of a
frivolous monarchy which had just been liquidated. The
pietas and *gravitas* of Rome attracted upholders of Republic
and of Empire. Moreover, this revival of interest in antiquity
did but continue a movement which had already affected the
arts in the closing years of the *ancien régime*. The writings of
Winckelmann in Germany, the *Voyage du jeune Anacharsis* by
the Abbé Barthélemy in France (1788), the successive discoveries in the cities of Herculaneum (from 1719) and Pompeii
(from 1748) aroused a new interest in the daily life of Greece
and Rome, reflected in the poems of André Chénier. In
painting, Hubert Robert (1733-1808) was a precursor of the
classical painters of the First Empire by his synthetic pictures
of Roman buildings in picturesque ruin.[2] Joseph Vernet (1714-

[1] Musée Fabre, Montpellier, which contains several pictures by Greuze.
[2] The Museum at Valence has a number of these.

1789) painted Italian scenes and sea-pieces, and, as a disciple of Claude, was interested primarily in light, though he tended to dramatize and sentimentalize his pictures.

The dominant painter of the Revolution and Empire was Jacques-Louis David (1748-1825), and the Davidian school remained in power for a quarter of a century. For the second time, as critics have pointed out, political absolutism synchronized with classical art. Under Napoleon, David played the rôle of Le Brun under Louis XIV, devoting himself to adorning and recording the greatness of his master. The art of David, like that of the Le Brun group, was neo-classical, with a certain preciseness and stiffness, a conscious and almost theatrical nobility of attitude, with little attempt at depicting movement. The human figures appear to have been modelled on the statues of antiquity. Landscape and light are not of great importance to David, for his figures are studio-lighted.

His best-known pictures are either scenes from classical antiquity, like 'Le Serment des Horaces', 'La Mort de Socrate' and 'Les Sabines', or from the epic adventure of Napoleon: 'La Distribution des Aigles' [1] and the colossal picture of Napoleon's coronation, 'Le Sacre'. David, like all the neo-classical painters, cared more for draughtsmanship than for colour, yet a magnificent display of red and gold brings glamour to the Napoleonic pictures. Though not primarily aiming at the expression of emotion, he had temperament, as he showed in his active revolutionary career. He painted some masterly portraits, the best known being that of 'Madame Récamier', Chateaubriand's muse, reclining on a couch of antique design. Two grim and pathetic portraits are the pictures of the dead 'Bara' [2] and 'Marat'.[3] A. J. Gros (1771-1835), the painter of Napoleon's battles and of 'Les Pestiférés de Jaffa', belonged, in theory, to the school of David, but put much more colour and movement into his canvases and used light more effectively.

The most famous of David's pupils and thirty-two years younger than the master was Jean-Auguste-Dominique Ingres

[1] Versailles.   [2] Musée d' Avignon.
[3] Musée Moderne de Bruxelles.

(1780-1867), who is supposed to have had a hand in helping David with the portrait of Juliette Récamier. Ingres appears to have been, like Gustave Flaubert, a Romantic by temperament who forced himself to adopt the discipline of the Classical tradition. He declared himself a pure classic and showed his classicism by his preference for subjects taken from Greek and Roman antiquity, by his preoccupation with design—he was a magnificent, an inspired draughtsman—and by his lack of interest in colour. His pictures of classical subjects, 'Jupiter et Thétis', 'Stratonice',[1] 'L'Apothéose d'Homère' (this last picture inspired Puvis de Chavannes), owe more to the paintings on Greek vases than, as in the case of David, to statuary. In both cases the ideal was perfection of form.

The Romantics looked upon such perfection as mere elegant serenity without life or movement, and found it lacking in atmosphere and in light. The classical painters' ideal of absolute beauty has its parallel in the literary ideal of the age of Louis XIV. Both the literary men of the Grand Siècle and the Davidian painters believed that the Ancients had achieved perfection of form, that perfection of form is founded on reason, on symmetry, and that, given inspiration, the perfection found once and for all by the Ancients might be reached by application and infinite study. Just as Racine in his tragedies adopted Greek subjects and observed the rules of Aristotle's *Poetics* as he understood them, so the painters applied themselves to reproducing the themes dear to the Greeks. In both cases success depended on having enough inspiration to make of the imitation something other than a mere copy of Greek art. Racine's tragedies are not like those of Euripides even when he treats the same subject—*Phèdre* and *Hippolytus* as tragedies are very different—and Ingres did much more than copy figures on Greek vases. Ingres' best-known picture is 'La Source', begun in 1807 and finished in 1856; he painted a magnificent series of 'Odalisques' and a number of portraits, an exceedingly attractive one of 'Madame de Senonnes'[2] and an outstanding one of 'M. Bertin' in the Louvre.

[1] Musée de Montpellier.   [2] Musée de Nantes.

Eugène Delacroix (1798-1863) provides a striking contrast
to Ingres. He was the chief of the Romantic school, and his
rôle among the painters resembled that of Victor Hugo among
the poets. The poets, and other writers too, who found everyday life dull and disappointing after the great days of the
Revolution and the Napoleonic victories, turned to exotic
countries with strange customs and picturesque costumes, or
went for their subjects to the past, not the past of Classical
Antiquity but to the Middle Ages and the Renaissance, ages
in which discipline and convention had not taken the colour
and the adventure out of life. More important still, they took
as their subject their own passions and emotions and gave
lyrical expression to their own personality. In painting, much
the same happened. Design and composition, of paramount
importance to the Classics, meant less to the Romantics, whose
interest was in colour. Not, however, that Delacroix neglected
these classical qualities. His technique is classical, it is by his
subjects and by his treatment of them that he is a Romantic.
His first picture, 'Dante et Virgile aux enfers', with its human
forms writhing in agony, made a sensation by its novelty of
treatment, its dramatic power and energy. Delacroix had had
a predecessor in the short-lived Géricault (1791-1824), whose
'Radeau de la Méduse' shows the twisted bodies of the dead
lying on the tragic raft around the handful of survivors who
think they descry a sail which may bring help in their last
extremity. Delacroix goes further than Géricault in suggesting
horror ('Médée') [1] and despair ('Le Tasse en prison'), this
last the subject of Baudelaire's sonnet:

> Le poète au cachot, débraillé, maladif,
> Roulant un manuscrit sous son pied convulsif,
> Mesure d'un regard que la terreur enflamme
> L'escalier de vertige où s'abîme son âme . . .

Delacroix's 'Les Massacres de Scio' shocked the classicists by
its lack of symmetrical arrangement, its neglect of beauty and
its vigour of dramatic expression. His African pictures, made
after a visit to Spain and Morocco, reflect the Romantic's

[1] Musée de Lille.

Matisse, *The Music Lesson*

Renoir, *Two Little Circus Girls*

interest in the colourful East, and colour and passion give the keynote to all his numerous and varied compositions. Though he became almost the official painter to Louis-Philippe, he remained anathema to the Classicists who formed the jury for the Salons. On one occasion, it is said, seventeen pictures by Delacroix were refused. The young Romantic painters, who considered the Classicists as utterly frigid, had their revenge when they passed in front of a Classical canvas—they affected to turn up their coat collars lest they caught a chill!

Delacroix painted landscapes, though it is not as a landscape artist that he is best known, and, following the tradition of Poussin, introduced human figures into them, as had been the tradition ever since the seventeenth century. Landscape was a setting, a *décor* for human figures or decorative divinities, and had to be worthy of them, just as, according to Boileau, pastoral poetry, when it evokes the country or the woods, must make them worthy of a consul. Partly under English influence, particularly that of Constable (1776-1837), whose 'Hay Wain' was well known to French painters,[1] landscape was beginning to be looked upon as worthy of being treated, not as a mere decoration, as a background, but as the main theme of a picture. Moreover, instead of painting landscapes in the studio, as was the tradition from Claude to Delacroix, painters began to paint out of doors.

Jean-Baptiste Corot (1796-1875) belonged to a group of artists who lived in the little village of Barbizon and painted in the forest of Fontainebleau. He was first and foremost a landscape painter and the first to recapture an art lost in France since the days of Claude and Poussin. He was a poet in paint—like Claude—and his landscapes are dreamlike idyllic visions, bathed in immaterial light. He loved the spring, he preferred the magic and the mystery of dawn or dusk and he gives to the twilight moods of the countryside an atmosphere of other-worldliness. He used delicate tints, pale greens and blues and pearly greys to evoke his visions, veiled in the mysterious half-light of dusk or dawn. General impression is what interests him most. As he

---

[1] Delacroix proclaimed that Constable was the father of French landscape painting.

P

wrote himself: 'I am never in a hurry to get down to detail. The masses and the character of a picture interest me most of all.' There is nothing grim, nothing violent or melodramatic about his pictures, nothing of Delacroix's fire and fever. When he places figures in his landscapes, they are decorations for the landscape, not a justification for it; man is not more important than nature. In his pictures, as in Claude's, the most striking feature is the trees. Among his best-known canvases are 'Souvenir d'Italie' and 'Les Etangs de Ville-d'Avray',[1] and he painted innumerable landscapes of Picardy and Italy. The Louvre contains an incomparable portrait by him, the head and shoulders of a young woman, called 'La Femme à la perle', a picture so seductive that it has even been compared with Leonardo's 'Mona Lisa'. Corot's friend Henri Harpignies (1819-1916) was also a remarkable painter of trees, as he proves in 'Les Ilex à Villefranche' and 'Lever de lune'.

While in Corot's canvases the landscape was all-important and the human figures secondary, in those of Jean-François Millet (1814-75) man is seen as essentially and intimately a part of the landscape. 'When you paint a picture', wrote Millet in one of his *Letters*, 'whether it be a house, a plain, the ocean or the sky, always think of the presence of man, of his affinities of joy or suffering with such a scene . . . when creating a landscape, you will think of man; when you create man, you will think of the landscape.' Millet was a peasant and had worked on his father's farm in his youth; peasant subjects came nearest to his heart and his interests. The poetry he discerned in rustic toil furnished his real theme, not graceful posturings of Arcadian shepherds nor yet peasant weddings and rural junketings. For Millet, life is real, life is earnest; the emotion aroused by his pictures is melancholy, none of his peasant scenes is gay. A list of his pictures (we may leave aside the early imitations of Boucher undertaken to gain his bread and butter) reveals the story of the ordinary, dull, daily round of work on a small farm: 'Le Semeur', 'Le Berger', 'Les Moissonneurs', 'La Tondeuse de moutons', 'Paysan greffant un arbre', 'Les Glaneuses', 'Femme faisant paître sa vache', 'Les

[1] Musée de Rouen.

Planteurs de pommes de terre', 'Femme battant le beurre'. Millet's evocation of rustic scenes illustrates La Fontaine's reflection on the peasant's life in the Fable of 'La Mort et le Bûcheron' (of which Millet exhibited, unsuccessfully, a picture in 1859):

> Quel plaisir a-t-il eu depuis qu'il est au monde?
> En est-il un plus pauvre en la machine ronde?

The most popular of all Millet's pictures is 'L'Angélus': a young peasant couple stand in a potato field, where they have been lifting the crop and where fork, basket and wheelbarrow have momentarily been abandoned while they listen, in an attitude of prayer, to the church bell. This picture has been reproduced so often that it has become almost hackneyed. Its appeal is emotional, and some critics declared that Millet's painting was heavy and thick, wanting in free and airy tones, that his landscapes were empty and devoid of charm. He made pictures of rustic scenes, indoors as well as out-of-doors, more authentic than any that were painted before his time; he sought, in his own words, truth before beauty. Though ruthless realists accused him of idealism and his peasants have been compared unkindly and rather unjustly to those virtuous and idyllic beings who people the rustic novels of George Sand, modern critics admire his use of light and the 'allure monumentale et sculpturale' of his canvases.

Gustave Courbet (1819-77), the 'sublime plebeian', represents in painting the same realist tendency as Emile Zola in literature—naturalism. Courbet held the view that 'the art of painting can only consist in the representation of objects visible and tangible to the painter.' He paints his scenes with the rough directness of the artisan who puts down on the canvas what he sees and puts it down with such crude realism that the work of his predecessors seems too civilized, too idealized, almost conventional, almost genteel. Courbet was not untaught—he learned much from the pictures of the Bolognese school which he saw in the Art Galleries; that he painted his landscapes in his studio from memory is suggested by the famous picture of himself at work, 'L'Atelier', a large composition in which he intended to express his social views. He was a follower of Proudhon, the socialist writer, and his stone-breakers in 'Les Casseurs de pierres' [1] are intended to have a propaganda value. A typical composition is the 'Enterrement à Ornans', a striking realist picture of a contemporary funeral in his native village. In addition to these realist works, he painted sea-pieces like 'La Vague'—he is accounted an out-standing French painter of sea-pieces—and incomparable landscapes like 'La Remise de chevreuils', a wonderful vision of a forest glade. His social views led him to join the Commune in 1871, and the last years of his life were spent in retirement in Switzerland.

At that moment a revolution was taking place in French art. It was the work of a group of painters known as the Impression-ists. The chief of the group was Edouard Manet (1832-83), whose 'Déjeuner sur l'herbe' and 'Olympia', painted in the early 'sixties, startled Paris. The most outstanding of the others were Edgar Degas, Claude Monet and Auguste Renoir. Though all were called Impressionists, each of course had his own particular style and his own preferences in the matter of subject. These artists were also referred to as the 'pleinairistes', since they painted, not in their studios, but in the open air. Up till that time, painters of landscape usually, like Claude, made notes and sketches of the scene they intended to paint and did the actual painting later, in the studio. Manet's picture 'Le Jardin' made a sensation as something quite new. 'The most important person in any picture', announced Manet, 'is the light'. The picture, like all the impressionist landscapes, was made in the garden depicted.

The aim of Manet and the Impressionists was to see things as though they were looking at them for the first time, and to depict them without any distortion due to thought: to paint what they *saw* in the landscape, not what they knew was there. The impression was to be instan-taneous and passively received, uncontaminated by imagina-tion, judgment or memory. They sought to capture, very much as Edmond and Jules de Goncourt had sought in such

[1] Dresden.

descriptions as that of Bas Meudon, the 'la vérité du moment', to note down exactly what they saw at such and such a spot at, say, ten o'clock on a June morning. What they would see on a September afternoon, or even on the same June morning an hour afterwards, at the same spot, would be quite different because the lighting would not be the same.

To seize and retain this 'truth of the moment' it became necessary to represent sunlight and movement more adequately, the light being the element which changes the aspect of the landscape most rapidly. Painters had long before noticed, and Delacroix had pointed out, that the human body has a different colour in sunshine and in shadow and that shadows themselves have colour. This became the central element in the Impressionist doctrine. By laying side by side on the canvas touches of colour which contrast, they reproduced the colour cast on objects by the sunshine. The idea is that light is made up of a combination of the colours of the rainbow which may be separated by a prism. In the impressionist paintings it is the eye of the observer that has to look at the colours on the canvas in such a way as to see *in combination* the colours placed side by side. Various painters used different methods of laying on their paint, some made comma-like strokes, others applied dots of colour (*pointillisme*), others preferred mosaic squares. To give the 'rainbow atmosphere', light colours are used—orange, blues, pearly greys. Flesh takes on a mother-of-pearl hue. Instead of mixing the colours on the palette, the impressionist put side by side patches of pure colour, his object being to give the observer's eye a sensation of greater brightness than if the colours had been mixed. Moreover, bright hues were contrasted with other bright hues instead of being put against dark ones.

The result of this technique is that in any gallery the impressionist pictures, if they are near old masters or pre-1870 paintings, make the other pictures appear dark and gloomy beside their own luminosity. The Impressionists saw little to charm them in dark browns and blacks, and these colours are noticeably absent from their canvases. The absence of contours is not less noticeable, and recalls Turner's later luminous landscapes. As Manet said 'There are no lines in nature'. Form, structure and balance tend to be sacrificed by the Impressionists, who also show a marked preference for subjects drawn from life and scenery in the city and suburbs.

Among the characteristic paintings by Manet are 'Le Bon bock', [1] a very fine study of a stout jovial man smoking a pipe, 'La Servante de bocks', 'Canotage' (a study in light and colour) and 'Un Bar aux Folies-Bergère'.[2] His subjects were very diverse and his manner varied, but he devoted a good deal of his talent to depicting the aspects and scenes of La Ville Lumière. Edgar Degas (1834-1917) also took as his subject the life of Paris, with its dancing girls and its horse-racing. Though not particularly interested in the impressionists' obsession with light, he adopted their method of painting the immediate view, seizing upon the momentary mood, the significant gesture of the ordinary man and woman, in his case often the gesture of a ballet dancer caught in a flash. His paintings and drawings of the ladies of the ballet show them off stage, with nothing of the pretty-pretty about them; they are plain hard-working creatures as he paints them in most of of his pictures, e.g. 'Miss Lola au Cirque Fernando', 'Danseuse', at the Tate Gallery. 'L'Absinthe', in the Louvre, shows a forlorn-looking couple sitting in front of their apéritif before a large expanse of marble table.

Claude Monet (1840-1926) is the painter of shimmering and glowing colour, a musician in colour (his pictures call to mind Debussy's music), interested in light to an even greater degree than Manet, and more exclusively. He reminds one irresistibly of Turner. He is an eye, and his pictures are visual sensations —there is no story, often no human figures at all. He painted twenty pictures of 'La Cathédrale de Rouen' in different lighting, fifteen pictures of haystacks, 'Les Meules', showing light effects at different hours of the day. The Tate Gallery possesses some fine landscapes, including the highly decorative 'Le Bassin aux Nymphées'. It was a picture by Monet, called 'Impression, au soleil levant', that gave its name to the Impressionist movement, a name first applied in derision. Pierre Auguste Renoir (1841-1919) is the great portraitist of woman,

[1] Philadelphia.   [2] National Gallery.

not in studio lighting, but with the play of real light and in a natural pose. His best-known pictures that are specifically Impressionist include 'Le Moulin de la Galette' and 'Le Déjeuner des canotiers'. [1] Both these are examples of *genre* painting of contemporary Parisian life, and particularly the frivolous or vulgar aspects of life in the capital. Most of the Impressionists tended, like Zola in the novel, to stress the more sordid aspects of the life of their time and to avoid anything suggestive of idealism of any kind. The Lyons painter Puvis de Chavannes (1824-98), inspired by Ingres and Millet, represents idealism. He brought back the art of mural painting, executed frescoes in the Sorbonne, in the Paris Hôtel de Ville and in the Panthéon, pictures of monumental simplicity, executed in greys, blues and whites with Corot's limpidity and Millet's poetic emotion. One of his pictures, 'Le Pauvre Pêcheur', shows the pathetic figure of a fisherman standing in his boat gazing at his tackle while the mother picks flowers on the bank, keeping an eye on her small child.

Paul Cézanne (1839-1906) began as an Impressionist and exhibited his pictures with the other members of the group. While adopting the impressionist method of painting in terms of light, he was not fully satisfied with the vagueness of form which the Impressionists affected and declared that his ideal was to go back to Poussin—'Poussin all over again, but after Nature,' said Cézanne. He meant that he wished to return to the more formal organization characteristic of the classics, to give the art of composition a greater place in his canvases while retaining Impressionist colour. With him the line, which had tended to disappear in the pictures of the contemporary school, came back into painting, if in a new kind of way. For many years Cézanne worked alone and forgotten in his beloved Provence, and was rediscovered only in 1904, two years before his death. He painted a great number of landscapes; the most impressionistic, and perhaps the best known, is 'La Maison du pendu'. He executed striking portraits and a group called 'Joueurs de cartes', which is really a group portrait of four Provençal peasants. According to some critics, Cézanne's

[1] Chicago.

faulty draughtsmanship explains the tendency in some of his followers to reach back towards the primitive. Like Gauguin and Van Gogh he wished to achieve a primitive vision, that is, simplification and concentration. He is also credited—or debited—with having, in spite of himself, been the inspirer of the Cubists, who were impressed by his geometrical design, by the 'solid volume' of his landscapes.

Paul Gauguin (1848-1903) began as one of the Impressionists, then turned from their doctrine of instantaneous truth of impression to preoccupation with design and decoration. Colour and pattern were what interested him most. When he went to Tahiti in 1891 he did his best work, and painted in brilliantly splendid colour the exotic landscapes and the copper-coloured natives he had before his eyes. Among his most notable pictures are 'Te Rerioa', 'Feo Iheiho', and 'Nevermore', all in the Tate Gallery, which also contains a number of flower pieces—marvellous poems of colour and pattern.

Georges Seurat (1859-91), a pointilliste, gave more attention to composition than did the Impressionists, and was known as a Neo-impressionist. He died young and left few pictures, but these are looked upon by critics as works of genius, e.g. 'La Baignade' [1] and 'Le Dimanche à la Grande Jatte'.[2] In these two large canvases he uses landscape as a setting for human figures.

Henri de Toulouse-Lautrec (1864-1901) is one of the most strangely arresting figures in the history of French art. The scion of an ancient aristocratic family, he was crippled by a childhood accident which stunted the growth of his legs, making him the undersized, grotesque being revived in 1953 with commendable insight in the film 'Moulin Rouge'. He found a derivative in the Parisian underworld, and particularly in the garish, agitated glitter of that most celebrated of Paris night-clubs, the Moulin Rouge. Night after night he sat there, his tiny legs dangling from his chair, drinking, sketching the habitués and the artists. His colour is stark, some of his best-known works being posters for the Moulin Rouge. His incisive and caustic line reveals an extraordinary

[1] Tate Gallery.   [2] Chicago.

sense of life and movement, reducing with masterly and ruthless simplification a silhouette or a face to a few significant traits.

The end of the nineteenth century was a period of great diversity of inspiration, as may be seen from the few examples noted above. The new century with its schools and movements offers no less variety: Fauvism, Cubism, Surrealism, Neo-primitivism, to name only a few. The Fauves were a group including, among others, Matisse, Rouault and Derain (b. 1880) whose pictures were exhibited in 1905 and whose creed was that painting should express only sensation and should express it brutally. A critic referred to the gallery in which these pictures were hung as 'la cage aux fauves', 'the wild beasts' cage', and the name stuck. The Fauves, true to their kind, worked independently. Their chief exponent, Henri Matisse (1869-1954), a reflective and methodical painter, towers over the others. His colourful 'Liseuse sur fond noir',[1] his 'Liseuse distraite',[2] and 'La Forêt [2] may be compared with the haunting 'La Sainte Face',[3] 'Les Trois Juges [4] and 'L'Italienne' [4] of Rouault, and with Derain's landscapes and portraits in the Musée d'Art Moderne in Paris. The Fauves, exuberant colourists, affected to despise composition and nuances.

The Cubists, whose theorist was the poet Guillaume Apollinaire, include Picasso and Georges Braque (b. 1881). They created a strange world in which the artist may show a human head seen, at the same time, from several angles, or decompose a face into its constituent cubes, cylinders and cones; in either case the effect disconcerts the profane. Cubism, initially a reaction against Impressionism, still flourishes—even the Second World War did not destroy its vitality. Pablo Picasso (b. 1881), a many-sided genius, always experimenting—not only painter, etcher and engraver but sculptor and ceramist —ranges from the almost orthodox 'Portrait de Madame Eluard' [5] and 'Femme assise' [6] to the 'Femme nue assise', [6] which looks more like a puzzle in solid geometry. This

---

[1] Musée d'Art Moderne, Paris. [2] Tate Gallery.
[3] Musée d'Art Moderne. [4] Tate Gallery.
[5] Musée d'Art Moderne. [6] Tate Gallery.

intensely serious and imaginative artist occasionally appears to be deliberately poking fun at his public, as when, with the remains of a scooter and a feather, he represents a bird.

Neo-primitivism sought its inspiration in the naïve-looking pictures made by an ex-Customs officer, Henri Rousseau, *le douanier* Rousseau (1844-1910), such as the very decorative 'Singes dans la forêt'. Rousseau appears to have originally been hailed as a master in pure derision, but his vogue has lasted and some affirm that to-day an artist who can claim proletarian origin as navvy, mason, gardener or simply employee enjoys in the eyes of many a privileged position.

Paris still remains, in the twentieth century, what it has been for a hundred years—the Mecca of the artist. Experiment and research were carried out in the congenial climate of *La Ville Lumière* not only by Frenchmen but by Spaniards like Picasso, Dutchmen like Van Gogh—whose strong colour-contrasts appeal to modern taste—Slavs like Kandinsky or Marc Chagall (b. 1890), whose 'Poète allongé', strange but decorative, adorns the Tate Gallery. More than half of the seventy thousand painters who exhibit their works in the two hundred galleries and twenty 'Salons' of Paris are reported neither to be Parisians nor even French.

Much modern French art, abstract or non-representational, no longer attempts to copy or reproduce nature. Our grandfathers and great-grandfathers not only liked a picture to show a piece of the exterior world that they could recognize as such, and preferred a painted tree to look like a tree, but many of them looked for a story and, best of all, a story with a moral. The modern French painter has quite a different view of what constitutes art. He sets out to paint in full independence whatever his temperament or the nature of his mind impels him to express. The copying of external nature has, he believes, been done too often already; that kind of art may be left to the photographer, since no painter's brush can, in that task, vie with the camera. The modern painter very often shows less interest in Nature with a capital N than in his own nature; and it is this he takes as his subject. He may, like the Surrealists (whose origins were literary), plunge into the obscure inner world of the unconscious and evoke strange visions which afford valuable material for the psychologists. The precursor of the Moderns in this field was Odilon Redon (1840-1916), the painter of the strange 'Caliban endormi'. [1]

Some modern artists, intent on spontaneity and concentration, may shun the sophistication of the industrial cities and look for inspiration to the art of the African negro or to the primitive decorative design of remote South Sea islands, striving to capture some of the magical qualities achieved by sculptors and painters whose vision was unspoilt. Others may seek their subject in music, or take as their ideal *la peinture pure*, painting that has no obvious human significance. The modern view, formulated by Chagall in 1947, holds that beauty, style and order are no longer what matter. 'An entirely new art must correspond to an entirely new epoch, and this art itself is begun anew by each artist, whose adventures will be unique.' The complete individuality of the artist implies that the spectator must make a particular effort to understand what the artist would be at. The works of Picasso and his emulators represent, in the words of a contemporary critic Jaime Barbarès, 'the transformation of the grotesque into visions made possible by a certain condition of the soul. They are studies of realities observed from a constantly changing point of view.'

The most significant group of contemporary French painters calls itself the Jeune Ecole de Paris—a cosmopolitan group despite its name, for quite a high proportion of its members hail from outside Paris and outside France—from Belgium, Canada, China, Denmark, Germany, Greece, Persia, Portugal, Spain and Turkey. They can claim, however, to have been formed in and by Paris. The productions of these young painters—some of them born after the First World War—at first appear novel and disconcerting, but on reflection it appears that they are not new in the sense that they have flowered spontaneously and in isolation, without reference to the schools that preceded them. The new school shows clearly enough, by its manner and choice of subject, that it continues and develops the trends of the schools that flourished at the open-

[1] Paris, Private Collection.

ing of the present century, particularly the Fauves, the Cubists, the Neo-primitives and the Surrealists. Among the outstanding names in the Jeune Ecole de Paris may be mentioned Hans Hartung (German), Nicolas de Staël (Russian), Maurice Estève (French) and Pierre Tal Coat, who hails from Brittany.

To appreciate the work of contemporary French painting, one must keep in mind what the painter is trying to do and not blame him for not doing something else. When he declares —as several artists of the Jeune Ecole de Paris most emphatically do—that he desires simply to combine form, colour and rhythm into a pleasing pattern which means something to him and which he hopes will mean something to us, it is unfair to complain because we cannot recognize a landscape, a domestic scene or portrait. Why should we ask him to tell us a story when he offers us the expression of a mood? The modern painter no more thinks a story essential than a modern composer will admit that his tone poem must have a melody that can be identified and learned immediately. The Victorian father liked to hang on his drawing-room wall a painted story on which he—and his family—might usefully meditate. An Orchardson was ideal. The contemporary painter offers not a story but a pictorial pattern of line and colour, because he is convinced that the artist can do nothing of greater value as art. The provision of stories he regards as the domain of the poet and the novelists. His own conception of painting implies nothing more than the love of colours and forms for their own sake—*et tout le reste est littérature*. As for those who demand qualities that the picture does not supply, the artist would liken them to the Philistine who condemned poetry with the brutal question, 'What does it prove?'

In contemporary painting, with its geometrical compositions, its violent colour contrasts, its unusual rhythms, some see the expression or the symbol of the disorganization of the modern world, adrift from its moorings and no longer knowing whither it is bound, a world in which the traditional values are no longer recognized. Others envisage modern painting—and art in general—as undergoing a period of groping experiment from which will emerge, perhaps, an art less enigmatic and more universal in its appeal. It is not without relevance, and to some it may possibly be a consolation, to remember that the art of a century ago proved equally disconcerting and perplexing to the French public. French art in 1848 was summed up by Alfred Rambaud, the historian of civilization, in words that might be applied to the art of to-day. 'There are no longer', he wrote, 'any dominant schools of painting; one might almost say there are no schools. Each artist seeks with full independence the road pointed out by the nature of his mind, his temperament and, one might almost say, the structure of his visual organs. It is an anarchy in the best sense of the term: it is the reign of individualism.'

READING LIST

Note.—It is more important to see paintings than to read about them.

Short Histories of French Painting

Bell, Clive. *An Account of French Painting*. London, 1931. Useful and readable.

Dorival, B. *La Peinture française*. Paris, 1946. An up-to-date account. An excellent manual, but the vocabulary is occasionally abstract. Bibliographies. Ninety-six excellent reproductions.

Gillet, L. *Histoire de l'art*. Chapters I-XIV in Volume XI of *Histoire de la nation française*, edited by G. Hanotaux, Paris, 1922. French painting, architecture, and sculpture from beginnings to *c.* 1920. Eighteen coloured plates and one hundred and ninety-five black-and-white illustrations.

Hourticq, L. *France* in the 'Ars Una' Series. Paris, 1911. An extremely well written and attractive account of French painting, architecture and sculpture from Roman times up to end of nineteenth century. A thousand small illustrations and some coloured plates.

Underwood, E. G. *A Short History of French Painting*. Oxford U.P., 1931. A very good summary, in non-technical language. Very readable. Gives life-story of the more important painters. Contains bibliography and useful list showing where French paintings can be seen. Fifty illustrations.

Wilenski, R. H. *French Painting*. London, 1931. From Gothic times to *c.* 1930. Useful list of important pictures. Two hundred and forty illustrations.

Masters of Modern Painting. A useful series published in London deals with individual painters including: Cézanne, Corot, Fantin-Latour, Gauguin, Manet, Millet, Monet, Toulouse-Lautrec. Each volume contains forty reproductions. The Phaidon Press, London, has a volume on the French Impressionists and volumes on individual French painters, e.g. Ingres, Cézanne, Renoir, Van Gogh.

COLLECTIONS OF FRENCH PAINTINGS

France
Paris

The Musée du Louvre has the greatest collection of French pictures in the world. The Musée National d'Art Moderne, quai de New York, contains a fine collection of works by recent and contemporary artists. The Bibliothèque Nationale, rue de Richelieu, in which frequent special exhibitions are held, has a permanent collection of 2,500,000 engravings. The Musée Condé in the Château de Chantilly and the Palais de Versailles should also be visited.

Provinces

Lille, Lyons, Dijon, Nantes and Montpellier (Musée Fabre) have particularly fine collections in their museums, and there are also art galleries of interest in most towns of any size.

Great Britain
London

The National Gallery has works of Claude Lorraine, Nicolas Poussin and others. The Tate Gallery (Millbank) includes a fine collection of the impressionists and other moderns. The nineteenth century is well represented in the Victoria and Albert Museum. The Wallace Collection possesses many seventeenth, eighteenth-and early nineteenth-century pictures, and the Dulwich Gallery has some fine works.

Provinces

Glasgow Art Gallery has works by the Barbizon painters. The National Gallery of Scotland, in Edinburgh, contains pictures by Poussin, Watteau, Lorrain, five by Greuze and two by Chardin. The Barber Institute of Fine Art in Birmingham has some outstanding works, including several by the Impressionists. The National Museum of Wales at Cardiff (Gwendoline E. Davies Bequest) has five examples of Renoir, Monet, and three Cézanne paintings.

U.S.A.

The Metropolitan Museum of Art and other galleries and collections in New York contain fine examples of French painting, which is also well represented in collections in Baltimore, Boston, Chicago and Washington.

CHAPTER XI

THE CINEMA

In the film world France early won for herself a predominant place, and from 1907 to 1914 Paris held the key position in Europe. It was not without significance that, in 1912, the Gaumont Palace in Paris could boast of being the biggest picture-house in the world. Before this brief period of leadership, and indeed since, French technical and artistic contributions to cinematography were numerous and important. In 1914, when the First World War came, partial enemy occupation and the bending of all the national effort towards the liberation of the territory meant the eclipse of her cinema industry, and Hollywood seized the unparalleled opportunity to plunge into production on a colossal scale. To-day Hollywood films fill no less than sixty-five per cent. of the screen time available in the world's cinemas. Neither France nor any European country could hope to compete with the United States in scale of production, but competition in quality was not ruled out.

French cinema production has always provided copious evidence of ingenuity and of sensitivity to beauty, or, as some would prefer to put it, to plastic values. As one might expect in view of their achievements in other fields—painting and the theatre, for instance—the French favoured individual initiative and personal effort. Experiment in the cinema, as in the sciences, made a stronger appeal than team work; co-operation between a directorial group and a multitudinous army of actors and supernumeraries, mobilized to realize a gigantic and spectacular picture, has not been a marked feature of French output. Moreover, French production companies have frequently complained of the too vigorous action taken by the State tax-gatherers, who never, they allege, leave at their disposal that copious stream of capital found necessary elsewhere to irrigate the giant plants of large-scale production.

Scene from *Les Jeux Interdits* with Brigitte Fossey
and Lucien Hubert
(*Miracle Films Production*)

In Paris much has been achieved in film-making, but the scale of operations has been modest. In the early days it occasionally happened that one and the same man carried out the whole task himself: he thought out his subjects, directed, made and cut his own picture, sometimes even using a borrowed camera. Though these experiments no doubt brought into play original techniques, they did not often achieve popular success in France; their reward must have come most frequently from large-scale production abroad, which utilized the newly devised methods. Plenty of ideas occurred also to the directors who were working on a more elaborate scale, and some of the most brilliant among them, including René Clair and Julien Duvivier, succumbed for a time to the temptation of Hollywood. They left Paris in quest of more copious resources and the opportunity of working in a far wider field. The new environment, with its unlimited material possibilities, its tendency to standardization, its financial preoccupations, usually proved less stimulating and inspiring to the newcomers than had been the intellectual and artistic ferment of Paris. The fervent and sometimes effervescent individuality that had welled up so spontaneously in the magic atmosphere of the French capital, tended to lose part of its vigour when transported to an alien land and to a more luxurious and commercialized setting. When these directors had been working in Paris, the distinguishing features of their work had been the simplicity of its setting, a near-to-life realism both in acting and in décor, beautiful effects obtained inexpensively and, most important of all, an individualism far removed from the large-scale standardization needed for capturing the attention of the infinite multitudes of the common man.

In France, as in the United States, the beginnings of the cinematograph date from the last decade of the nineteenth century. In 1894, the year after Edison, who was trying to perfect a visual accompaniment to his phonograph records, had presented his kinetoscope for the first time commercially in New York, Louis Lumière (1864-1948), working in Lyons with his elder brother Auguste (1862-1954), patented his 'appareil servant à l'obtention et à la vision des épreuves chrono-

Q

photographiques'. That same year he showed a film, 'La Sortie des ouvriers de l'Usine Lumière', to the first cinema audience. Before the year 1895 was out, he had made half a dozen films of the type that would now be called 'documentaries' and, exhibited in Paris, they had been seen by the first paying audience.

It was a Frenchman, too—George Méliès (1861-1938)—who founded what is claimed as the first film-production firm, Star Film, and who built in 1896 the first film studio. Méliès, spending a year in London in his early twenties, frequently watched the performances of the great illusionist Maskelyne; on his return to Paris he bought the Robert Houdin Theatre and started up as an illusionist himself. Gifted with a lively imagination, he perceived that Lumière's new invention offered an even more fertile field than the stage for presenting those mysteries in which he had become an adept during his circus and music-hall career. To this pioneer work he brought immense ingenuity and built up his scenes into studio-made stories. He ranks as the creator of trick photography in film-making: 'fades' and 'dissolves' (*le fondu*), the printing of scenes over a black background, the doubling of rôles (*le dédoublement*), fast and slow motion, and other clever devices. In 1900 he was already trying to synchronize the phonograph and the cinema. He made no less than four thousand films and sold them at 1 fr. 50 (then 1s. 3d.) a metre. His own favourite film was his 'Voyage dans la lune' (1902), one year before the American 'The Great Train Robbery', frequently exhibited as the beginning of the modern film. Others worth remembering are 'Vingt Mille Lieues sous les mers', 'Le Voyage à travers l'impossible', a fantasy looked upon at that time as a phenomenally long film since it lasted no less than twenty-five minutes!—and 'Les Quat'cents Farces du diable'. Though by 1901 he became President of the first International Film Congress, he afterwards fell on evil days and was reduced to hawking toys outside Montparnasse Railway Station, until rescued and fêted in recognition of his outstanding film achievements.

To Méliès must go the credit of having made the film tell

a story—his stories were no doubt far-fetched, artificial and fantastic, but they were stories. Most French film-producers in the active period preceding the First World War, far from following Méliès' example of creating a new story made for the film, specialized in making screen versions of plays that had been successful on the stage. This seemed safer and easier. Leading lights from the stage of the Comédie Française were recruited for films and, bringing the celluloid version of their favourite rôles before the provincials and foreigners who had rarely before had the pleasure of watching such acting, increased by thousands the number of their fervent admirers. The cinema was still a minor art, dominated by a highly perfected stage technique, theatrical *jeux de scène* and stage perspective. To realize how far it had to travel in order to find its own technique, one need but compare the screen version of 'La Dame aux Camélias'—played by Sarah Bernhardt—with any modern film. The difference is the same as between the most elegant vintage car, complete with high-perched driving-seat and road lanterns, and the streamlined, chromium-plated modern version.

With the new art thus applied to plays which had been successful on the stage and to actors who were known already, production leapt forward, and by 1911 Léon Gaumont was turning out daily about ten thousand metres of film, an impressive figure for that early date. Though much of his work comprised the filming of stage plays, he also turned out some popular melodramas more specifically cinematographic: 'Fantomas', 'Vampires', etc. Many popular classics among French novels were presented in a screen version, including, in Pathécolor, Victor Hugo's *Les Misérables*. (This film had a great success among the industrial classes when it was shown in Great Britain under its French title, as often as not read and pronounced as 'Less Miserable'!). Meanwhile Max Linder, a hilarious comic, was disporting himself on the Continent, to the intense joy of young and old. His example was not lost on Charlie Chaplin.

Though the general public found satisfaction in the screen versions of their best-loved stage plays and novels, French film-makers, like Paris painters, felt impelled to create something new. Thus when René Clair, in 1923, made a film, 'Entr'Acte', on a dadaist scenario, he invented ingenious camera devices, such as slow motion, the reversal of the ordinary method of pictorial composition, the photographing, from below, through a sheet of glass, of a ballet dancer. His originality was recognized and his inventions were later adopted by large-scale producers abroad. René Clair won world-wide fame by his 'Chapeau de paille d'Italie' (1927). Film critics credited him (or debited him) with all the satire of the middle-class world served up so brilliantly in the film, forgetful that the original stage-play is none other than Labiche's lively farce, which delighted boulevard Paris in 1851, and of which Clair was very reluctant to make a film. This is very much a period piece, but none the less amusing. Clair followed this up with 'Sous les toits de Paris' and 'Le million', regarded as the best musical film ever made, 'Le Quatorze Juillet', and 'A nous la liberté' (1931). These films, still extremely popular and deservedly so, are widely shown abroad as well as in France. There is about them a note of piquant wistfulness, of poetical *je m'en fichisme*, of not unkindly irony—helped by the sensitive acting of Albert Préjean and Annabella. They have, too, a host of minor parts, the great charm of which is the naturalness found in the *commedia dell'arte*, seemingly unrehearsed, also a new perspective, photography at unexpected angles (for instance the nocturnal pavement and two pairs of walking feet). At the very moment when Clair was scoring an unprecedented success with his silent films: 'Sous les toits de Paris' and 'Le million', with musical accompaniment, the silent film was being swept away by the advent of the 'talkies' (1927). Clair, a few years afterwards, was working in London, and scored a resounding success with his rollicking farce 'Fantôme à vendre' ('The Ghost Goes West') (1936), less fine-textured than the silent films of the 1927 period.

René Clair's work was indeed outstanding, and 'A nous la liberté' evidently had its effect on Chaplin, whose excellent, entertaining and thoughtful film, 'Modern Times', shows its influence. But Clair was by no means the only French director whose reputation was international. Jean Renoir, son of the illustrious painter, achieved fame with 'La grande illusion' (1937), which treated the theme of war, fear of which was harrowing the menaced generation of the inter-war period.

'La grande illusion' is set in a German prison camp during the 1914-18 war. Its underlying theme is the futility of war, more or less obliquely hinted at in all the subordinate themes. It stresses the subtle affinities, in spite of enmity, between a French and a German aristocrat, between the tough French airman and the German peasant-wife who shelters him. On the other hand, an invisible gap separates the aristocratic officer and the 'temporary gentleman', each grudgingly aware of the other's merits. The film draws attention to barriers of incomprehension between allies, between Gentile and Jew, broken down now and again by a spontaneous gesture of human sympathy. It abounds in moving or wryly humorous incidents, and the acting of the protagonists, Pierre Fresnay as Capitaine de Boeldieu, Erich von Stroheim as the German commandant, Jean Gabin as Lieutenant Marchal, makes it one of the classics of the cinema.

Jacques Feyder, a Belgian, who directed a striking silent film on Zola's grim drama 'Thérèse Raquin' (1927), had made a popular hit with the joyous costume film, 'La kermesse héroïque' in 1935, which brought fame to Feyder's wife, the actress Françoise Rosay. That same year, Jules Renard's story of childhood martyrdom, 'Poil de carotte', furnished Julien Duvivier with the subject for a very moving and very artistically rendered film, with remarkable acting by Robert Lynen as the tousled, unlovely, appealing hero. Two years later Duvivier was equally fortunate with a picture made from Louis Hémon's novel, 'Marie Chapdelaine', evoking Canadian landscapes and scenes of rustic life. Though Duvivier scored another success with his gangster films, e.g. 'Pépé-le-Moko', a first-rate melodrama of the Kasbah of Algiers, magnificently acted and photographed, most popular with the British audiences was his 'Carnet de bal', a series of episodes in the lives of people whose only link with each other is that they had all signed their names on the same dance-card.

The theme of 'Carnet de bal' is poetical. The charming features of Christine (Marie Bell) recall their youth—to some a welcome, if bitter-sweet memory, to others an unbearable contrast with present reality. Raimu, as a southern country mayor, Françoise Rosay as an insane mother, Louis Jouvet, as a night-club manager with a past, are unforgettable. Duvivier's 'La fin du jour' tells the half-touching, half-farcical, and wholly entertaining story of the eventide life in common of a group of superannuated actors.

Mention must be made of two fine spectacular films produced in France in the 1920s, 'Koenigsmark' (from Pierre Benoît's novel) and 'Monte Cristo' (from Alexandre Dumas's novel), both adventure stories, both considered by critics to have taste and accuracy, but both blamed, a trifle strangely, for lacking the dramatic action of such large-scale American productions as 'Ben Hur'. Some critics think French directors concentrate more on the pictorial elements than on the problem of movement and action. Carl Dreyer's 'La Passion de Jeanne d'Arc' has been cited as an example, though Dreyer was a Dane—in Denmark he had directed the gloomy but striking film, 'Day of Wrath'. Like many foreigners (e.g. Jean Epstein, the Polish director of the magnificent 'Finis Terrae', set in Brittany), Dreyer did much of his work in Paris.

Among the younger directors of French films stand out the names of Marcel Carné, Jean Vigo and Jacques Prévert, though many others have remarkable talent. Carné came into prominence with 'Les Enfants du paradis' (1944)—a long film, over-luxuriant and shapeless, but relieved by the magnificent *mime* of Jean-Louis Barrault, and, in the duel scene, some lovely shots of dawn in the Bois de Boulogne.

Jacques Prévert discovered new subjects and new scenes in the grim haunts of ports and waterfronts. The melodramatic happenings in this underworld of poverty and crime provided the material for his best-known films: 'Quai des brumes' (1938), a tragic police-hunt; 'Le Jour se lève' (1939), with Jean Gabin as the tough, moody hero; and 'Hôtel du Nord' (1939), where Louis Jouvet portrays, as often, the inscrutable and sardonic man of the world with a murky past and Arletty

the cheerfully disillusioned woman of the underworld. The
settings—a poor Paris suburb, a seedy hotel, the canal, the
sluice-gates—have a Utrillo-like quality.

The early death of Jean Vigo robbed the French cinema of
one of its most promising young directors, who had already
made his mark in 'Zéro de conduite' (1933), a school story of
difficult boys, and in 'L'Atalante' (1934), a whimsical, dream-
like tale of a barge, an elderly skipper, his bewildered young
wife and an eccentric deck-hand. Both films have been considered surrealist fantasies because of Vigo's use of large masses
of light and shadow and crazy aimless pursuits, reminiscent of
'La coquille et le clergyman' (1928). But Vigo applied them
to real life and not to dreams.

Film production continued in France during the Second
World War, although under German occupation it assumed
a definitely 'escapist' character, both in the choice of subjects
and in their treatment. Among the most notable films produced were 'L'éternel retour' (1943—director, Jean Delannoy),
a modern version of the Tristan and Isolde theme, Nordic,
poetical, magnificently icy; 'Les Visiteurs du Soir' (1942—
director, Marcel Carné), a mediaeval tale of two evil spirits in
the guise of wandering minstrels, is relieved by the irrepressible
impertinence of Arletty as the she-demon; 'Le corbeau' (1942
—director, Henri G. Clouzot), a sarcastic, wryly funny poison-
pen story in a small town.

The post-war years have shown that France has lost nothing
of her vitality in the film world. René Clément's 'La Bataille
du Rail', a war-story of the French railways, and Jean Cocteau's
'La Belle et la Bête' and 'Orphée' are outstanding. René
Clair's 'Le silence est d'or' shows that he can still compete
with his younger rivals, and 'Belles de nuit' (1952), a fantastic
dream drama shows him quite in his old form. Georges
Rouquier's 'Farrebique' (1945), which took three years to
complete, might serve as a masterly documentary on French
peasant life.

The French cinema has produced a number of outstanding
successes during the last few years: in 1950 the moving and
grim story of an island in Brittany deprived of its priest, 'Dieu

a besoin des hommes', and Nicole Védrès's 'La vie commence demain', a comment on contemporary life and thought magnificently acted by Pierre Fresnay. The following year appeared Robert Bresson's 'Journal d'un Curé de campagne' (based on Georges Bernanos's famous novel); and a particularly good crop in 1952: 'Casque d'or' directed by Jacques Becker; 'Jeux interdits', by Clément, an extremely sad and moving story of a little girl orphaned during the flight from Paris in 1940 who, with a young boy, takes refuge in a morbid game with crosses taken from the local churchyard; 'Belles de nuit', mentioned above.

'Monsieur Vincent', with Pierre Fresnay's magnificent portrayal of St. Vincent de Paul, should modify the views of those who doubt whether any religious feeling exists in France. Outstanding among the gay films are 'Jour de fête', a delightful fantasy in a realist setting, directed by the excellent comic Jacques Tati, who also played the leading rôle, and Noël-Noël's brilliantly funny 'Les Cassepieds', an entertaining comedy on the same theme as Molière's 'Les Fâcheux'.

There is a strong trend to treat filmcraft as an independent art evolving its own technique, and scripts are specially written for the screen ('Orphée', 'Les Belles de nuit', etc.). But there is no denying that some of the greatest successes of recent years have been adaptations of well-known plays or novels: for instance 'Les Parents terribles' from the play by Jean Cocteau, 'Gigi' from Colette's novel, the 'Symphonie pastorale' from André Gide's novel, with Pierre Blanchar as the Protestant minister whose rescue of a blind orphan wrecks his home-life and Michèle Morgan giving a touching interpretation of a blind girl. 'Touchez pas au Grisbi' (from Albert Simonin's novel) adopts a tough, slangy, Villon-like manner to give, for the delectation of the law-abiding, glimpses of the *apache* world.

A feature of the 1950s in French film-making is the co-operation for large-scale pictures between France and Italy. Twenty-three films were made jointly by the two countries in 1951. Italian films—such as Roberto Rossellini's 'Open City' (1945) and 'Paisa' (1946)—has won world-wide

applause for the simple, sincere presentation which has some
of the qualities so successful in French films around 1927 (e.g.
René Clair). Among the outstanding achievements of the
Franco-Italian group are: 'La beauté du diable', with René
Clair as director; 'Au-delà des grilles', with René Clément;
'Les miracles n'ont lieu qu'une fois', with Yves Allégret; and
'Le petit monde de Don Camille', with the French actor
Fernandel in the title rôle.

Not all recent French production has been in conjunction
with the Italians. Henri G. Clouzot, who scored a success
with 'Manon' (1949), a modernized version of l'Abbé Prévost's
'Manon Lescaut', was even more admirable with 'Le salaire
de la peur' (1953), the enthralling and terrifying story of the
nightmare drive of two lorries loaded with nitro-glycerine
in the wilds of Central America. The story is based on a novel
by Georges Arnaud.

Special mention must be made of at least some of the outstanding artists whose talent has allowed French films to hold
their own against severe competition. The reputation of the
French cinema owes a great deal to the late Raimu and the late
Louis Jouvet. Raimu, with nothing of the 'jeune premier' appeal,
was probably the greatest figure on the French screen between
1930 and 1940. With the bulky frame, the heavy thoughtful
features and the homely solidity of an ageing country mayor,
he symbolized an element in French life almost destroyed by the
hecatombs of the First World War. With a minimum of *jeux de
scène* he contrived to invest his parts with an extraordinary depth
of feeling, pathos and homely dignity leavened with humour.
No one can forget him as the middle-aged husband of a
flighty young wife in 'La Femme du boulanger', as the country
mayor in 'Otages' and in 'Carnet de bal'.

Louis Jouvet, saturnine, romantic and poker-faced, created
a totally different type with an equally wide appeal, that of
sensitiveness hidden under the dry, flippant, disillusioned
façade of the man of the world.

Among the dominating figures of the present day one should
mention Pierre Fresnay, an extraordinarily versatile artist,
ranging from the refined aristocratic aloofness of Capitaine de

Boeldieu in 'La grande illusion' to the intense human feeling and religious fervour of 'Monsieur Vincent'.

Jean Gabin, the soft-hearted 'tough guy'; Gérard Philippe, with his mischievous smile; Fernandel, the guileless well-meaning blunderer dear to the heart of Parisians; Michel Simon, whose prodigious ugliness and incredible grimaces achieve striking effects and whose performance as a disgruntled comic on the decline in 'La fin du jour' is not easily forgotten. And mention must be made of the benign and suavely caustic, wise-cracking, ineffably Parisian Sacha Guitry.

As regards actresses, one is faced with the continual emergence of new talent. Edwige Feuillère, who gave such an impressively moving performance in 'Olivia', a finishing-school drama; Michèle Morgan, wistful and appealing; the piquant and sprightly Danielle Darrieux; the young and charming Danielle Delorme (Gigi); Arletty, smart, astringent and worldly-wise; Pauline Carton, the irrepressible and forthright *femme du peuple*, a Mrs. Mopp-like figure, are a few of the galaxy of French stars who have retained their originality and individuality without succumbing to the temptation of becoming box-office puppets. Nor must we entirely forget the child-actors, the appealing naturalness and the childish intenseness of the girl and boy in 'Les Jeux interdits', or the Parisian mite with the tightly plaited hair in 'Sous le ciel de Paris coule la Seine'.

Cinema is international to a much greater degree than any other art, except perhaps music. In none other is international rivalry carried so far. Yet each of the countries now holding a leading place in the art has retained well-defined national characteristics in its film production. It might even be said that these characteristics are each country's best asset. The United States, Great Britain, France and Italy each has its own 'lane' in this international race—the lane, in the case of the United States, being a broad avenue! French film directors, like the legendary French cook, often have to make much out of little, and, at times, something out of nothing. The grandiose productions in which the Americans excel are not for them—they simply cannot afford the enormous cost. Most French directors harbour no ambition to stage super productions, for they do not do them well, as a few examples have proved conclusively. Nor are they particularly successful in period pieces, which have become an English speciality. Though they have never been very fond of nature films, they have achieved some superb documentaries.

The special province of the French director is the observation of human reality, observation touched with poetry, leavened with wit, softened by humour and imbued with a sense of beauty that gives the French film its characteristic tone and colour. Striking examples are the recurring theme of the Paris roofs in 'Sous les toits de Paris', and, in 'Les Jeux interdits', the glimpse of the landscape under a wonderful summer sun contrasted with the scene of horror as bombs rain down on the crowded bridge.

The French cinema has achieved the ideal mixture of pathos and humour that was the hallmark of Shakespeare, the ambition of the French Romantic dramatists, and the subject of Victor Hugo's thunderous argumentation in the *Préface de Cromwell*. No mere mechanical device whereby tears in one scene are automatically compensated by guffaws in the next, the mixture implies a sense of the complexity of life, a sense which allows for life's absurdities and balances the expression of diverse emotions. This French conception does not exclude artistic finish or the traditional trimming of rough edges. Theme and general effect come first; all the parts are subordinated to achieve a composite whole.

READING LIST

Bardèche, M., and Brasillach, R. *Histoire du cinéma*. Paris, 1935. English translation by Iris Barry (with plates). London, 1938.

Clair, René. *Reflections on the Cinema*. London, 1954.

Duca, L. O. *Histoire du cinéma* (Collection Que Sais-je?). Paris, 1951. A short history of the cinema throughout the world, amusingly illustrated with sketches.

Rotha, P., and Griffith, R. *The Film till Now*. New ed., London, 1949. A full and interesting, though rather discursive account of world cinema production; gives lists of films with dates and indications of names of directors, etc.

Sadoul, G. *Histoire générale du cinéma*, 4 vols. Paris, 1946-52. Covers period 1832-1920, with illustrations and bibliography. *French Film.* London, 1954.

Spencer, D. A., and Waley, H. D. *The Film To-day.* London, 1940.

CHAPTER XII

THE THEATRE

EVERY first-year student of French learns something about a dramatic tradition very different from Shakespeare's, for he early makes the acquaintance of Corneille, Molière and Racine. If he continues his studies, he delves into the mediaeval mystery and miracle plays which, with the still older tradition of Roman comedy—Terence and Plautus—form the basis of the dramatic tradition in France. The student generally finds as much pleasure (many find more) in his incursions into the eighteenth century; the delicate psychological *nuances* in Marivaux's exquisite comedies, the sprightly wit of Beaumarchais's irrepressibly satirical Figaro in the *Barbier de Séville* and *Le Mariage de Figaro*. Students are young enough to find delight also in the melodramatic extravagances, the lyrical sentimentalism of romantic drama: the (pseudo-)historical pageantry and rhetorical flourishes of Hugo, Vigny's divine discontent (or is it morbid?) in 'Chatterton', the elder Dumas's skilful handling of melodramatic themes. They may be more enchanted by the romantic dreams evoked so delightfully in Musset's comedies, which caught more Shakespearian magic than any of the other Romantics could achieve. Another world, where 'life is real, life is earnest', is opened by the bourgeois dramas of Émile Augier and Dumas the younger and Henry Becque, who contrive to include many amusing or witty scenes with the moral lessons they offer us. The living dramatists of the present century may be represented in the student's syllabus by Cocteau's *La Machine infernale* and Claudel's *L'Annonce faite à Marie*.

By this time the student, who from a personal interest in drama may have delved into many plays, realizes that for centuries France has possessed an official national theatre and that no nation has paid greater attention to drama than the French. The Comédie Française (Théâtre-Français or Maison de Molière), with its Salle Richelieu and its Salle Luxembourg (once the Odéon), which recruits its actors and actresses from the Conservatoire National, sets a very high standard for dramatic achievement, just as the French Academy represents the national standard for literature and language. The Théâtre-Français aims not only at literary merit in the plays accepted by its reading committee but at perfection in production, in scenery and in elocution, and it displays this perfection not only in Paris but in its performances in foreign countries—London, Edinburgh, America or, as in April 1954, in Moscow and Leningrad, where a company of French actors played as long ago as 1742.

The Comédie Française has a double rôle: the production of new plays which are considered to be of artistic merit, and the performance of repertory plays, according to the ancient acting tradition. Not that it is closed to innovation; it has even gone so far as to renew entirely the setting of Corneille's and Racine's tragedies in the years preceding the Second World War, thus bringing back life—as some consider—to the classics, and—according to others—giving meretricious adornment to plays which appeal best when the traditional décors, extremely simple, are maintained. The stagnation, the unpopularity of the classical repertory of the Théâtre-Français, of which Musset complains in *Une Soirée perdue*:

> 'J'étais seul, l'autre soir, au Théâtre-Français,
> Ou presque seul; l'auteur n'avait pas grand succès.
> Ce n'était que Molière, et nous savons de reste
> Que ce grand maladroit, qui fit un jour Alceste,
> Ignora le bel art de chatouiller l'esprit
> Et de servir à point un dénoûment bien cuit.
> Grâce à Dieu, nos auteurs ont changé de méthode,
> Et nous aimons bien mieux quelque drame à la mode.
> Où l'intrigue, enlacée et roulée en feston,
> Tourne comme un rébus autour d'un mirliton'

is a thing of the past, and not only provincials, and foreigners bent on *la culture française*, flood to fill the theatre's red-and-gilt seats, but Parisians also, particularly, of course, for the production of new plays (André Gide's 'Les Caves du Vatican in 1952). One can even occasionally identify in the boxes statesmen watching a renewed Molière comedy (M. Edouard Herriot, ex-President of the National Assembly, at *Monsieur de Pourceaugnac* in the 'fifties). The audiences of the Théâtre-Français take the performances very seriously (often parents bring their families in the cause of general education) and at times betray something of the breathless awe which opera-goers, in Vienna and German cities, bring with them to a performance of Wagner. The audiences, extraordinarily mixed, give as good a cross-section as any of the theatre-going public in Paris. Revolutionary and unstable as they are so often accused of being, the French manifest enduring respect for national institutions that represent the deep cultural tradition which looms so large in their vision of the outstanding merit of their country and people.

The Comédie Française, though it stands on a plane of its own, is but one of the fifty theatres in Paris; one of them, the Palais de Chaillot, a state-controlled institution like the Comédie Française and, like it, producing classical plays, is the largest theatre in Europe. Altogether no less than forty-six thousand seats (to say nothing of those in the music halls and cabarets, etc.) are available in the capital, a figure surprisingly high when it is remembered that the population of Paris is less than a third of that province-covered-with-houses called London. Though the Comédie Française stands aloof from ordinary commercial production, it would be a grave error to assume that all the other theatres preoccupy themselves entirely with provision of amusements on commercial lines. The vast majority of foreign tourists in Paris seek most frequently, and most willingly, the spectacular, elaborately presented, decorative musicals, with their well-drilled bevies of beautiful chorus girls (often British, for English girls, it is said, take more willingly to that kind of exacting team work). What the French theatre so often indulges in, the drama of thought, turning on the problems which beset people who try to understand why life is what it is, must naturally be a closed book to those whose knowledge of French is rudimentary. If the ear finds little, except the musical accompaniment, in a foreign theatre, the pleasure of the eye must be thoroughly exploited, and it is with this in view that the huge Châtelet Theatre and the music halls like the Folies-Bergère and the Casino de Paris must serve an 'eyeful'. In addition many theatres—like the Palais Royal—provide plays intended for an audience which possesses mastery of the French language and which wants to be amused, not to be called upon to reflect deeply on the enigmas of life. A long succession of French dramatists from Labiche to Robert de Flers and Caillavet, from Bernstein to Robert de Létraz, have specialized in intriguing and amusing the spectator and sometimes shocking him pleasurably. They have polished and perfected the technique for providing the Palais-Royal Theatre with its latest risky but harmless comedy. Some of the most successful authors of to-day, like André Roussin, who had three plays running at the same time in London in 1950 and the translation of whose 'La Petite Hutte' soon proved a success with the London theatre-goers, provide more gaiety than provocation of deep thought—as the Rattigan of 'French Without Tears' provided in England.

During the hundred years that preceded the First World War, and in spite of many political upheavals, the society which was mirrored in the French theatre had undergone no fundamental transformation since the Revolution of 1789. It was governed by a set of well-established moral values, as changeless and stable, it seemed, as the value of the *louis d'or*. Its structure was an internal hierarchy, not so rigid as to divide society into water-tight compartments but which presupposed the principle of authority: authority of parents over their children, of the husband over his wife, of the master over his servant, of the employer over the workman. This solid bastion was surrounded on all sides by a wall of accepted social conventions and a moat of decorum.

Around this external barrier the lighter-hearted and wittier among French playwrights carried out a great deal of frolicking, happy skirmishing, dart-throwing and ditch-jumping. One need but mention the delightful, often delightfully naughty, comedies of Meilhac and Halévy, Courteline, R. de Flers and Caillavet, and Francis de Croisset.

Inside the fortress, however, the spirit of evolution was slowly making itself felt. In this evolution, the theatre played a double part: it reflected changes and it spurred them on. On the one hand foreign influences, notably those of Ibsen and Strindberg, on the other the logical development of French Revolution ideals, led French playwrights to probe into such problems as social inequality (as in François de Curel's *Le repas du lion*), inequality of the sexes (as in Henry Bataille's *Marche nuptiale*, Maurice Donnay's *L'Affranchie*, etc.), divorce, strikes, family relationships, etc. The *théâtre d'idées* of the 'nineties and of the first years of the twentieth century centred mostly around Antoine's Théâtre Libre (1887). It registered a great deal of fluttering and beating against the bars of the cage—now and then some hero or heroine managed to squeeze through the bars, generally to his or her damage. Jean, in *Le repas du lion*, is killed by the strikers whom he wanted to befriend; in *La Marche nuptiale*, Grace de Plassans, disillusioned about the man for whom she has braved convention, kills herself—a reminiscence of Strindberg's *Mademoiselle Julie*. That was 'the revenge of society'.

The First World War shook the bars of the cage and they fell off at the Second. The whole structure of society was shaken, the principle of authority weakened, while the moral values of the past were subjected to ruthless reassessment. This change reflects itself in the theatre, in the radical transformation which has come over it since 1920, and especially since 1940.

In some respects the modern theatre outstrips reality. Not only does it spurn social conventions as mere vestigia, but it takes an aggressive pleasure in tramping down decorum and making the bourgeois shudder in his boots. It blurts out, unblushingly, what genteel folk prefer to leave unsaid, and if possible unthought, and it expresses the stark truth in even starker terms. It is illuminating, in that respect, to compare the first scene of the two versions of Jean Anouilh's *Colombe*, that given in Paris, and the softened version given in London. In the first one, Julien is a harsh, boorish, thoroughly unpleasant young man, Mme Georges, the dresser, is a well-

R

meaning old bore who blethers for ever about her infirmities, and Colombe, shy and unhappy, hardly opens her mouth. In the second, Julian and Colombe are a couple of cooing doves, the dresser a garrulous but harmless old thing, and this, incidentally, falsifies to some extent the dénouement of the play. Julian, more lovable, becomes less pathetic, since it is Julian's tragedy that no one can love him, except perhaps—and this is the unkindest cut of all—his charming, careless, universally popular brother who supersedes him so effortlessly in the heart of Colombe, his young wife.

Among contemporary French playwrights there are at least three well-marked trends, according to whether the play is conceived primarily as a symbol, as the illustration of a philosophical, moral or psychological problem, or as the development of a dramatic situation.

'The world', says Paul Claudel (1868-1955), 'is a temple where man moves through a forest of symbols.' To him, the only possible answer to human problems is a religious, even a mystic one. It lies in communion with the divine forces which are at work in every human and behind every event. Under the extraordinary luxuriance of his dramas always looms the stern doctrine of redemption at the expense of self-renunciation. These dramas are set against a highly stylized background which gives them, as it were, their moral atmosphere: the mystical, cathedral-building Middle Ages of *L'Annonce faite à Marie*; the sense of world adventure and discovery which pervades the sixteenth-century Spain of *Le Soulier de satin*; the antagonism between past and present under Napoleon's reign in *L'Otage*. His characters are hieratic and symbolical; their language has a Biblical rhythm, an easy flowing poetry with sudden familiar twists, everyday images and expressions that give it a peculiar and inimitable flavour. Claudel's plays—written in the moments of leisure left by his life as an ambassador, and not primarily intended for the stage—run counter to all the traditions of the French theatre with the apparent looseness of their plot, the multitude of characters, the extravagant stage-directions. Their success has been tremendous, especially in the case of *Le Soulier de satin* (thus named because the sorely tempted heroine places one of her satin shoes in the hands of the Virgin as a symbolical pledge), which was produced for the first time in 1943, in German-occupied Paris.

Among those contemporary dramatists who see the world in terms of philosophical problems which they try to solve or at least to resolve into terms of human reality, the most representative are perhaps—one a Catholic and the other an atheist —Gabriel Marcel and Jean-Paul Sartre. Both belong to the Existentialist movement, of which all that need be said here is that it claims to have evolved a new system of ethics implying a novel conception of being and of liberty.

Sartre, who with Camus and Simone de Beauvoir forms the core of the Existentialist group, came into prominence as a talented dramatist with the end of the Second World War, and his first plays reflect the bitterness engendered by German occupation. After the war, Sartre was the first contemporary French writer whose plays were performed on the London stage. His *Huis clos* ('Vicious Circle') was broadcast several times in the B.B.C. programmes. The play takes place in Hell, symbolized by a room furnished in hideous Victorian (Second Empire) style. It consists of a single uninterrupted scene in which the three characters—who are dead—talk together for an hour and a half, discovering gradually who they are, what has brought them there, and what insidious form eternal punishment is going to take. That is Sartre's conception of Hell: three people locked together, like three square pegs in one round hole, expiating the crimes of their earthly existence by the perspective of an eternity of mutually inflicted frustration and boredom. They cannot help each other. If they could, they would have to be different, and if they were different, they would not be in Hell. As one of the characters, Inès, puts it, 'in this labour-saving Hell the inmates have to do the work themselves, as in a self-service restaurant'.

In *Les Mains sales* (1948), Sartre turns the searchlight on the abnormalities resulting from the resurgence of barbarous instincts in the fabric of civilized life. The problem is whether or not a man has the right to kill another man for the ultimate benefit of humanity as decided by the political party to which they both belong. The issue is further complicated because Sartre, apparently throwing a spanner in the wheels of his own argument, gives his hero an intimate personal motive for the assassination he has undertaken on the orders of the party. Has the murderer acted from idealistic motives, or has he yielded to a purely animal instinct in eliminating a rival? For his own self-respect he clings wildly to the first theory, but the only means he has of proving it is his own death. For reasons easy to understand, these *débats de conscience* loom large in the post-war French theatre.

Gabriel Marcel, a Catholic but not a mystic, excels in reducing a complex situation to a neat philosophical problem. His strongly marked moral preoccupation is probably one of the reasons for his success in England, where many of his plays have been broadcast. A good example of his technique is *L'Homme de Dieu*. Problem: What happens when a man whose mission in life is to preach forgiveness of injuries—in this case a Protestant minister—finds himself the victim of an unforgivable injury? The fact that the core of Marcel's plays is a philosophical problem gives them perhaps at times a touch of mechanical artificiality, but does not detract from the subtle observation and brilliant, if sinuous, argumentation.

Other dramatists, faced by the same perplexities, have tried to solve them in a different way. They turn to the eternal, essential patterns offered by the ancient Greek myths and legends through which they endeavour to decipher the baffling complexity of contemporary reality. The theme of man's blind struggle against an incomprehensible and relentless fate appears through Jean Cocteau's revised version of the legend of Oedipus in *La Machine infernale* (1934). The theme of Antigone—sublime devotion to duty impersonated by Antigone versus public order personified by Creon—appealed to Cocteau and to Anouilh: Anouilh's play, performed during the German occupation, took from the circumstances a particularly deep and immediate significance. This is also true of Sartre's *Les Mouches*, which revives the story of Orestes and the eternal problem of patriotic murder. In this rather obscure and diffuse play, Sartre exposes in a dialogue between Jupiter and Aegisthus his conception of liberty: 'Men are free, Aegisthus. You know it, and they don't.' Free, that is free to choose between any two courses of action without being answerable to any one but themselves.

In a different mood, a few years before, in 1935, Jean Giraudoux had treated a not dissimilar question. In *La Guerre de Troie n'aura pas lieu* he ironically reduces the theme of war to the smallest common denominator, applicable both to the Trojan war and, among others, to Franco-German relations. The cogitations of the Greeks, the perplexities of the Trojans, the diplomatic see-saw, the eternal arguments in favour of war and against war, are given added urgency and piquancy by the lingering illusion that things are still in the making, that the Trojan war, after all, is not inevitable, that a commission may still be appointed to settle the dispute, that Greek wisdom or Trojan humanity may still find a way out.

That the future of Franco-German relations haunted Giraudoux is apparent in another play of his: *Siegfried et le Limousin* (adapted from the novel of the same name). Siegfried is a Frenchman who, wounded and having lost his memory, becomes a German and attains a high position in his new country; he finds himself faced with the problem of rediscovering France and his former self through his acquired German self. It needed Giraudoux's whimsical and charming turn of mind—which later gave itself full play in *La Folle de Chaillot*—to tread lightly upon such burning ground.

Both *Siegfried* and *La Guerre de Troie*, like so many of the best plays between 1928 and 1950, were produced by the great actor and manager Louis Jouvet, one of the most important figures of the French stage during that period. Among other successes, he created the title-part in Jules Romains' *Knock*, a robust comedy in the true Molière vein. (*Knock* is probably, together with René Fauchois' *Prenez garde à la peinture* adapted in English under the title 'The late Christopher Bean', the most widely appreciated and most often performed French play in Great Britain. They are both in the French tradition of the *comédie de mœurs*, a rich and apparently inexhaustible vein.

Alone, and practically equidistant from the two principal groups already mentioned, stands Henry de Montherlant, aristocrat, matador, playwright, the conscious high priest of pride and strength. His themes are not unlike Claudel's, but he solves them by pride, not by saintliness. His language aims at, and sometimes attains, a dark, lyrical magnificence. Spain, the last stronghold of feudal pride, is his land of predilection. In *Le Maître de Santiago*, set in sixteenth-century Spain, he evokes the figure of an impecunious and intensely proud grandee, Don Alvaro Daro. His poverty, besides being infinitely galling to a man of his rank, stands in the way of the happiness of his daughter Mariana, unable to marry the man she loves. There are gold-mines in Spain's American colonies —why not do as many have done, sail westward and make a fortune? His daughter, his friends, urge him to do so. He refuses angrily, hating colonization on principle and scorning what he would consider an ill-acquired fortune. But the crux of the matter is that Mariana, against all the forces of youth and love, rallies to his point of view and voluntarily resigns herself to share his haughty life of solitude and penury. The success of the play was mostly due to the character of Mariana, whom one critic called 'the most ideal figure of the contemporary theatre'.

Equally apart stands François Mauriac, who turned to the stage rather late in life, after having made a reputation as one of France's foremost novelists. His plays, *Asmodée* (1938), *Les Mal aimés* (1945), *Le Passage du malin* (1947), show the same qualities of grim, relentless intensity, the same deep psychological insight as his novels, and generally develop the same kind of theme, that of a set, stable, conservative *milieu* in which a new and disturbing element is suddenly introduced.

The younger generation of French dramatists, well known in Great Britain since the war, brings a much more complex and often strikingly original contribution. The war, the profound cleavage and the bitterness engendered by the German occupation, left a deep mark on the post-war theatre.

Sartre's *Les Morts sans sépulture*, Salacrou's *Les Nuits de la colère*; *L'Etat de Siège*, by Camus; and indirectly *Montserrat*, by Emmanuel Roblès, which evokes the drama of hostages under enemy occupation, are a few of the plays which reflect the post-war mentality.

Armand Salacrou's *Les Nuits de la colère* (broadcast by the B.B.C. in 1946 under the title 'Men in Darkness') is a grim Resistance drama, beginning with a gangster-like scene in which a couple of pro-German collaborators are shot. The whole story—how a man can be brought to give away his oldest friend—is worked out by the flash-back, retrospective method which films have made familiar to us. Much of the dialogue turns on the problem of different conceptions of patriotism under alien occupation, but the dramatic handling is so skilful that abstraction is avoided. A definite concreteness is given to the problem by the contrasting pictures of friendship between two families before 1941 and their enmity after the occupation. The play, surprisingly, ends on an optimistic note rarely found in Salacrou's plays, whether pre-war or post-war. His pre-war plays, among which *Une Femme libre* (1934), *L'Inconnue d'Arras* (1935), and his post-war plays, *Les Fiancés du Havre, L'Archipel Lenoir, Dieu le savait* deal with moral problems to which he finds no answer in religion or anything else—'little closed worlds', as he calls them. He is astringent and not afraid of being unpleasant; his dialogue is witty, often extremely funny, with more than a touch of satire towards the middle-class conception of life, but this does not deflect from the intense seriousness of his themes, nor from the shrewd observation that goes to the making of his characters.

Jean Anouilh—who had in recent years the unusual experience of having as many as three of his plays performed simultaneously in London—has, on the contrary, sedulously avoided any reference to actuality. He has himself divided his plays into *Pièces noires* and *Pièces roses*, which gives a fair idea of his two-sided conception of life—although there is definitely more *noir* than *rose*. He excels in clothing painful situations under a disguise of sparkling wit and debonair invention; his plays give the impression of being etched out with acid and daubed over with poster paint, an unusual but effective combination. A recurrent theme is that of escape, escape from the fetters of self, family and society. It is the subject of *Y avait un prisonnier*, the story of the home-coming of a liberated convict whose respectable family immediately attempts to imprison him in a sort of moral jail; it is also the subject of *Le voyageur sans bagages*, where a man who has lost his memory and is claimed by tearful relatives feels nothing but aversion for the past which is thrust upon him and yearns for the freedom of forgetfulness. *Colombe*, already mentioned, is based on the story of Sarah Bernhardt, but whether by design or by chance it is the blonde heroine who steals the show, and not the tragedy queen. Among his *Pièces roses*, one must mention *Le Bal des voleurs*, a dazzling and most deftly handled fantasy, and *L'Invitation au château* ('Ring Round the Moon') which revolves round the formidable Mme des Mermortes in her wheel chair, while the twin brothers, Horace and Frédéric, keep up a whirlwind of imbroglios, mystification, mistaken identities, and the rival beauties, Isabelle and Diane, flutter tantalizingly in and out.

One of the most striking traits in most of the contemporary plays on the French stage is the apparent looseness and carelessness of the construction, all the more remarkable if one compares it with the solid structure and careful finish of the nineteenth and early twentieth centuries. Henry Becque, one feels, or even Maurice Donnay, would have thrown up their hands in horror at the incursions of the scene-shifters, the sudden impudent and disconcerting changes of time and place, the different scenes acted simultaneously in various parts of the stage, the jolts, the flash-backs. The whole technique certainly owes a great deal to the technique of the cinema, but probably also to the Impressionist and Surrealist schools of painting.

While it is impossible in this brief study to treat all to-day's dramatists as they deserve, it is equally impossible not to mention the names of such successful writers as Jean-Jacques Bernard, whose *Martine* was so popular that lots of little French girls born at the time were christened with her name, or Marcel Pagnol, whose *Topaze*, and Marseillais heroes, Marius and César, brought so many guffaws to theatre audiences before setting out on their hilarious career in the cinema.

In contrast with the relative eclipse of the novel in France since the Second World War, the contemporary French theatre shows great vitality, originality and daring. This is, of course, primarily because of a fortunate chance: the simultaneous presence of authors endowed with an original mind. But other elements are involved: the French attitude to the theatre. Frenchmen take the stage seriously—let us not forget the battle of the *Cid* and the battle of *Hernani*. A performance is really a creation of something 'précieux et ardent', as Jules Romains said, 'a communion between the author, the actors and the public, a fever of expectation, a thrill in common.'

Moreover, there was the war and the German occupation, that gave theatrical performances a new meaning and a spiritual significance. In this atmosphere of repression a play would sometimes stir up latent electricity, phrases would take on an edge that maybe the author had not intended. The French public, always ready to perceive allusions, would release its pent-up feelings by thunderous applause at a phrase of which every Frenchman understood the double meaning, applause which left the 'visitors' vaguely uneasy. Some plays, like Anouilh's *Antigone*, derived from the circumstances a deep significance that has since vanished.

The theatre serves both as a safety-valve and as a pressure gauge. Under the baffling variety of subjects, the ephemeral and the eternal, the frivolous and the serious, the definitely naughty and the uncompromisingly stern, one may discern the will of modern men and women to adapt themselves, not only to a new world, but to a perpetually changing world, and to get hold of what eternal values may have escaped the great slump.

READING LIST

Ambrière, F. *La Galerie dramatique.* Paris 1949.
Bellesort, A. *Le plaisir du théâtre.* Paris 1938.
Dussane, B. *Notes de théâtre.* Paris 1951.

Gautier, J. J.   *Paris sur scène.*   Paris 1951.
Hobson, H.   *The French Theatre.   An English View.*   London 1953.
   An excellent work.   After a preliminary survey it deals with
   Sartre, Salacrou, H. de Montherlant and Anouilh.   Useful
   list of Works on contemporary French drama.
Lalou, R.   *Le Théâtre en France depuis 1900.*   Paris 1951.
Pillemont, G.   *Anthologie du Théâtre français contemporain.*   3 vols.
   Paris 1945-48

CHAPTER XIII

LITERATURE: FIVE VIGNETTES

LITERATURE is not only the flower of civilization but part of
its tissue and its most enduring asset. It is not our purpose, nor
would it be possible in the limited space of one chapter, to give
a history of French literature. We can merely indicate one
or two distinctive features and take 'soundings'—cast into the
form of vignettes—of five French writers. Selection is perforce
arbitrary and cannot be expected to satisfy everyone. We
have taken samples in depth as well as on the surface. While
Montaigne and Proust are universally valid—like Molière,
Chateaubriand or Balzac—and represent a point of view that
could easily shape itself into any other European consciousness, Racine, Flaubert and Mauriac represent something that
could hardly have grown anywhere east of the Rhine or south
of the Pyrenees. The perpetual effervescence of literary
schools and coteries tends at times to obscure the persistent
characteristics of the French mind. The two outstanding
features are the humanist tendency and the high standard of
literary expression.

Every literature, of course, has man as its main object.
English literature gives much attention to man and nature,
German more to man and the infinite, while Russian stresses
the conquest of himself by man. French literature is interested in man (including woman), for himself, a vast and ever-
renewed curiosity, devoid of inhibitions, as to all the forms of
human life and aspects of human consciousness. It is the development of the classical French tradition of the moralists
and psychologists, distrusting the display of sentiment, and
often pessimistic lest they appear naïve. This curiosity reveals
itself as not averse to cynicism, scepticism or scoffing. Nowhere has it been so difficult as in France to confine writers
in the strait-jacket of conventions. Even at a time when
religious passions were still smouldering and ever ready for an

opportunity to burst into flame, Racine found a useful alibi in Greek history and perhaps even in Athaliah's outrageous challenge to God.

However unwilling to submit to any other kind of convention, French literature has respected the rules of art. The French literary genius has flourished because art has traditionally imposed a measure of constraint. Some may consider that the 'Celtic tendency' to dispersion and discursiveness has been checked by a classical sense of form. French writers are averse to indulging in vagueness as synonymous with depth. Mystery and the twilight atmosphere are comparatively rare in French prose literature. The ideal is the clear, limpid sentence without repetition or digression. In this respect Proust is not typical, but is as much preoccupied with literary art as the traditional French prose-writers.

MICHEL DE MONTAIGNE, 1533-1592

'C'est un sujet merveilleusement vain, ondoyant et divers que l'homme.'

Montaigne, speaking of books, says: 'C'est la meilleure munition que j'aie trouvée à cet humain voyage.' After more than three and a half centuries, his own Essays remain an eminently companionable choice for the 'humain voyage' because, as his 'spiritual daughter', Mlle de Gournay, said, 'il désenseigne la sottise'.

Among the foolish notions of which he purges the human mind are intolerance and fear. Unfortunately, they crop up again at each generation, foolishness being inherent in human nature. Our own generation, heavily beset with such evils, resorts in despair to drugs, frontal leucotomy and psychoanalysis. Montaigne's method is more leisurely and also less humiliating for the patient. At no time does he assume the attitude of the veterinary surgeon to a sick beast. Kindly, painlessly, ironically he lifts the burden off the soul of man and sets him free.

The Essays enjoyed from the first a notable popularity in

England, where their empirical and unsystematic spirit did them no disservice. (Also, the fact that Montaigne appears to have been a cat-lover may well have endeared him to English hearts!) Ben Jonson had read the Essays; Florio's English translation is one of the two books known for certain to have belonged to Shakespeare.

Into an age resounding with the clash of fierce theological disputes, Montaigne brought a modern spirit of amused, sceptical, almost experimental detachment. His charm lies in his friendliness and spontaneity, his delightful way of telling anecdotes, his shrewd irony, the infinite variety of his subjects, and still more in the engaging and disarming frankness with which he takes us into his confidence, with details that in another might seem trivial: how he always dressed in black or white, never was much good at husbandry, never tired on horseback, had excellent teeth, of which he lost one in his fifties, and suffered grievously at times from gallstones. These details spring up in the course of argument, not so much out of sheer egotism as because he is after all the specimen of humanity nearest at hand and which he knows best.

This knowledge of himself, nourished with the wisdom of the ancients, was backed by a wide experience of men. He had not always viewed life from the beloved seclusion of the library in his manor; he had travelled, he had been a magistrate, mayor of Bordeaux, the friend and adviser of princes and kings. (Nowadays, he would be a senator, *centre droit*, ex-minister, and he would probably be prevailed upon in a time of national stress to head a coalition government!)

Beneath the pleasant disorder of the Essays (much of which is due to successive additions), and under their appearance of leisurely detachment, they are more militant than would seem at first sight. They could not have been written by a cold philosopher, and Montaigne was humane. The piteous cry of a hare under the hound's teeth went to his heart; he hated to see children maltreated, and it is with sincere indignation that he condemns the treatment of the native American populations by their Spanish conquerors. Yet he lived in times of intolerance and cruelty. His own province of Périgord, like the rest of France, was torn by religious strife and ablaze with civil war. He refused to take part in the struggle; he was himself a Catholic, his brother had become a Protestant—that, he considered, was no reason for cutting each other's throats.

Back in his manor of Montaigne, up in his tower and alone in his library with his friends—Seneca the Stoic, Lucretius the Epicurean, Plutarch and many others—his readings and his thoughts organized themselves around his dominant preoccupation: intolerance, the source of fanaticism and cruelty.

Montaigne is no Don Quixote and tilts no lance at any windmills. He much preferred sapping the ground unobtrusively under the enemy and laying delayed-action mines. At the same time he sedulously avoided trespassing on religious ground, and his point of view is strictly *laïc*. Instead of denouncing intolerance as criminal, he ridiculed it as absurd. The amiably perverse delight he took in piling up examples of grotesque and contradictory opinions, beliefs and customs, his sarcastic parallel between human and animal intellect, all tended to expose the futility of man's stubborn pride in his own opinion. It is not in the power of man, argues Montaigne, to attain absolute certainty about anything—unless, he adds piously, human reason be enlightened by divine revelation. We may remember that Montaigne, although a Catholic and to all appearances a devout one, belonged to that long-civilized and cultured south-west of France where various heresies—the Arian, the Manichean—had flourished until driven underground by persecution. Dogmatic creeds are apt to lose some of their value when several have appeared in succession. Doubt, philosophic doubt, which takes in every possibility and rejects none *a priori*, suited Montaigne's easy-going temperament as well as it satisfied his shrewd mind. He would say with St. Augustine, 'qu'il vaut mieux pencher vers le doute que vers l'assurance en choses de difficile preuve et dangereuse créance'.

Therefore, since nothing is more precious than life and more futile or changeful than men's opinions, what justification is there, asks Montaigne, for burning a man alive for a matter of opinion? The question, pertinent in the sixteenth century, is not less so in ours, where burning at the stake has been replaced by more perfected methods of mass destruction. For, among general uncertainty and perpetual transformation, one thing is certain, at least temporarily: it is life, and life is good, although hedged with pain and death and with their natural consequence, fear.

It was with the intention of fortifying himself against the idea of death that Montaigne began writing extracts from his favourite authors, particularly the Stoics, and adding his own comments. He soon found that the art of living was a pleasanter and more profitable subject of meditation than the art of dying. He refused to see life as a valley of tears. A great many evils, he argued, exist merely in our opinion, and why fret to death about them when a gentle, reasoned dose of scepticism would go such a long way to alleviate or even nullify them? There remain pain and death, both unavoidable. One may steel oneself to face them unflinchingly. That is the way of the Stoics, whom he admired. He himself, when 'marvellously tormented' by his nephritic pains, endeavoured to bear them smilingly or at worst 'gémir sans brailler'. In the thick of the civil war he went on living in his manor without guard or garrison. (He even tells a very pretty story of how one of his neighbours once nearly took advantage of it.)

Even then, the Epicurean comes, as it were, to the help of the Stoic. The same gentle scepticism which does away with 'evils of opinion' can rob pain and death of most of their terrors. Nothing in the Essays is more entertaining than Montaigne discussing the pros and cons of his own painful disease and concluding that on the whole it has its points, if only the delightful moments of abatement. In any case, the mind of the sage, he affirms, should be his inner citadel, where he should be sole master and where no evils could reach him.

A selfish ideal, some may object. And since no cause is worth burning a man alive for, does it not follow fairly logically that no cause is worth dying for? Pascal, whose soul was that of an ascetic and a hero, looked down upon Montaigne's endeavours to pad with scepticism the rough edges of life. Yet, those who taunt Montaigne with his famous remark that any disguise, even a calf's hide—meaning, it may be presumed, feigned stupidity—is legitimate to save oneself from blows, forget that he holds intrepidity to be the best safeguard in danger, and those who charge him with selfishness forget with what depth of feeling he spoke of friendship and of his long-lost friend Etienne de la Boétie. The Essays are not a handbook of sanctity; they have been more justly called 'le bréviaire de l'honnête homme'. Montaigne holds that nature is good and that one cannot err by following her guidance; he proposes an ideal of quiet stoicism tempered by irony, of broad-mindedness and justice, of reasonable optimism. Even now, it is not unworthy of a trial.

Villon, Montaigne, Rabelais all laboured under a similar difficulty: that of a language in the making and as yet unequal to its task. Villon's language is only just emerging from mediaeval French, it has the charm as well as the angular naïveté of primitive paintings. With Rabelais and Montaigne, the problem was slightly different; the French language of their times was but a promising sapling, not strong enough yet to carry the weight of philosophical thought and psychological research. It had to be bolstered up with Latin props.[1] It was also subjected to a variety of experimental graftings and prunings by Rabelais, Montaigne and the poets of the Pléiade. Towards the middle of the seventeenth century it had reached its full growth; it had shed its mediaevalisms, Latinisms and provincialisms, as well as the angularities of its syntax. Words had attained the full strength of their meaning at the same time as the French mind was reaching the adult state, emerging from the obscurities of the Middle Ages and from the heady ferment of the Renaissance.

> Ce que l'on conçoit bien s'énonce clairement,
> Et les mots pour le dire arrivent aisément,

wrote Boileau in his *Art Poétique*. Flaubert, the 'martyr of style' at a later period of language transformation, must often have pulled a wry face at this dictum. But indeed the 'mot

[1] In Calvin's *Institution Chrétienne* the Latin shows clearly under the French.

juste' which cost Flaubert such agonies of seeking and waiting seems to flow effortlessly from the seventeenth-century quill pens. And this is not only true of professional writers. Louis XIV, who had had so little schooling, wrote with concision and a natural dignified elegance; his letters, his Instructions to his grandson, Philip V of Spain, are models of style as well as of mature political thought. Saint-Evremond, Gilberte Pascal,[1] Mme de Sévigné, the elder Mademoiselle,[2] Saint-Simon all wrote with a natural ease which is sometimes perfection itself.

The trend of the language is all towards concision, elegance and clarity. Pascal, in one of his *Provinciales*, regrets not having been able to make it shorter, owing to lack of time. La Rochefoucauld distils his maxims, lopping off a word here and there, while La Fontaine knows better than anyone how to obtain a maximum of effect with a minimum of words.

JEAN RACINE, 1639-1699

There exists at Langres, a portrait of Racine in his early thirties, probably about the time of his *Mithridate* and therefore at the height of his glory, before age had imparted to his features a ponderous majesty reminiscent of his august patron Louis XIV; a handsome face, refined and aristocratic, and yet full of torment. A depth of bitterness, of repressed longing lies behind the cool ironical glance with its faint suggestion of supremely well-bred insolence, while the fine, sensitive, disdainful mouth seems about to fling a stinging retort. He had, in fact, the most mordant wit in France, and his epigrams were deadly.

Given the necessary equipment, there are few better schools for a future psychologist than a youth spent among mystics with an exacerbated sense of sin. Racine's youth was spent among the Jansenists—those puritans and mystics whose disputes with the Jesuits have been immortalized by Pascal's *Provinciales*. From sixteen to nineteen, he studied, mostly the classics, at Port Royal, fountain-head of Jansenist doctrine

---

[1] Blaise Pascal's eldest sister.
[2] This is Mlle de Montpensier, author of entertaining *Mémoires*.

S

in France. His masters were kind and immensely learned; later he railed bitterly at them in revenge for their outspoken disapproval of the career he had chosen—one of them even going so far as to denounce all playwrights as 'public poisoners, not of bodies but of souls'. Yet, Port Royal and its 'vallon solitaire' ever remained in his thoughts as a haunt of holiness and peace.

Much of his subsequent life is a matter for conjecture. though recent research has brought further light. Thanks mostly to a few allusions in Mme de Sévigné's letters, one can more or less reconstitute a picture of the ten most brilliant years in his career: his successes, starting with the triumph of his tragedy *Andromaque*, which overnight eclipsed Corneille's glory; his love-affairs; echoes of cabals and rivalries, and then, at the age of thirty-seven, his sudden, surprising and never fully explained renunciation. He gave up play-writing and sought a reconciliation with his former Jansenist friends; he even thought of entering monastic orders, then, on second thoughts, married a good, pious woman who had never read and apparently never did read a line of his. The most important events of his later life were the court performances of *Esther* and *Athalie*, two Bible plays which he wrote at the request of Mme de Maintenon, Louis XIV's consort, for the young ladies' school she had founded at St. Cyr. During his last years the King's partiality for him had cooled; his dying wish was to be buried at Port Royal, at the feet of one of his former masters—a gesture of fidelity but also a tacit protest against a disfavour which had been deeply felt.

A man of intense and passionate feelings, he was always guided and often led by his emotions. In fact, the Jansenists, for all their rigidity, lived in an atmosphere supercharged with emotion; it was their friend, Pascal, who said that the heart has its reasons which reason does not know. There are two sides to the seventeenth century: one, with Corneille and Descartes, believes in logic and the triumph of human reason, while the other seeks to humble the pride of reason and to stress the need for divine guidance. Yet Racine's name remains indissolubly linked with that of Corneille, his illustrious elder and predecessor, not only because they are France's greatest tragic poets, but because, in their totally different ways, they so penetrated, more than any other writers, into the French national mind as to be inseparable from it.

To the average Anglo-Saxon, French classical tragedy, with its almost empty stage on which characters in antique garb explain their *états d'âme* in Alexandrines, without so much as the irruption of a troupe of strolling players or of an occasional drunkard to brighten up the proceedings, is the least accessible form of French culture; his first reaction is to contrast it to its detriment with the English Elizabethan drama. On closer acquaintance he may relent in favour of Corneille, but Racine's genuine admirers have been few on this side of the Channel before the twentieth century, even though they include such names as that of Meredith. Contrarily to what happened in England, French drama had not found its highest expression in the unfettered exuberance of the sixteenth century; it found it under a slowly evolved system of voluntary restrictions. French tragedy, tense and sharply focused, concentrates upon the crucial moment of the story; its climax arises from the inner debates and decisions of the characters, and it drives straight to its end, unrelieved, but also unhampered, by jocular soldiery or playful peasantry.

Corneille made the tragedy a drama of conflicting loyalties in strong and resolute souls, on the theme of self-fulfilment through self-renunciation. The choice—love or duty, martyrdom or happiness—might be agonizing, but still it was free, guided by reason, sustained by will-power. He rather sidetracked that most unruly of emotions, love, by granting it merely secondary status, so to speak, and placing it under the strict tutelage of reason. Racine restored it to its despotic independence as the dominant interest in drama. Moreover, in his view, human behaviour depended far more on temperament, inclinations and passions than on reason, which he sees as the dupe or the slave of passion. Yet most of his characters are highly intelligent people who know exactly what they are doing. Passion may deprive them of their judgment, it does not impair their lucidity. With the impartial accuracy of the seismograph needle, their conscious mind registers the flutters of hope, the convulsions of jealousy, the paroxysms of vengeance. In this sense, Racine could define his *Phèdre* as 'the most reasonable thing I ever put on the stage': Phaedra, carried away by a passion stronger than her will, still sees herself and judges herself like a tortured but lucid patient noting the progress of an inexorable disease.

The plots as well as the characters reflect this unequal struggle. Except in the case of *Athalie*, which stands in a class apart since its hero Joad, the inspired prophet, fights God's own battle with God's own arms, the pattern of Racine's tragedies is invariably one of cold calculations or wise forethought either foiled by the sincerity of sentiment or wrecked by the wild incalculability of passion. Thus Acomat's astutely woven conspiracy in favour of Bajazet is wrecked by Roxana's insane jealousy, while, in *Britannicus*, Agrippina's long-term diplomacy crumbles like a card castle in a draught. *Phèdre* alone has next to no plot; it is a solitary flare-up, the last stage of a consuming passion. Such a conception excludes any notion of free choice: Racine's plays are like gathering thunderstorms. While he cared little for the bludgeonings of logic, a fascinated curiosity led him to probe into the motives of those unwarrantable acts of violence or despair which the Ancients attributed to fate or to divine vengeance and which nowadays justify a plea of temporary insanity. In spite of the title, the principal female character of *Andromaque* is not so much Hector's widow, gentle Andromache, as fierce, fiendish and yet pathetic little Hermione, maddened by jealousy for Pyrrhus to whom she is betrothed and who has forsaken her for Andromache, his captive. The situation is rather different in Euripides, but Racine disliked the idea of his Andromache reduced to the condition of concubine. In vain does Hermione endeavour to touch Pyrrhus's heart, in vain does she beat her fists against an invisible wall, rave, storm, cajole, threaten:

> '. . . Perfide, je le voi,
> Tu comptes les moments que tu perds avec moi!
> Ton cœur, impatient de revoir ta Troyenne,
> Ne souffre qu'à regret qu'une autre t'entretienne.

Tu lui parles du cœur, tu la cherches des yeux,
Je ne te retiens plus, sauve-toi de ces lieux:
Va lui jurer la foi que tu m'avois jurée.'

In sheer violence, nothing on the French stage goes beyond
the dreadful scenes in which Hermione, trembling with jealous
fury, urges her unwanted lover, Orestes, to kill Pyrrhus,
threatening him with a possible reversion of her feelings:

'S'il ne meurt aujourd'hui, je puis l'aimer demain.'

and then, once Pyrrhus is dead, turns with frenzied despair
against his murderer:

'Pourquoi l'assassiner? Qu'a-t-il fait? A quel titre?
Qui te l'a dit?'

Even then, Racine remained Port Royal's spiritual if erring
son. The essence of his drama is passion conceived as a force
of corruption and decay, a cancer of the soul which destroys
every feeling, even the instinct of self-preservation, and leads
through intense suffering to crime and death. There can be
found in its entirety the pessimistic Jansenist doctrine of the
essential fragility and corruption of man unless redeemed by
special divine grace.

Corneille's psychology is the psychology of victory, with all
its eventually crippling limitations. The word victory had no
sense for a Jansenist mind: the only victory that mattered
being the victory of God, and all other triumphs being un-
desirable, a source of satanic pride.

Racine liked Greek legends with their aura of fabulous
poetry. Euripides was his model for *Andromaque, Iphigénie, Phèdre*.
His contemporaries blamed him for making his Greeks and
Bajazet's Turks too modern and too French, but it does not
seem to have worried him unduly. Human traits, he thought,
alter but little through the ages.

In *Esther* and *Athalie* he introduced a modified feature of
Greek tragedy: music and choral singing as a link between the acts. 'Athalie' has a tragic grandeur: the story
of Joash, the child-king miraculously snatched from death and
secretly brought up in the Temple of Jerusalem, perhaps

stirred memories of his own pious childhood; but he reached
the greatest height of his inspiration in the characters of
Athaliah, the cruel and idolatrous old queen, and her adversary
Joad the prophet, incorruptible and inflexible, without illusions, a sort of Cardinal de Richelieu, and yet not without
compassion and tenderness in his exhortation to Joash:

> 'Entre le pauvre et vous, vous prendrez Dieu pour juge,
> Vous souvenant, mon fils, que, caché sous ce lin,
> Comme eux vous fûtes pauvre, et comme eux orphelin.'

A diplomat's anecdote gave him the idea of *Bajazet*. The
character of Mithridates, the old pirate-king, appealed to him
by its mixture of greatness and savagery. Madame, sister of
Charles II of England, suggested to him the subject of
Bérénice, a tender and melancholy idyll of love versus the
raison d'Etat where the initiated could read under the names of
Titus and Berenice those of Louis XIV and Marie Mancini.
The only other time he dipped into Roman history he chose
one of its darkest pages, the poisoning of Britannicus on Nero's
orders. Except for Burrhus, Nero's tutor, his Romans are no
longer the same breed as Corneille's. The Roman Empire,
like an over-ripe fruit, is beginning to show signs of decay,
one of them being the covert power of the nimbler-witted
Greek freedmen, Pallas and Narcissus.

Racine did take some liberties with history when treating the
age of Britannicus and the character of Junia, but his Agrippina
and his Nero, the 'monstre naissant' are such as he found them in
Tacitus: she, autocratic, bold and unscrupulous, an ageing
tigress snarling at her cub fast outgrowing her; Nero, emerging
from adolescence, still subdued by force of habit but impatient
and longing for power. Though she still retains a few shreds of
imperial insight, neither has any moral sense. Yet these
monsters compel interest because they suffer, monsters as they
are, and because they are so alarmingly normal. One may
even perceive under the tight-lipped sarcasm of Nero's answer
to his mother's recriminations:

> 'Je me souviens toujours que je vous dois l'Empire:
> Et *sans vous fatiguer du soin de le redire. . . .*'

what may well be an echo of young Racine's cold exasperation under the well-meant reproofs of Mother Agnes.

In fact, his orphaned childhood, surrounded by kind, puritanical womenfolk, may account, as much as his later associations with actresses, for his extraordinary insight into feminine psychology. Corneille's women characters are all but virile; Racine's are drawn with unsurpassed variety, tenderness and delicacy. They are wholly feminine, serenely illogical because perfectly consistent with themselves: Andromache, through all her vacillations, is never actuated by anything else than her love for Hector and for her son; Hermione, by her unrequited love for Pyrrhus, Agrippina, through her tortuous diplomacy and apparent contradictions, by her passion for power and distrust of her son:

'Je le craindrois bientôt, s'il ne me craignoit plus.'

Racine was blamed for introducing a love interest in *Britannicus* and for making Hippolytus, in *Phèdre*, Aricia's lover. In this last case, his justification lies less in the authorities he invokes than in Phaedra's heart-rending cry:

'Ah! douleur non encore éprouvée! . . .
Ils s'aiment! Par quel charme ont-ils trompé mes yeux?'

His characters are poetical creations and his renown depends primarily on the fact that he is a poet even more than a dramatist or a psychologist. It is as a poet that he is most difficult to define. Strange as it may appear, he brings to poetry, apart from occasional touches of stilted formality, the best qualities of prose: the clarity, elegance and agility needed in dramatic dialogue. He handles irony with deadly accuracy and economy of words. One must read him aloud to realize the delightful harmony of his verse, the pure music of Phaedra's lament:

'Ariane, ma sœur, de quel amour blessée, . . .
Je le vis, je rougis, je pâlis à sa vue.'

Or Bérénice's:

'Que le jour recommence, et que le jour finisse,
Sans que jamais Titus puisse voir Bérénice.'

Some writings, even masterpieces, have in a sense an opaque quality: they mean nothing beyond what they say. Racine has the gift of evoking infinitely more than he says; several depths lie below his deceptive, shimmering transparency.

GUSTAVE FLAUBERT, 1821-1880

Cynicism being the fruit of disillusionment, it is not unusual for a generation of idealists to be followed by a generation of cynics. In the case of Gustave Flaubert, a belated Romantic who became eventually the flag-bearer of the Realists, realism was a sort of revenge ('People imagine that I *like* reality; I loathe it!') coupled with a nostalgic resentment for the world of lost illusions.

His first published work, *Madame Bovary*, brought his name into the full glare of publicity, and himself before the courts, for alleged 'offences against public morality and religion'. It is a closely woven, astringent study of middle-class provincial life, the story of a country doctor's young wife, bored by the dullness of her surroundings, yearning for romance and glamour and seeking them in illicit love affairs which bring her to disaster and suicide. It was not so much the realistic approach which jarred contemporary susceptibilities—Balzac, before Flaubert, had given them some pretty severe shocks. It was the deliberately detached and dispassionate tone with its undercurrent of caustic irony. Flaubert, however, was acquitted, the whole incident having if possible increased his angry contempt for the stupid nineteenth century in which it had been his misfortune to be born.

There is something enchantingly truculent about Gustave Flaubert, his powerful frame, defiant look, and long trailing moustache 'à la Viking', his fits of wild exuberance and his moods of hopeless gloom, his fanatical devotion to art, his rabid hatred of the bourgeois (as opposed to the artist), the sadistic relish with which he collected samples of smug platitude for his *sottisier*, the ogrish manner, which hid an almost morbid sensibility and the tenderest of hearts. A Norman by birth, the son of a distinguished surgeon (Dr. Larivière in *Madame Bovary*), he liked to think of himself as a barbarian, a throw-back to the ancient sea-rover stock from which he had inherited his fair-haired northern type and also, as he thought, his restlessness, moodiness and spleen. Chateaubriand, the father of Romantic pessimism, once humorously deplored the all-too numerous progeny of his gloomy hero, René. Flaubert is a late offshoot of René, with whom the hero of *Novembre*, one of his earlier works, bears a marked resemblance. The glorious attack of intense gloom in which he revelled as an adolescent was in full conformity with his temperament.

So was the carefully nurtured sense of maladjustment which is part of the Romantic complex and which he analysed penetratingly in *Madame Bovary*. How he hated the too, too familiar green Norman landscape, and how he execrated the comfortable, self-satisfied mercantile bourgeoisie of Rouen! In spite of himself, Flaubert owes much to the scientific and medical atmosphere in which he grew up: the matter-of-fact, unemotional familiarity with physical suffering and death, the scrupulous attention to accurate detail, and also the inside knowledge of the medical profession that gives such authenticity to his picture of the country doctor—a plain, hard-worked man —compared for instance to Balzac's apostolic *Médecin de Campagne*.

All his ambitions turned towards an ideal of literary perfection. He had no other aim in life, and, since his father's death had left him comfortably off, no material cares. After a few years in Paris and a journey to Italy, he had at last realized a life-long dream and spent four years exploring Egypt, Palestine and Asia Minor. Although it is known through his friend Maxime du Camp that he was occasionally subject to some sort of nervous fits, perhaps epilepsy, the exigencies of his temperament as a writer may have accounted as much as health or family reasons for his retirement to his house in Croisset, near Rouen. There he spent most of his life, shut up, like an alchemist, in his study built on a terrace overlooking the Seine, from which he could gaze nostalgically on the outgoing ships. His mother, his niece Caroline, his friends with whom he kept up a lively correspondence, composed the background of his existence. His unhappy adolescent passion for Mme Schlésinger cast a shadow over his whole life, but the 'Muse', to whom much of his voluminous correspondence is addressed, was a Provence-born Parisienne, blonde, beautiful Louise Colet, who held a *salon littéraire* in Paris and wrote a great deal of not very good poetry.

The word which best expresses Flaubert's method of work is 'distillation.' Every artist who takes his work seriously learns in time how to use to the best purpose the gifts allotted to him. Flaubert's mind functioned like an alembic: out of a mass of facts, sentiments and sensations, he strove to extract the few drops of imperishable essence. He had to serve a hard apprenticeship after coming to the unwelcome conclusion that his tastes lay one way and his gifts another. His tastes did not attract him to Balzac, who was just then carving out with such gusto great slices of contemporary life, but rather to the school of Art for Art's sake which still occupied the southern slopes of Romanticism under the leadership of Théophile Gautier.

Flaubert was a heavy-weight compared to Gautier, whose spirited, colourful and rapidly executed sketches he admired without being able to emulate, burdened as he was by an introspective and philosophical turn of mind. His *Tentation de Saint Antoine*, a philosophical prose-poem on which he had lavished all his gifts of pageantry and colour, was frigidly received by his friends, to his bitter disappointment, although he admitted later that the 'extirpation of the lyrical cancer' had been timely. The subject of *Madame Bovary* (a recent small-town tragedy) was suggested to him by one of his friends as a sort of counter-irritant. He disliked it intensely till he perceived in it a theme of sentimental frustration germane to his own.

To that extent he could say 'Madame Bovary, c'est moi.' There were two sides to him, Flaubert I, the Romantic, the artist, and Flaubert II, cold, observant and caustic, who kept a sharp eye on the first. His heroine also has two personalities, the cleavage between them becoming radical after the episode of the ball at the château, which gives concrete reality to the world of her dreams. As Emma she is the twin of Flaubert's romantic self. He gave to her, as to Mme Arnoux, in *L'Education sentimentale*, Mme Schlésinger's dark eyes and lovely features. But as Mme Bovary she is as she appears to the other people around her, to her blind and adoring husband and to her homely neighbours, among them the unforgettable Homais, a model of bourgeois pomposity and self-satisfaction.

This duality extends to the composition of the novel, in itself an extraordinary achievement, which Flaubert never equalled again: a tale of two worlds moving simultaneously at a different pace, radically foreign to each other though their basic elements are the same, connected only by Emma, who lives in the one and vegetates in the other.

The current of duality ran strongly in Flaubert's work—his historical novel *Salammbô* is also a tale of two worlds: Carthage and the Barbarians, connected by the love of Mâtho, rebel leader of Carthage's foreign troops, for the Carthaginian princess Salammbô.

The stern discipline he had imposed upon himself for *Madame Bovary*—the hours spent tracking *le mot juste*, pinpointing the sensation, checking the smallest reference—still held when he wrote *Salammbô*; a subject after his own heart, exotic, colourful and violent, for which he exhausted not only historical sources, but anything that could give him a clue to the particular flavour of life in Carthage in 241 B.C. In the pages of his novel, the Phoenician city, Rome's dreaded rival, comes to life, with its crowded streets and sea-girt citadel. Carthage, no longer queen of the seas, is still redoubtable: a complex of highly civilized greed, cruelty, and Oriental mysticism. Though *Salammbô* may not be everybody's book, the present-day conception of the historical novel is due to Flaubert.

For all that, Flaubert's outlook, even in his modern novels, is that of the entomologist rather than of the psychologist. Emma is the one exception, a projection of himself. While Balzac threw himself hotly into the fray, Flaubert (in his novels at least, for his correspondence reveals a totally different frame of mind) remains on the brink, describing with absorbed interest the evolutions of extraordinarily interesting insects; some magnificent: Salammbô, Hamilcar, Salomé—some drab: Homais, Charles Bovary. His irony grew more caustic as the years went on. In *Madame Bovary* it is well under control: either in grotesque but plausible juxtaposition, as in the Agricultural Show scene when Rodolphe makes passionate declarations to Emma under a barrage of proclamations of prizes for fat cattle; or in the apparently guileless, word-for-word reproduction of Homais's asinine speeches. In *Bouvard et Pécuchet*, his last work, left unfinished—the dreary saga of two well-meaning imbeciles in search of knowledge—irony is relentless, bitter and oppressive.

Madame Bovary and *Salammbô* represent the extreme swings of the pendulum. His other modern novel, *L'Education sentimentale*, a story of Parisian life, is a curiously negative book; the literary, fashionable and revolutionary Paris of 1848, seen through the intelligent eyes of an idle and sceptical young bourgeois, Flaubert. But it is Flaubert less his *raison d'être*, the empty shell of the man, with a stiffness due to self-consciousness, apparent in the dry, crumbly texture of the style. His *Trois Contes* is probably his work best known in Britain. With less genius than Balzac, he is a greater artist; from him both artistic realism and brutal realism in great measure derive. He has left an imperishable tradition, of objective truth, of uncompromising probity. He has set generations of French writers seeking for *le mot juste*. His own prose provides a model of harmonious perfection, so studied that it looks natural except in some over-written passages. To appreciate his natural gifts as a writer, free from the 'throes of style', one must turn to his stimulating correspondence.

Flaubert exerted a profound influence on such English novelists as George Gissing and George Moore, in their adoption of a more objective point of view and more artistic care in writing. Perhaps even more, his influence was exercised through his disciple Guy de Maupassant, a Flaubert less profound, in no sense philosophic, but striking his instrument with a sure hand.

MARCEL PROUST, 1871-1922

The most influential of twentieth-century novelists was without doubt Marcel Proust, whose reputation was established in the last decade of his life, after the publication of his 12-volume *A la Recherche du temps perdu* (from 1912). The length of the work and its new technique had disconcerted publishers' readers, and it was at his own expense that Proust published *Du Côté de chez Swann*, the first of his work destined to world-wide success.

Twentieth-century psychology, by its incursions into the subtle play of external influences on every man at the very beginning of his separate existence, has done much to stress the individuality of men instead of considering them as exemplars in a biological sequence. Much light, too, has been thrown on those elements in man on which he once kept silent.

In his most penetrating analysis, such as the evocation of Emma Bovary's adolescence in his search for symptoms of her new personality Flaubert had not gone beyond the data supplied by her conscious memory. Not for a moment did he plead that Emma was not really responsible. At most he indicated the sentimental and epicurean streak in her father. Proust is the first novelist in a France imbued with the classical tradition of consciousness and reasoned clarity, to have penetrated into the obscure domain of the unconscious beneath the realm of reason, though the mystics of Port Royal and Racine had of course been aware of it as early as the seventeenth century long before Nodier, Huysmans, Barbey d'Aurevilly, not to speak of others.

Endowed with an extraordinary faculty of analysis, Proust could penetrate deeply into the arcana of himself and of others. He dissects with uncanny skill his own feelings and the modifications that these show when they find outside expression. He observes at the same time with unparalleled acuity. Almost imperceptible details attract his attention, and many of them reveal to him the existence of something hidden. For example, the almost invisible green line in M. de Charlus's tie, or the equally inconspicuous red line in his socks, give him a clue to some oddity in Charlus's hidden personality. Proust's mind may be compared to one of those delicate precision instruments of which the needle registers minute oscillations which to the eye of the profane appear simply as a uniform line. One can attribute, if one wishes, this hyper-sensitiveness in Proust to his mixed parentage—his father was a distinguished Parisian doctor, his mother an extremely intelligent, witty and cultured Jewess. This double heredity gave him the key to two worlds—the French world which he observed with the passionate attention of a foreigner, an Oriental sensitive to nuances of all kinds that a Frenchman might miss—and the Jewish world particularly represented by the hero Swann, whom he examines from the point of view of a Cartesian Frenchman.

Proust's mother and his maternal grandmother constituted the major influences on his life: a mother and grandmother fixation if ever one existed. The child was intelligent, highly nervous, of delicate health; to this sensitive boy the missing of the accustomed evening kiss from his mother brought an agony of suffering. His trouble was asthma, a malady with a psychological side which may make of the sufferer a hypo-chondriac in self-defence. Coddled and indulged by his adoring mother, the child led an existence morally as well as physically cushioned. Strangely enough he was able to do his short period of military service (to which he refers in *Jean Santeuil*, a recently discovered novel begun in 1896), though he must have been what the French call 'un drôle de soldat'.

The youthful writings of Proust, showing a certain precio-sity, were welcomed in the literary and social groups in which he figured as the wealthy dilettante, quite the dandy and not entirely without snobbery. During this period he frequented more than one social class—the aristocracy, the bourgeoisie with literary pretensions (the Verdurins), and the higher reaches of the demi-monde (Odette de Crécy)—and, perhaps unconsciously, stored up a rich harvest of obser-vations.

The death of his parents brought to an end this golden age

of childhood and youth during which he had been adored and petted. It freed a hidden side of Proust's existence and extended his investigations into zones so far hardly touched. Henceforth his chief aim in life was to recapture, by memory, the vanished paradise and thus live again, in ecstasy, lost moments of this golden past.

One most fleeting sensation—the taste of a sponge-cake dipped into an infusion of lime-leaves, the awareness of uneven flagstones on which one stumbles—recalling a sensation of a moment in the past—can unlock to a flood of memories: his memories of childhood, adolescence and youth, seen again in the light of acquired knowledge, but without losing their divine freshness and their magic. An outstanding example of the magic that Proust can evoke around a memory is the passage about the three steeples at Martinville as they appear to him by chance while he is travelling along the road: gliding one behind another, coming together again, and again separated, as though they were animated by a mysterious life. Proust shows an extreme acuteness of impression and analyses a sensation into component parts—one part belonging to the outside world and the vital part which is in us—enriched in Proust himself by a shimmering poetry of associations. In the many pages devoted to his idolized grandmother, for one bleak instant the ecstasy fails and he sees her as she appears to other people— a red-faced, stout, ageing woman.

Proust's book is a world and a diverse one. He paints for instance the aristocratic group—*le Côté de Guermantes*: a small, closed group calling each other by names unknown to the outsider. Proust loves to dissect the motives underlying grandiose appearances. When Swann pays his farewell visit to the Guermantes, who are going to a party, they are in far too much of a hurry to spare a word for a dying friend, feigning incredulity about his illness; but they are not in too great a hurry for Mme de Guermantes to go and change her shoes, which offend her husband's sense of colour, from black to red to match her dress.

The most successful portrait is probably that of Swann, a wealthy, cultured, intelligent, very sensitive Jew. His life is coloured by his disillusioned yet tormenting love for Odette de Crécy, a demi-mondaine not very intelligent, and, more serious still, without much taste. In the varied circle of somewhat decadent aristocrats, the principal figure is the Baron de Charlus, enigmatic, complicated, tormented.

A delightful scene of comedy figures is the bourgeois group: the ridiculous dinner party at the Verdurins—the hostess, a snobbish, managing bourgeoise, dying to have a literary salon and striving to lord it over her band of second-raters enlivened only by Dr. Cottard's unforgiveable puns.

Some of the most delightful of Proust's visions are inspired by nature and by architecture. In translating Ruskin he had learned much, but Proust creates his own poetic pictures: the river Vivonne, with its flowers and its reeds, the apple-blossom of Normandy, the unforgettable, almost heart-rending vision of a hawthorn bush in all the fragility of its beauty. Then there are his visions of the sea—a luminous fluidity reminding one of the luminous world in which his characters move. His whole memory-world, like the Martinville steeples, is fleeting, unstable, making and unmaking itself. There is no plot, no ultimate solution: the crisis passes and life continues.

Proust describes his strange world in a new style created for this purpose, a style which is complex, luxuriant even, loaded with clauses and digressions, and following the tiniest folds in a subtle and complicated tissue of thought. The style is part of the magic which evokes his visions, for he chooses his words with the same skill with which a painter chooses his colours.

How can one explain the great success of Proust in the Anglo-Saxon world? It may be that his viewpoint, though French, is that of an outsider—just as the Russian Mme de Ségur gave particular charm to her not-yet-forgotten pictures of French château life. Is it not perhaps Proust's racial duality as well as his acute sensitiveness which enable him to put into words such things as the special summer Sunday morning atmosphere in a village in the Ile de France, the slate-covered steeple shining like a 'hot black sun', the faint fragrance of buns and incense, the draper's ingratiating smile, even the crisp fresh smell of a new handkerchief?

Du Côté de chez Swann, A l'Ombre des jeunes filles en fleur—these opening sections with their freshness, compared with the more heavily laden, more introspective later sections, remind the reader how luxuriant is *A la Recherche du temps perdu.* The change of tone reminds him that Proust became more introspective, more completely shut away in his cork-lined, heavily curtained room, working in bed, growing more and more ghostlike, pale and thin, with his dark eyes more enormous, till he died, devoured by the world he carried within himself. For him the justification of living was the re-creation, in an artistic form, of transient and never fully lived experience.

François Mauriac (*b.* 1885)

While Proust, partly owing to Scott Moncrieff's masterly translation, scored an immediate success in Britain, some refractoriness was shown towards Mauriac until the translation of *La Pharisienne* brought him to the fore and was succeeded by translations of most of his other novels. Perhaps this tardiness must be imputed to the very qualities that led to his being acclaimed as one of France's leading novelists and that are in many ways diametrically opposed to those of Proust: the extraordinary economy of style with which he obtains his most striking effects, the tautness of his characters, the atmosphere of tense, unspoken tragedy, the severe and indeed pessimistic outlook, the feeling perhaps of being driven willy-nilly to a conclusion imposed by the author.

Proust can occasionally muster a wry smile at himself; his meanderings did him no disservice with the English, accustomed in their great novelists to a certain incoherence; they enjoyed his discreet, piquant irony, his sense of the real, the reappearance of the same characters. They no longer quailed at psychological investigation carried out at unusual or abnormal levels, since such investigations were just acquiring scientific value under the aegis of Freud. Proust, in short, does not set moral problems: the vagaries of M. de Charlus, the equivocal

T

character of Albertine are, among others, studied from a
morally neutral point of view.

Mauriac, on the other hand, is a moralist and a Roman
Catholic, a Roman Catholic with some leaning towards
Jansenist severity. Proust's world is limited by suffering on
one side and a refined consciousness of pleasure on the other.
Mauriac's is hedged between sin and atonement, his work is
imbued with an idealism austere and mystic, as tense in its
conviction as is, on the politically opposed side, the severe
idealism, humanitarian and revolutionary, of André Malraux.

Few authors have been marked to the same extent as François Mauriac by their native land and early surroundings.
The striking originality of his novels is due in a great measure
to their atmosphere: that of the extreme south-west of France,
the immense pine forest that covers the sandy, monotonous
stretches of the Landes, south of Bordeaux, an unsmiling,
sparsely inhabited, secretive land, already akin to Spain by
the white heat of its summers, the shrill note of the cicadas and
also by the temper of its people who have all the intensity of
passion and nothing of the wonted exuberance of the south.

This world of sharp contrasts finds an unforgettable expression in Mauriac's novels. His is the blinding flash, the ruthless
conflict between light and darkness in souls that are at once
severe and incoercible. He does not explain so much as illu-
minate. His style is concise, vigorous and incisive; he builds
up a character in a few lines, sometimes in a few words. Even
Flaubert's much-vaunted opening of *Un Cœur simple* does not
equal the first two lines of *Genitrix*, a whispered conversation
between Mathilde's husband and her mother-in-law, in the
room where Mathilde is lying dangerously ill:

'She's asleep.'

'No. She's just pretending. Come away.'

Mauriac's scope goes far beyond that of the regionalist novel.
He puts clearly, and before all else, the problem on to the moral
level, that of sin and atonement. The governing idea of his
work is the inner conflict in man, the eternal struggle between
the flesh and the spirit. There is a passage in which he recalls
his feelings as an adolescent during the Easter celebrations:

the contrast between the stern, spiritual exaltation of the sacrifice being solemnized by the Church, and the heart-breaking, sensuous sweetness of a southern spring. His adoration of the beauty of the world is mingled with a burning consciousness that this beauty prompts man to sin. Perhaps no other writer except Pascal—'l'usage délicieux et criminel du monde'—has felt and expressed this conflict with so fierce an intensity.

He takes no easy view of either sin or atonement. Atonement cannot be bought except with one's own soul, even for secret sins that exist only in the sinner's conscience. No one could accuse Noémie (in *Le Baiser au lépreux*) of having killed her husband Jean Peloueyre, a pitiful cripple to whom she, young and beautiful, was wedded in a marriage of convenience. She has not been unkind to him, she has pitied him, she has tried to force herself to overcome her repulsion, but her pity hurt him more deeply than her scorn would have done. She has not killed him, but she has made life impossible for him, and therefore it is for her to expiate what was in fact a moral murder. This is not the only case in Mauriac which deals with the theme of the moral murder. In *Genitrix* it is Felicité Cazenave, with her daughter-in-law, and also with her deeply beloved son. In each case, as also in *Le Nœud de vipères*, it is the slow choking-out of life in *l'étouffoir familial*.

In these books Mauriac seems to come very near to Jansenism. Like the Jansenists he admits that there are souls for whom redemption is impossible. The soul without God strives in vain. Such is Thérèse Desqueyroux, an exceptionally intelligent, attractive and cultured woman, brought up in a totally agnostic atmosphere. When the novel opens Thérèse has just been released from preventive detention for the attempted poisoning of her husband. The prosecution has withdrawn its action and Thérèse is on her way home—to his home. Night has come. As the carriage rolls through the endless pine-forests of the Landes, she endeavours to see clearly into herself. She was in love with Bernard when she married him. What has happened? Her reflections only reveal one thing to her: an inner wilderness. She finds nothing to which she can

T*

attach herself, not even her child, no Christian humility and no hope in God. When Bernard, still baffled but half-forgiving, releases her from her quasi-imprisonment in a lonely country house and lets her loose in the wilderness of Paris, it is like an untamed animal being released into the jungle. For all her culture, charm and intelligence, she is a parched soul, longing in vain for the comforting dew of faith, humility, the sense of sin and of redemption.

What gives the work of Mauriac its vigorous originality in French literature is the constant parallelism between inner life and nature. For him nature is the endless forest of the Landes, the pine trees growing in the barren soil, each bearing in its flank the wounds from which the resin flows, as if permanently in anguish. Mauriac personifies them and his books are impregnated with the perfume of the pines. In one passage of souvenirs of his early days he tells how he sometimes looked with wonder at a pine tree surrounded by a shallow trench that isolated it from its fellows and cut through the deep intertwining of the roots. Its yellowing foliage revealed that it was diseased. It was dying alone, cut off from the others which it might have contaminated. There Mauriac sees an image of the solitude of the individual man—whom he sees as isolated even in his family, even in his social group. But for grace, the soul is isolated and he might have taken as his theme *Solus inter solos*. The forest again serves as a symbol in its mass as well as in the individual isolated tree. The forest, so alive, is now and then ravaged by those destructive fires that, even after they appear to have been extinguished, linger, smoulder secretly and flare up again. As Mauriac says, 'The human heart knows those ruses of a half-stifled passion.'

Mauriac's characters are well defined, standing out in sharp relief and with none of that luminous fluidity in which the Proustian characters seem bathed. Nor have the men and women in Mauriac those shimmering facets of the subtle and complex characters who circulate round Swann. They are characters set in a strong one-piece mould, they have an inner being which knows no compromise.

French prose literature continues to provide infinite variety.

The novelist, however, is so preoccupied with a diversity of problems—ethical, psychological, regional and exotic—that he at times forgets that the essential element in a novel is the story. Those who still desire to find a real narrative more often turn to the drama or the cinema, both of which, for excellent reasons, must tell some kind of story. In any case the impression remains with the observer that French culture penetrates abroad at the present time, more vividly on the stage and on the screen than between the yellow paper covers which assured readers in an earlier generation that they would enjoy a new adventure.

INDEX

NOTE.—The more important page references are set in **bold type**.

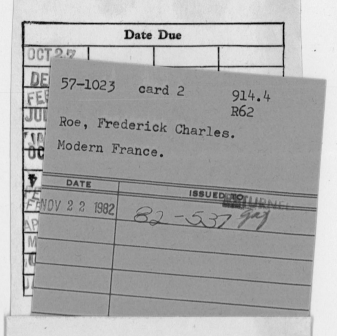

Roe, Frederick Charles.
  Modern France.